So, You Want To Be A Project Manager?

Mindset and

Habits for Growth

By Jonathan L. Isaacson
The Intentional Restorer

Printed in the United States of America
First Printing, 2021
Revision 1, 2022
IBSN 978-1-7356227-5-0

Published by The DYOJO
thedyojo.com

Library of Congress Control Number: 2021919081

Early testimonials for this book

"I like what I saw from the mediocre book. Jon puts into words things veterans of the industry should know and shortens the learning of those new to the industry. Most of us learn by on-the-job training with some guidance. His books provide guidance for those willing to take the next steps at raising their knowledge." - David Watts (New York, NY)

"Jon Isaacson's commitment and passion to develop intentionally is shared throughout this book. This book serves to advance the Be Intentional mantra that Jon embodies in all that he does." – David Princeton, Principal Consultant, Advocate Claim Service LLC (Muskego, WI)

"This book is incredible. It's like you've written a 'How To' guide on my life over the past 20 years. I just wish I had access to this when I was going through it. Definitely doesn't suck." - Rob MacPherson, Manager of National Estimating Services, DKI Canada (Orangeville, ON)

"I like Jon's style and the unique way he is presenting these thought leadership ideas." - Jeff Cross, Media Director, ISSA Media (Pataskala, OH)

"This third book by Jon Isaacson is arguably his best yet. In an industry facing greater hiring struggles than ever, it is imperative to connect the dots between hiring and recruiting, and leadership and retention. Don't be deceived by the title. With real stories of real restorers and other leaders woven throughout, So, You Want to Be a Project Manager? is for any leader looking to dial in on leadership, and the importance in restoration of creating a team with the right balance of technical skills, personal skills, and a desire to serve." - Michelle Blevins, Owner and Publisher, C&R Magazine (Troy, MI)

"I liked most of what I read." - Charles Cassani, CR, Analytical Specialist, Restoration Management Company (Sacramento, CA)

"Well written and very relevant to where we are currently in the development of our company." - Kevin Hussey, CEO & President, United Fire & Water Damage (Baton Rouge, LA)

"Engaging and flows very well." - Luke Draeger, Outside Sales, Aramsco (Seattle, WA)

"Practical and real information." - Ken Larsen, CR, Senior Consultant, IDSO family of Companies (Santa Rosa Beach, FL)

"Some great pointers in there." - Josh Winton, IAQ Josh (Fort Lauderdale, FL)

"Great job of communicating that it's all about mindset. I saw mention of the book as a great tool for owners and managers who are developing PMs and I think we are in need of help in this area." - Katie Smith, CEO, PHC Restoration (NC)

"I liked the content that I got to read, excited to read the whole thing." - Gabriel Kellogg, Claims Specialist, Just Right Cleaning & Construction (Moses Lake, WA)

"Good stuff." - Thomas McQuire, Founder & Owner, Large Loss Mastery (Melbourne, FL)

"Good points are made in this book with great examples that I don't recall reading anywhere else. Jon has a unique way of looking at things." - Michael Knaack, Sustainability Manager, Tacoma Public Schools (Tacoma, WA)

TABLE OF CONTENTS

FOREWORD

Around 2007, restoration professionals began to take notice of Purdue University's Construction Management (CM) program. The industry was excited that it was being received and included in academia with opportunities to earn recognition in our area of specialization. In 2008, Dr. Randy Rapp announced the first official college-level courses offered in the Disaster Restoration and Reconstruction Management (DRRM) concentration of technology after school.

Dr. Rapp stated, "This unique opportunity has kept us very busy for the past year, as we met with numerous Restoration Industry Association (RIA) professionals and continue diligently gathering relevant materials for course text and reference development."

In an article published in Restoration & Remediation[1] Magazine, he noted that BCM and the RIA partnered to research and verify the body of knowledge essential to the consistent development of professional restorers. The first courses included Introduction to DRRM Management, DRRM Project Management, and DRRM Industry Problem Investigation. During the summer of 2009, 275 RIA Certified Restorers (CR's) were surveyed with funding support from RIA, and the results were presented at the RIA's fall conference in St Louis that year.

In 2011, Dr. Rapp reported on these survey results, stating, "We were able to establish the structure and content of a Certified Restorer body of knowledge. The International Journal of Construction Education and Research published the results last year."

---

[1] Cox, R. & Rapp, R. (2009, September 2) *Disaster Restoration and Reconstruction Management Move Ahead at Purdue*. Restoration & Remediation Magazine.
https://www.randrmagonline.com/articles/83668-disaster-restoration-and-reconstruction-management-moves-ahead-at-purdue

The RIA Certified Restorer Body of Knowledge (BoK) is available for free[2] to all members. It is organized to cover primary knowledge sections that follow core competencies and levels of understanding. Pete Consigli has represented RIA On the BCM Construction Advisory Council (CAC) in support of collaboration with Purdue University including guest lectures to the DRRM students assisting with internships and employment in the industry.

Some naysayers spread the misnomer that those who can't do, teach, but Dr. Rapp is proof that you can do both at a high level. Working with a worldwide firm on projects ranging from Hurricanes Katrina and Wilma, as well as the Restore Iraqi Oil program.

Readers of this book likely will find a lot of value in Dr. Rapp's book which goes into greater detail on the topic, *Disaster Recovery Project Management: Bringing Order from Chaos.* His book compiles, "Insights acquired through decades of real-world experience, as well as from his academic research and teaching responsibilities, the author explains pertinent requirements and methods for the contractors and other professionals who bring order from chaos."

From January 2009 through December 2018, Dr. Rapp said, "We delivered formally scheduled undergrad courses, three different courses of 8-credits total, in disaster restoration and reconstruction management. By his count, about 60 students completed at least one of the courses and another 40 students earned the concentration designation on their transcripts. As the Purdue team shifted their focus to graduate students, a number of Ph.D. students, including two from the US military, have earned their doctorates by researching disaster recovery topics.

---

[2] Restoration Industry Association. *Certified Restorer Body of Knowledge.* https://www.restorationindustry.org/certified-restorer-body-knowledge-0

The Purdue team focuses on instruction, keeping Bob Bonwell's words in mind: "You cannot outperform your knowledge." In the summer of 2020, the prior work was compiled into a professional development online course[3] to prepare people with conventional construction experience for disaster work. The following summer, Dr. Rapp and the team compiled an asynchronous online master's course for the MSCM online program.

Dr. Rapp notes, "The course emphasizes differences between conventional construction projects and disaster recovery work. Nuances of understanding can make the difference between the mediocre and strong performance of the disaster recovery project team, without needing to learn 'the hard way.'" Or said another way, as many of you have heard me say on The DYOJO Podcast, this knowledge will help you shorten your DANG learning curve.

In 2011, Pete[4] composed the following White Paper which many have referred to as a timeless outline for intentional project managers. This paper was used as a reference and resource for DRRM students to supplement guests' lectures. Coincidentally the document has also been used as a training resource in the industry for estimators and project managers entering the restoration sector.

With Pete's blessing and Dr. Rapp's review, I am including this work, in its entirety, to open this book. I hope it will wet your appetite for expanding your knowledge as well as your hunger to know more about the history of this amazing industry.

---

[3] Purdue's Disaster Recovery Certificate course - https://www.purdue.edu/newsroom/releases/2021/Q1/online-course-from-purdue-hastens,-heightens-disaster-recovery-planning-and-execution.html

[4] Dr. Rapp reviewed thas chapter prior to publishing and noted, "Pete was closely involved helping Purdue get Rusty Amarante and the IAQ Radio duo, Cliff [Zlotnik] and Joe [Hughes], as well as some of the demolition industry leadership to the May 2014 I3R2 conference. Downloads of parts of the Proceedings of that three-day event, which captured the industry panel discussions and 30-plus academic articles now numbers over 20,000. Much favorable impact."

Pete wanted me to make sure that we included this disclaimer: At the time of the publication of the white paper, Pete Consigli was a consultant and Advisor to RIA from 2007. After 10 years of serving the association in that role, in 2017 Pete's contractual duty ended. He is an RIA Honorary member and widely considered the association's historian.

Insurance Restoration Terminology and Damage Repair Project Sequence

A White Paper by: G. Pete Consigli, CR, WLS – RIA Industry Advisor

Purdue University DRRM Concentration Guest Lecture September, 26th 2013

Preface

Various nomenclatures are used in the Restoration Industry to describe the work that restoration contractors perform. The word "restoration" can be a diluted term to mean everything from drying and cleaning a partial room of wet carpet to complete demolition and rebuilding a structure. That leaves a wide chasm that can be confusing to the various stakeholders involved in a disaster including insurance companies and other entities that provide funding for the repairs.

Restoration at its root meaning is described by Webster's as: "To return something to its nearly original state or form". Generally speaking, those in the industry classify restoration into 3 phases, mitigation, restoration, and reconstruction. This paper will expand on those 3 phases, offer a model for the sequence of a restoration project, and provide some clarity behind the meaning of industry jargon.

The project sequence has parallels to general construction or remodeling work but is differentiated by the "unplanned" nature of a disaster. This dynamic offers unique supervisory challenges to the project, including agreeing on the scope of work, determining who will pay for what, and dealing with assurance issues that the property has been returned to a safe and habitable state while maintaining its pre-disaster usability and market value.

Insurance Restoration Terminology

Damage Repair: Restoration is often referred to as Damage Repair, a term that distinguishes the restoration process from general remodeling (normally elective and planned) or renovation (a term used for urban rehab work or in the weatherization industry sector). The term damage repair may have a prefix inserted and be called "Insurance Damage Repair". All damage repair work is not always paid for by the proceeds of an insurance policy!

Insurance Restoration: What normally starts the "insurance repair" process to determine if there is coverage is language in a standard insurance policy that the policyholder has to inform their carrier they had a loss. This will "trigger" a duty by the insurer or their agent to commence an investigation to determine causation. An insurance policy has various components that clarify what is covered and what is not but generally, coverage is defined by named "perils" affecting the dwelling" (building) and the "contents" (personal belongings of the occupant). Covered perils can be defined as a one-time burst or explosion from water, wind, fire, or other causes. Special coverage is available for flood and earthquake-prone areas through insurance companies and government entities.

Homeowner policies may also cover clean-up from unique kinds of events such as damage caused by a trauma scene, drug lab, teargas, fuel oil, vandalism, and skunk emissions.
Damage caused by a lack of "normal and customary" maintenance tends to be non-covered damage. Additionally, specifically named exclusions to a policy may be environmental contaminants known as "pollution exclusions" as well as damage from rats and squirrels which falls under the "rodent" exception. Insurance policies may also have provisions for code upgrades after a loss.

The latter should not be confused with a property owner's desire to upgrade their property as part of an insurance claim because they have a desire to do so and want their insurance company to pay. This dynamic often comes about from a feeling of victimization due to the loss, or a feeling of entitlement one may have because they have paid premiums for years. These "emotional" aspects of damage repair present unique challenges to restorers and insurers alike.

A thorough inspection and agreement of the scope of repairs by all the stakeholders will clarify what should be covered by the insurance policy as a result of the loss and what other work the policyholder may desire that would require a separate agreement with the contractor doing the work. This dynamic is no different than buying a new house that comes with "standard" finishes and appliances, etc. The buyer then has an option to upgrade as part of the post-sale contract formalities with the builder.

Restoration Contractor: Those in the industry often refer to themselves as Restoration Contractors. Using the term "contractor" may have legal implications governed by the contractor licensing laws of states or various jurisdictions. The restoration industry is made up of many specialty service providers and generalists who normally refer to themselves as "Full-Service Restoration Contractors". The specialty providers use a wide range of terms to differentiate themselves in the marketplace but the general term "Restorer" is often used by the industry either by itself or in conjunction with a specialty service niche. The word "certified" may also be used to show the achievements of a company's proficiency or an individual's competence.

Mitigation Phase 1: The first phase of a restoration project is Mitigation, a term used in insurance policies and is part of a mandated obligation the policyholder has to take steps to mitigate the loss. A damage event in the insurance vernacular used by the restoration industry is defined as a "loss". Therefore the term "per loss damage" is used to define something that existed before the occurrence and might not be covered under a standard insurance policy.

Mitigation is defined as: "To minimize, prevent or secure from further damage". The term mitigation is often interchangeable with "Emergency Services"; the difference being emergency service is normally a first response activity (usually defined by hours) versus mitigation which is a "process" that might take multiple trips over several days to a project site.

Restoration Phase 2: After the mitigation phase of a project is completed, then restoration can be performed once all the stakeholders of the project agree on the scope of work, project logistics, and cost. This process allows the customer; restorer, insurance adjuster, and other potential stakeholders to arrive at a "meeting of the minds". Meeting of the minds is a legal term used to signify an agreement by parties to a contract. The execution of a contract is an underlying concept that characterizes the work of a general contractor, and in many states regulates the work professional restorers perform.

This phase of a project might also include "Remediation" work, an interchangeable term the restoration industry uses which can be confusing. The use of the term "remediation" generally refers to remedial procedures for mold, sewage, and abatement of asbestos, lead or other contaminants using engineering controls and HEPA devices.

When this type of work is required, an independent 3rd party (often called an Indoor Environmental Professional or IEP) is normally needed for their special expertise to help specify the scope of work, provide project oversight, and verify the efficacy of the remedial process. Clarifying the need for an IEP is an important component of the "meeting of the minds" and it should be determined to whom they have their primary duty, who pays them, and what project stakeholders are involved in the reporting process of their work.

Reconstruction Phase 3: Not all restoration work involves reconstruction, as many projects professional restorers handle require only cosmetic type repairs such as painting, flooring replacement, and minor structural repairs to drywall or hardwood floors. These types of services, whether handled in-house or by a subcontractor, are part of the restoration phase. Phase 3 projects are normally associated with major structural damage caused by a single site large loss from a fire or water main break in a high-rise building or multiple losses due to an area-wide disaster from a hurricane or tornado.

In the event that a project requires phase 3 reconstruction, mitigation, and remediation work should be completed enabling an accurate scope of repair for the reconstructive phase. It is not uncommon in the industry that even on projects where a full-service restorer performs phases 1 and 2, a different "general contractor" or "builder" might perform phase 3. This can be due to customer preference, competitive bidding, or area-wide workloads and scheduling bottlenecks. In the case of some commercial, industrial or institutional projects, contractors who are familiar with the original design and construction of the building might be considered more "qualified" to perform the work.

Damage Repair Project Sequence

1. Starting Point:
   a. Receive inquiry/assignment
   b. Assess the situation/evaluate prospect
   c. Determine Emergency Response vs. Non-Emergency

2. Dispatch:
   a. Emergency Service crew vs. Estimator/ sales function
   b. Clarify use of Work Authorizations, Contracts, and Assignment of Benefits with "direction to pay" clause

3. Site Inspection:
   a. Determine the type and degree of damage (DOD)
   b. Mitigate damage using appropriate consent forms for emergency work, use waivers as appropriate
   c. Agree on Scope and develop the Estimate for non-emergency work

4. Close the Sale:
    a. Arrive at a "Meeting of the Minds" with the property owner, insurance adjuster, and other stakeholders
    b. Execute contract using "right to know" customer briefing info to communicate risk and reduce liability

5. Perform the Project:
    a. Establish performance benchmarks and project phase timelines
    b. Set production schedules
    c. Use of In-House Crews vs. Sub-Contractors
    d. Use of photographs, industry forms, and standards for communication and documentation purposes

6. Intangibles: Addressed upfront, during the meeting of the minds or execution of the contract
    a. Permit requirements
    b. Vetting of sub-contractors and change order policy
    c. Determine the need for and use of outside consultants or IEP's
    d. Determine if a mortgage company endorsement is required and decide on a payment schedule
    e. Project-specific issues: access, security, client concerns, insurance and bonding requirements, etc.
    f. Discuss restorer's role in project if not performing full service (areas of responsibility and "hand-off")

7. Project Close-Out:
    a. Restoration effectiveness verification (when specified and agreed to)
    b. Punch list, partial and substantial certificates of completion

     c. Final walkthrough and execute Certificate of Satisfaction with customer
     d. Send final invoice

8. Post Restoration Follow-up/Issues:
   a. Ensure subcontractor and vendor invoices are processed
   b. Deal with multiple party checks and insurance draft endorsements
   c. Lien releases
   d. Customer follow-up (quality control, post "selling")
   e. Collection of funds
   f. Provide Warranty of Workmanship
   g. Procedure for handling warranty complaints
   h. Review project for quality control purposes and "lessons learned" insights, perform cost/profit analysis

Conclusion: Damage repair and reconstruction projects are different than remodeling work and general construction and present unique supervisory and management challenges. Understanding the nature of insurance coverage and the role insurance plays in the damage repair process is essential to a successful restoration contractor's operation. Restoration nomenclature can have interchangeable or multiple meanings so it is essential to understand and use industry terminology in a consistent manner.

Restoration projects may involve up to 3 unique phases and have benchmarks that define where one phase of a project is complete and another begins. This aspect of restoration work can be helpful in establishing partial phase completion with the customer and trigger progress payments to the contractor.

The use of industry standards establishing best practices is a critical part of supervising and managing a restoration project. Using standardized industry terminology and procedures to execute contracts will ensure a higher probability for a successful and profitable project. Diligent project documentation utilizing photography and written forms provide the ability to explain and/or justify emergency work procedures and project costs and will facilitate insurance-related payments.

Disclaimer: The information provided in this document and presented during the lecture is based on the personal experience of the author/presenter based on 35 years of experience in the restoration industry. It is meant to provide insights into the unique challenges faced when supervising a damage repair project. It is not intended to provide legal, insurance, or professional advice.

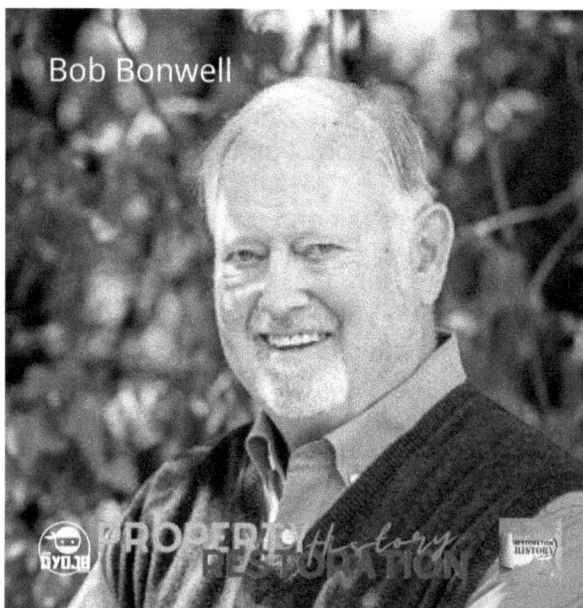

We discussed Knowledge and Skills for Project Managers with Dr. Randy Rapp on The DYOJO Podcast Episode 85, we also feature comments about Bob Bonwell who was pivotal in getting the DRR Program into Purdue. Learn more about Bob and many other characters who have contributed to the rise of our industry at **PropertyRestorationHistory.com**

PREFACE

You can know something to be true and choose not to act accordingly. I understand wisdom to be the application of truth. Wisdom is the result of being a lifelong learner. One of life's greatest teachers is a failure. If you never try something that pushes you out of your comfort zone, you may be able to reduce your failures. But if you challenge yourself to engage in something that has a strong risk of failure, are you really doing something worthwhile?

I do not consider myself to be wise, but I have demonstrated that I am a lifelong learner. One of the reasons I write is because I love seeing good people, like yourself, understand that the path to achieving your goals is closer than you think. If you want to grow your career, I am living proof that average people can make it happen.

When I say closer than you think, I do not mean to imply that the process will be easy.

If one of the benchmarks of your personal and/or professional growth includes project management in the skilled trades (and more specifically property restoration), then I believe this is a book for you. With the help of some wise friends, I have done my best to produce a book that has something helpful to say.

This book IS NOT a how-to or step-by-step guide for project management, but it does contain many of those foundational principles I believe will help you in your quest. Whatever your goals are, you must start with your mindset and habits if you want to make progress in the process.

Famed martial artist Bruce Lee approached his craft with a passion for mastery and the thoughtfulness of a philosopher. He was intentional in his actions and his intensity brought brilliance to everything he did. Many of his thoughts on martial arts are applicable to personal and professional development as well.

Bruce Lee says, "The successful warrior is the average man, with laser-like focus[5]." This is a helpful perspective on the importance of weeding out what is unnecessary. I believe Bruce would encourage you to prioritize the distribution of your time and energy to what is most important to you.

Your core values should not be compromised, but growth requires change. Your mindset will need to adapt and your habits will need to evolve. I hope what I have written will challenge and encourage you.

This Book is Intended For

- **Construction professionals** who seek to grow their career opportunities by pursuing the role of project management.
- **Project managers** who need some guidance to better understand leadership development and execute their position.
- **Managers and owners** who are looking for some assistance in helping their team members develop in their skills and responsibilities in project management.

Most of us grew up hearing, "You can do it."

Which is true, you can do it.

The question is, will you?

---

[5] Isaacson, J. (2020) *The Bruce Lee Mindset for Business.* Cleanfax Magazine. https://cleanfax.com/management/bruce-lee-mindset-prioritize-focus/

Bruce added what I call rapid practicality to his habit of focus. Something that he said applies so adeptly to career development in property restoration and the skilled trades is, "Knowing is not enough, we must apply. Willing is not enough, we must do."

- Some of you need some more knowledge to take the next steps.
- Some of you need to stop sitting on the knowledge you have acquired and put it to work for you.
- Some of you need to come down a notch on your ego so that you can build some real credibility before you can achieve.

I am excited to hear about those of you who needed a kick in the butt to gear up and scale higher on your life challenges.

If you are reading this book, you are taking Baby Steps[6] in the right direction. You can do it, what are you waiting for?

---

[6] Warning, I am a "90's Kid" so a lot of my references will inherently make sense to Geriatric Millennials like myself but will require some context for anyone outside of this generational distinction. Baby Steps is a reference from the movie, *What About Bob?* With Bill Murray. I used it as a reference for my article *Baby Steps and Estimating 2020* in Restoration & Remediation (R&R) Magazine - https://www.randrmagonline.com/articles/89249-baby-steps-and-estimating-in-2021. I encourage you to watch the movie, or you can check out this clip from the movie - https://www.youtube.com/watch?v=IqTy3Bc8m_s

Part 1

What Are You Waiting For?

The author, an average restorer, and his above-average family

CHAPTER 1

The Will to Prepare to Win

The will to win is not nearly so important
as the will to prepare to win.
Vince Lombardi

A key transition in my career happened while I was working past the feeling of being stuck in mid-level management to the more positive outlook of being planted in the middle of the organization. Developing your career is an ongoing process and a growth mindset requires constant vigilance. The question we all have to be asking is, what separates the dreamers from the doers?

Most people would say that they have the will to succeed. But, as famed Green Bay Packers coach and the namesake for the NFL Super Bowl trophy, Vince Lombardi said, "The will to win is not nearly so important as the will to prepare to win." Preparation is the differentiator. Through this book, I will try to help you develop a framework, a playbook of sorts, that you can utilize to continue to move your plan of action for personal and professional development down the field.

One day I was at a second-hand bookstore and I stumbled across the biography of one of the early head football coaches of my home team, the Seattle Seahawks. Like many coaches, Chuck Knox was known for his Knoxisms. He came into town at the helm of a losing team and took them to the AFC Championship in their first year. A feat that would not be repeated until their first Superbowl appearance under Mike Holmgren in 2005/2006.

Knox recalls that in his younger years he was in a St. Patrick's day parade when someone remarked that he and his friends looked like they were ready for anything. Chuck recalls that his dad responded, "Yeah, ready for anything, but prepared for nothing[7]." This echoes what Lombardi stated and should be something we take to heart if we want to achieve our dreams or be counted among the winners.

This book sparked in me an interest in reading biographies from coaches I respected. Think about it, the teams that win, especially those that sustain a championship caliber competitive edge, are not always the most talented teams but the teams that play together. I wanted to glean how these coaches were able to get through to convince millionaires that it was in their best interest to work as a whole rather than just pad their personal stats.

Like me, you may have rooted for years for a team that consistently underperformed. During the Knox years, there was a Monday Night Football game between the Seahawks and the Oakland Raiders with World Wrestling Entertainment (WWE) level hype for a showdown between two marquee players. Brian "The Boz" Bosworth was an All-American linebacker from Oklahoma University that was supposed to take Seattle to the promised land. He would have the task of stopping another highly touted rookie, running back Bo Jackson.

What many may not remember is that Bo Jackson was not yet an icon, he was the rookie back up to former MVP Marcus Allen. Bo opened the game with a fumble. In the anticipation of the clash between the two rookies, The Boz had declared that he would contain Jackson. Not only did Bosworth fail to deliver on his jeers, when the two squared up head-to-head Bo dragged Brian into the endzone. This play was the cherry on

---

[7] Farnsworth, C. (2018, May 13) *Remembering Former Seahawks Coach Chuck Knox And His Many "Knoxisms"*. Seahawks.Com
https://www.seahawks.com/news/remembering-former-seahawks-coach-chuck-knox-and-his-many-knoxisms

top of a Monday night breakout party for Jackson, who reached a then team record 221 rushing yards on their way to a 37-14 rout of the Hawks.

Like many teams and professionals who say they want to win (or be winners), Brian looked the part and even had great success while in college. The Boz had a pretty shell but ultimately failed to launch. Bosworth played 17 more games in the NFL while Jackson went on to be one of the most iconic players in history and a household name with his "Bo Knows" Nike campaign.

Bo Jackson was a baseball player who also played football. In his breakout season, the Raiders allowed him to complete his season with the Kansas City Royals prior to reporting for football duties. You could say that Jackson's football career was his side hustle. He learned from a master craftsman while initially sharing responsibilities with Hall of Famer Marcus Allen and continued to hone his craft.

If you want to prepare to win, I lay out many of the roles and responsibilities of project management in Chapter 3 so that you can work on those skills. Maybe you have done all of the things that people think they need to do, but you rarely have an opportunity to put those resources to the test. In property restoration, this might be the technician that has several certifications but hasn't made any progress with promotions. You are on the team but you aren't getting the ball. You need to be ready like Bo was to seize on your opportunities.

In order to properly prepare to win, you will need to face the facts of your current level of skill, conditioning, and aptitude for the game that you want to play. On one extreme, you don't want to be so confident (cocky) that you get run over when your opportunity comes. Humility is part of the process, but many aspiring professionals allow an unhealthy fear of failure to hold them back from taking necessary risks. We will discuss some resources to address this reality in the next chapter.

If you are reading this book, you likely are a weekend warrior who understands that in order to get anywhere you have to put the extra work in to create your chances for growth. You have invested in resources to help you tune up your mindset and habits so that you are better prepared to win. Whether that is taking courses after hours, reading growth-minded books on your breaks, and setting aside time for personal development on weekends.

You know the hard truth that life is about opportunity, not convenience. You know that if you want to achieve, you will have to make your own progress. I do my best to help you get your vehicle on the right track by helping you build skills for managing projects and people.

If you want to be a winner, you need to develop and consistently practice winning habits. Brian Hoyer, who was a back-up for then six-time Super Bowl champion quarterback Tom Brady, noted how **dedicated Tom was to practicing the basics**[8]. "Being around it makes you a better quarterback," Hoyer said. "You watch what he does and how focused he is with fundamentals -- front foot, shoulders, eyes, all those things. I remember going back to my first stint here (2009-2011) and I felt like I became such a better fundamental passer just by watching him and doing the same drills. He's obsessed with it."

In career development I believe there are three fundamental "plays" that you must master if you want to build a foundation for growth. These are the same three characteristics that I look for in potential hires. If you can bring these three elements to the table, you can learn to do anything. The will to prepare to win, or to be a winner, is built on the attributes of being honest, hardworking, and willing to learn. .

---

[8] Reiss, M. (219, January 6) *Tom Brady Spends Time With Throwing Coach During Playoff Bye Week* . ESPN https://www.espn.com/blog/new-england-patriots/post/_/id/4816289/tom-brady-spends-time-with-throwing-coach-during-playoff-bye-week

Play #1: Be Honest

> Potential (n.) *latent qualities or abilities that may be developed and lead to future success or usefulness.*

You may say to yourself, "I could do that," and maybe you are right. Perhaps your grandma is right and you have the potential to be something or someone great. But remember this, potential is worthless if it is not developed. You can sit on potential all your life or you can put yourself to the test. You have to start by being honest with yourself and earnest in the process of proving your potential into reality.

As a member of the Industry Panel at the Disaster Conference[9] hosted by Purdue University, industry founding father, Cliff Zlotnik shared this thought, "Situational experience is likely of greater importance than a certificate or card that implies competency." He is saying that there is no substitute for hands-on experience. You only gain situational experience by being in situations that test your abilities above and beyond their current levels.

Many current project managers think that they could manage a project of any size. While that may be true, there is a difference between confidence and arrogance. Cliff was asked, what is the minimum level of qualification a contractor should have before responding to catastrophic events (i.e. large scale losses), and he remarked, "Having done at least one previous project of the same type of peril of similar severity. The greater amount of situational experience the better." Again, nothing prepares you better for the role than the responsibilities of the role.

So, what do you do if you have never done it? You must be honest about your lack of experience and source means to

---

[9] Consigli, G. (2015, January 24) *Best Practices: Demolition, Restoration, and Reconstruction.* Purdue.
https://docs.lib.purdue.edu/cgi/viewcontent.cgi?referer=https://www.goo gle.com/&httpsredir=1&article=1034&context=i3r2

acquire relevant skills and experiences. As Cliff noted, you may have certifications that you think qualify you for advancement, but you have to understand that they are only part of the puzzle. Similar to a college degree, you can be "educated" to the gills, but if you don't have common sense or the ability to apply what you have learned to your unique situation, the letters behind your name have no value in the workplace.

Before you can grow you will need to admit where you are. There is a temptation to surround yourself with yes-people, those who will tell you what you want to hear. This will lead to confirmation bias, where you are not getting important feedback and criticism for your personal progress. You need to be honest with yourself and you need people who are rooting for you without sugar-coating reality.

Play #2: Be Hardworking

On a rowing team, the oars persons face the rear or stern of the craft. The only member of the team that does not row is called the coxswain. They alone sit facing the bow and see where the boat is headed. It may seem like it should be easy to get a bunch of well-trained athletes into a long narrow boat and be competitive. In his amazing book, *Boys in the Boat*[10], about the men's rowing team from the University of Washington that won the 1936 Olympics, Daniel James Brown remarks,

> *"What mattered more than how hard a man rowed was how well everything he did in the boat harmonized with what the other fellows were doing. And a man couldn't harmonize with his crewmates unless he opened his heart to them. He had to care about his crew."*

Brown helps the reader to understand how important the interpersonal dynamics and the harmony of the team were to the overall performance. He also demonstrates that without a coxswain, a powerful rowing team is not in sync or in rhythm

---

[10] Brown, D. (2013) Boys In The Boat: Nine Americans and Their Epic Quest
https://www.danieljamesbrown.com/books/the-boys-in-the-boat

even though everyone is driving forward. Similar to project management, the cox is responsible for steering the vessel, keeping the team member safe and on rhythm.

If you are honest and hardworking, it will be difficult for anyone to speak poorly of you. The position of project management may get you out of the field, no longer rowing, but that does not mean that you will not be required to work as hard as your team member to keep your ship on course. The coxswain may be the closest literal definition of leadership. To lead-the-ship, you will need to earn trust and connect with your teammates on a personal and professional level if you are going to be effective.

If you are honest and hardworking, it will be difficult for your supervisors to ignore you. As I have said before, I know that I was initially able to build some recognition as a mold remediation technician by doing my work well, being thorough with my documentation, and ensuring that my paperwork was legible.

You will learn to recognize that rowing hard isn't the only measure of progress. You must have oars in the water before you can go anywhere, but to ensure that you are not on an endless loop, you need vision. You need a rhythm for your personal development and you will need collaboration if you are going to build a strong team to help you achieve your organizational goals.

If you are spinning in circles or you can't quite get the rhythm down, these types of setbacks aren't for lack of effort, but for lack of vision for the steps to your destination and a lack of rhythm to optimize your labor. In business, you need to clarify the benchmarks that enable you to honestly track your progress. Similarly, when you are working as a team, it is important to clarify the vision and the goals, otherwise, well-intentioned people may find that they are all rowing with one hundred percent effort and yet as an organization, they are not making progress.

Play #3: Be Willing to Learn

My favorite proverb goes, "I applied my heart to what I observed and learned a lesson from what I saw[11]." I have to constantly remind myself to shut up and listen, especially when I am sitting with people who have forgotten more restoration truths than I am likely to obtain. In the search for doing things the right way, the internet has democratized information. This means that there are few barriers to anyone sharing their thoughts. This can be helpful but it has also created a lot of noise which can make it difficult to discern between harmful ideas and quality content.

In 2007 the Association of Specialists in Cleaning and Restoration (ASCR) rebranded as the Restoration Industry Association (RIA). At that point in history, the group was going strong at 60 years old and also unveiled their first motto, *"We make it better. We promise."* Reflecting on this time, Pete Consigli and Cliff Zlotnik cited the late Martin "Marty" L. King who characterized what we all do as "the business and profession of damage repair[12]."

The duo expanded on these mandates noting, *"The business of restoration is finishing projects on time and on budget while satisfying the stakeholders, often under adverse situations while remaining professional and making a profit."* This description also serves as the roles and responsibilities of a project manager. Finishing (1) on time, (2) on budget, and (3) satisfying stakeholders, all while upholding the highest standards for ethics and safety.

Intentional restorers, like yourself, have the high calling of "making it better" from wherever you are in the restoration ecosystem. We arrive at the worst times in our clients lives and we have the great opportunity to bring some assurance that we are there to "make it better". Your development should include learning about our rich history as many of the best practices in

---

[11] Proverbs 24:32 NIV

[12] Consigli, P. & Zlotnik, C. (2017, October 26) *Connecting Mission With Motto.* Cleaning & Restoration. https://www.restorationindustry.org/cleaning-and-restoration/connecting-mission-motto

our industry remain as true as they were when they were first being tried and tested over decades.

If you are reading this book, I would like to assume that means you are willing to learn. If you are going to "apply your heart to what you observe" you want to be around those whom you can observe doing things right and well. I would encourage you to learn from the best you can find. Surround yourself with some of those who have *been there and done that* (BTDT), they can help you to see that in order to move forward we often do ourselves a favor to look back at what has already been done. You also want to be around those who are still there and still doing that as you can work together to address modern variations of age-old problems.

Keep yourself in check by putting your career into perspective with the rich history of property restoration. Speaking of the value of organizations like the RIA, Cliff Zlotnik said, "The shortcut to growth is community." Go where there is momentum and find out how you can help. I have been encouraged by the momentum that the Advocacy and Government Affairs Committee (AGA) has been building by having earnest conversations with role players at Xactimate, Third Party Consultants (TPCs), and Third Party Administrators (TPAs).

As long as the RIA continues its commitment to hearing and representing restorers, we will continue to see momentum build. Those that are honest, hardworking, and willing to learn would do well to uphold and connect with fellow restorers that uphold high standards and best practices such as those expressed in the RIA Code of Ethics[13]:

As providers of property damage restoration, remediation, and cleaning services to the public, we subscribe to the following principles in our relationships with customers, employees, and business associates:

---

[13] Restoration Industry Association (2006, June 20) *Restoration Industry Association (RIA) Code of Ethics.* https://www.restorationindustry.org/RIA-code-of-ethics

- To treat our customers and their property with care and respect.
- To provide professional service in accordance with high standards of practice that will, where possible, restore the customer's property to its pre-damaged or pre-soiled condition.
- To operate in a manner consistent with ethical principles and sound business practices.
- To be proficient in our work through ongoing participation in education and training.
- To provide our customers with accurate information concerning the scope of work required and its costs, maintaining strict impartiality in our professional opinions.
- To disclose to the customer any connection we may have to their insurer or any other interested third party.

Put In The Work

I had the pleasure of supervising David Smith (Eugene, OR) and seeing him progressively develop his skills. Sometimes all you need is someone to believe in you or at least give you a shot. David took each opportunity that I gave him and kept asking for more. He grew from a disciplined technician into a thriving project manager. When we were co-managing, even though I was technically his boss, we built a high-functioning multi-disciplined team.

Currently, David is recovering from high volume program work and doing well working in an adjacent industry. As he reflected on his time in project management, he said, "It is one of those positions that you do not know what you are getting into because of all the work that takes place behind the scenes. One aspect of project management that does not get much mention for those entering the position is the preparation of the work."

If you want to be a project manager, you have to prepare for the role. If you want to succeed as a project manager you will need to recognize that, "Every aspect of being a project manager requires preparation and planning." David says this preparation of the work includes, "Everything from scheduling job walks, ordering materials, and scheduling manpower. Pieces do not just fall into the right place, you have to put them there."

Both David and I enjoy sports analogies, and even though he was born and raised in Oregon, he is also a Seahawks fan. Perhaps this helped us to work well together, the shared anguish of rooting for a losing team for so long. David said, "Project management is like being a quarterback. You are in charge of communicating to your team the plan and how it is going to be executed."

While we have talked about the will to win versus the will to prepare to win, David points to one of the biggest busts in recent NFL history, JaMarcus Russell. David says, "He had amazing talent but did not want to do the work. Russell's team caught on. Coaches worked to help him by having him study certain coverages to prepare for the week's upcoming game." Whatever the team tried, they could not seem to get through to the young talent.

To test his commitment to preparation, David recalls that the coaches gave him a blank tape to review[14]. When the QB came in for practice they asked him if he watched the film. Russell's response was that he had and he was out of the league a couple of years later. Another talented player who wasn't willing to put in the total work to take themselves and their team to the next level.

David contrasts this with the quarterback that everyone loves to hate, Tom Brady. Remember, he was a 6th round pick that was

[14] Wells, A. (2018, November 4) *David Diehl: Raiders Gave JaMarcus Russell Blank Tapes to See If QB Watched Film.* Bleacher Report. https://bleacherreport.com/articles/2804453-david-diehl-raiders-gave-jamarcus-russell-blank-tapes-to-see-if-qb-watched-film

not supposed to amount to anything. Yet, Brady has gone on to win 7 super bowls and with those numbers it is hard not to argue that he is one of the greatest of all time. The underdogs, with an unquenchable thirst, can outwork those that "look the part "and who may even be more talented. than them

David commented, "Most people say he is extremely competitive but what really stands out about him is his preparation. From his diet to the playbook, he is relentless in his preparation. Brady has been known to not only study his playbook in-and-out but that of the opposing defense as well. This extra preparation allows him to make the necessary adjustments to put himself and his team in a position to consistently be successful."

When we were working together to schedule mitigation, you have to recognize that you cannot plan for every event but you have to always be prepared for incoming emergencies. Our response should NEVER be chaotic. You plan your schedule to address your current work as well as hold contingencies for incoming work. David says, "Preparation is critical if you want to be a project manager. Without preparation you are leaving your success up to others. You have to be willing to put in the prep work, even when no one is looking."

Prepare to win by winning where you are. Chuck Knox often told his players, "Play the hand that you're dealt." If you want to advance in anything the playbook is simple:

- ## Be honest
- ## Be hardworking
- ## Be willing to learn

These characteristics do not guarantee success but they will give you a helluva chance. You can't cry about the opportunities you aren't getting, you have to get out on the field and make your plays.

Prepare to win and go get you some.

CHAPTER 2

What's Your Big But?

Everyone I know has a big but.
Come on Simone, let's talk about your big but.
Pee-Wee Herman

If you say that you want to be a project manager, follow up by asking yourself, why aren't you? If your response to your own inquisition is that no one has given you the opportunity, you should slap yourself and remember that no one is going to. Waiting around for something cool to happen is not going to get you across the goal line. We will be diving deeper into what it looks like to prepare to win in the position of project management, but first, you have to conduct some honest self-evaluation.

Pursuing a growth mindset requires asking difficult questions of yourself. One of the best questions you can ask yourself comes from an unlikely source; Pee-Wee Herman. It has been brought to my attention that some of our younger readers may not know who this is. As a Geriatric Millennial, Pee-Wee was a staple of the Saturday morning experience on his show Pee Wee's Playhouse which ran from 1986 through 1991.[15]

In 1985 Paul Ruebens, who plays Pee-Wee, wrote a script for the film Pee-Wee's Big Adventure. While it had some success at the box office, it developed a cult following as well as launched the directorial career of Tim Burton and introduced the world to composer Danny Elfman.

---

[15] If you like controversy, you may be interested in the events that led to, or at least contributed towards, the rapid end of the show.

In the film, Pee-Wee lost his most prized possession, his one-of-a-kind custom 1940's Schwinn bicycle. He suspects his nemesis Francis stole it from him out of jealousy. We wouldn't have to dig very deep to draw parallels between developing your career, working through adversity, and understanding that not everyone wants you to succeed. But I want to draw upon the great quote and subsequent application that we opened this chapter with.

Amidst a great personal setback, our main character launches out on an unknown journey in search of his missing treasure. Some people help Pee-Wee on his quest, many of whom become unexpected allies. Meanwhile, several of his friends fail to empathize with his loss or provide any constructive input. Take note, not everyone will understand what you are trying to accomplish. You have to know when to receive and when to push past criticism.

Midway through the film, Pee-Wee is particularly down in spirit as he has learned that the Alamo does not have a basement. You may ask yourself, why did he think this structure had a basement and why would Jon include this random factoid in this chapter? I use this moment to poke another barb in the cult of personal and professional development.

Mr. Herman consulted an "industry professional" who was not a practitioner in his field (a bit of a dig there). The "coach" he hired sounded wise but gave poor advice for an exorbitant fee (another dig). Pee-Wee thinks he is doing the right thing, he does the typical thing by consulting his friends, engaging in [the late 80's equivalent of] social media, and he even seeks out "professional" advice. Take note, he has to learn to cut through the noise in order to keep his mission moving forward.

He sets out on a mission to re-acquire the one thing he values more than anything. He craves success in his pursuit, but he is failing. His poor results are not for lack of effort. While he is distraught and feeling hopeless, Herman takes a job washing dishes in a dive restaurant to finance his debts. This is poignant as I know I have had to hold second jobs, earn additional income, and spend hours outside of my paid time, to pursue my ambitions.

To cheer him up, his new friend Simone takes him up to a movie viewing area in the head of a dinosaur statue. Simone shares her dreams of traveling the world and Pee Wee drops an insightful line that also serves as the opening salvo of this chapter. He says, "Everyone I know has a big but. Come on Simone, let's talk about your big but."

The ability to answer this question is what separates the doers from the dreamers. You may have the will to win and even taken steps to prepare to win, BUT. You have a dream and you have a "big but" that keeps you from venturing out to pursue that vision. Or you have taken some initial steps, but you have hit a wall and are struggling to push through. For Simone, it's a lumberjack of a man named Andy, her boyfriend, who is holding her back.

There is no supergene, no special training or magic pill that makes you an achiever. A growth-minded professional is one who has identified a dream and/or a vision and they are taking steps, no matter how small, to pursue that dream. A doer must face the opposition from within; the concerns of those who care for them, as well as the assault from those who oppose them, and continue to move forward (even if it's an inch at a time).

- The question is not whether there is a risk of failure but whether you will be nimble enough to navigate and pick yourself up after you face the multiple obstacles and setbacks that arise as you chase your dreams.

- The question is not whether you are the best able, most qualified, or expert enough to launch out upon your path, but whether you are willing to work your butt off, always be learning, and remain true to your values as you meet the obstacles between you and the end of your road.

My friend, author, and podcast host[16], Josh Zolin says it this way, "No matter what career you choose, true success is only earned by putting in hard work, getting up after countless failures, and doing sh*t you don't want to do." As we said in the last chapter, the playbook to prepare to win is rather simple: be honest, be hardworking, and be willing to learn. This does not guarantee success but it puts you in a position to seize upon your opportunities. The growth-minded achievers roam among us and if you want to be counted among them, you will have to fight against the fear of failure.

In my experience, it isn't as much the risk of failure itself, but the fear of failure, or *atychiphobia*[17] that holds most back from having the faith in themselves to grab life by the horns and enjoy the tumultuous ride. In that head of the dinosaur, Pee-Wee is encouraged by his new friend. Their discussion also inspires Simone to rise above her fears and to buy a bus ticket. She takes the first steps to pursue her dreams. Herman, on the other hand, is chased down by her former boyfriend Andy.

In the moment of the chase, Pee-Wee is scrambling from certain death. This unplanned run for his life leads him to his next opportunity, effectively jolting him from his depression and back onto his own journey. Herman faced setbacks. You understand that life isn't about getting over one hurdle and then the race is over but rather continuing to rise over hurdle after hurdle. We work hard. We are always learning.

When we can work hard and learn from our experiences we uncover simple truths that change our mindset and affect our habits. Unexpected allies like Simone can encourage us to move forward while we filter out the noise from hack professionals and naysayers. We want to shorten our DANG learning curve without dismissing the importance of learning through our journey.

---

[16] Check out the book and podcast by the same name, *Blue Is The New White*

[17] Isaacson, J.(2016, November 29) *How to Overcome the Fear of Failure.* http://www.izvents.com/words/how-to-overcome-fear-of-failure

If you don't want to get left behind with the I-would-buts, there are two limiting mindsets that you have to confront. I believe these two are the most common: (1) thinking too highly of yourself and (2) thinking too lowly of yourself. Both of these perspectives lead to limiting statements such as:

- How often have you said, "I would do this-or-that, but…" and failed to launch?
- How often have you started out on your journey but when you meet resistance you hesitate to take the next step? Saying, "I would move forward with this-or-that, but…" and stall your momentum through analysis paralysis.
- Have you been in a position of leadership, faced with daily decisions and said, "I would do this-or-that, but…" and you allowed fear of failure to prevent you from action?

If you think you are hot stuff and this means that you aren't willing to learn and don't put the hard work in, let's be honest; you're not going to move onward or upward. Shut your ego down and go back to Chapter 1. Success is not guaranteed and nothing will be handed to you. Often this bravado is masking deeper-seated fears. Don't let your yeah-buts get in your way or allow the fear of failure deter you from trying.

Fail. Learn. Repeat.

The fear of failure will hold you back if you feed it. You should always assess risks but the fear of failure should not have the final say. If you are tempted to say, "I would, but…I am scared to fail," let me share a time from my career when I had to start over. Starting over is usually what you do after you fail. I will share some of my story that proves that you can rebound after falling flat on your face.

I began my property restoration career in beautiful Ventura, California. I became a mold guy In the midst of the mold-is-gold era. I was fortunate to be teamed up with a great leader and was able to help build our remediation department into a thriving and profitable division within our full-service company. When I was first offered a role in leadership, I responded that I would, but... I was pursuing a career in law enforcement.

I loved what I did as well as the people I was working with. Eventually, I understood that the doors in criminal justice were not opening while opportunities were continuing to be presented to me in property restoration. As the sage *Forrest Gump*[18] once said, "I may not be a smart man, but I know..." an open door when I see one. We had a prior assistant manager that didn't understand our team dynamics or how to lead. When the position became available again I took it because I didn't want another knucklehead to ruin what we had built.

We eventually moved up the West Coast to Oregon. I was surprised by how many companies did not return my call or offer to interview me. I was sure that I had an impressive resume for a young person. I was applying to companies from the same franchise line that I had worked in so I was particularly disappointed thinking that somehow being a part of the global "family" would at least warrant an interview, but it didn't.

In later years, someone who worked for me was on staff for one of the companies that I applied to. This person informed me that when my resume came through the owners laughed, remarking, "Who spends that many years doing only mold remediation?" In my not-so-humble opinion, they missed out on a great opportunity to hire a motivated team member because of their limited perspective. They didn't know anyone in Oregon that was doing that level of mold remediation but they also didn't comprehend the scale of the market in California compared to theirs for some reason.

---

[18] If you don't know the name Forrest Gump, look it up. You can also watch the Oscar Award winning "documentary" about his life.

I think this is a learning moment for anyone applying to a new company or market. You have to understand who you are seeking to work with and communicate in terms that they can relate to. I discussed this topic with Andrew Golkin on *Benchmarks of Growth*[19]. Andrew joined his father's franchise when the Great Recession significantly reduced his engineering business. He saw an opportunity to help his family's company become full-service, meaning offering both mitigation and repairs, but had to learn the skills from the ground up.

One attribute that we agreed that a restorer should be proud of, and has become a catchword, is resilience. Nearly every situation that we respond to is something new and challenging. An employer would be hard-pressed to put you in a situation where you wouldn't be able to respond with a level of unparalleled calm (the chill). This calm under pressure is a characteristic that most employers seek and many in restoration have this nailed. The ability to scan, plan, execute, and document your work will help you to be a successful technician as well as a thriving project manager. We will talk more about this acronym SPEeD in the next chapter.

In my move to Oregon, because there was a disconnect between who I was applying to and how I had presented myself, the doors to something I felt I knew were not opening. I was not going to be able to transfer from known to known. But, I am thankful that it didn't happen the way I planned. I found an opportunity that would put my abilities to the test. I was hired by a construction company in Salem, Oregon to start a restoration division. They had dipped their toes in insurance work and saw an opportunity to grow this part of the business. We were able to make some great connections and rapidly grow a restoration division into a revenue center.

This is where I first learned you can be independent and you can get insurance estimates approved without the use of Xactimate. As I grew the division I was asked to take on a greater role which included overseeing repairs for the whole company. Things were

---

[19] The DYOJO Podcast, Episode 64

going well, but the market started to take a turn downward and there were some underlying issues within the organization so I pursued another uncomfortable dream, to go out on my own.

The owner and I are still friends to this day and he helped me get my entrepreneurial start. Things went well for the first few years but then the recession hit. In 2009 I went from regular growth and thinking I was just starting to do well, to the phone being dead; no work coming in. Deafening silence. For about a year I did whatever I could to put food on the table. Including working at a beef jerky factory and Big 5 (a regional discount sports retailer) due to the kindness of a family friend.

It seemed like the stars were aligning after a long period of scraping by. Finally, there was a job listing for an estimator role at a national company that I had initially applied to when I first moved to Oregon. Our family was so excited when I received an invite for an interview but I was devastated when I didn't get the position.

Then there was a big BUT. About a week later the manager called with another idea. I was invited to meet at "the Applebees" (that statement still makes me laugh to this day) to discuss a different role. Long story short, I would not be starting over completely but I would be back in the industry, working as the mitigation manager for a local branch. Many of the principles that I share come from this period.

It wasn't long before I was being given additional roles and responsibilities, but most of those came because I pushed myself to find opportunities and drive myself forward. If you think of yourself too highly, you are likely to miss opportunities because you are waiting for them to come to you. Don't let your I would-buts hold you back from taking risks.

Embrace Your Suck

If on the other hand, you are honest, hardworking, and willing to learn but you struggle with self-doubt, I would recommend you read Rachel Stewart's book *Unqualified Success*. Rachel reminds us that the key to success starts with understanding, "The only qualification to get better: **being willing to suck when you start**."

The author shares insights from her own journey as well as many relevant principles that will be helpful in shortening your DANG learning curve.

I had the pleasure of meeting a young man who had some experience being a write-and-run project manager for a landscaping company. While he didn't have much training and the company he had worked in did not have a defined process, I could see he had potential.

While Greg is doing well now, he literally learned the industry from scratch. He is proof that if you listen, learn (even when someone is yelling at you), and apply the basics you can make a run at career advancement in the skilled trades. At many points in the process, Greg had but-moments. My role in helping him develop his potential was to provide the space for learning from failure; encouraging him to embrace his suck.

One awesome story that came out of this period brought us into contact with a nationwide property manager that specialized in large-scale apartment complexes. The company that Greg and I were working for had really upset one of the high-up West Coast representatives of this particular management company. As hard as our company had tried to reach out and repair the relationship, this person had blacklisted our organization and there had been no response for several months.

Greg was still green in learning the industry and being a project manager, but because he did the core things well he was able to seize on an opportunity. A call came in for a property that literally had floating feces in an apartment complex. Greg could have said, I would, but...I don't have any experience in Category 3 work.

Instead, Greg made the appointment and we went out there together. We discussed the process on the way to the job and he took the lead in the conversation with the property manager and the maintenance lead. I was there to assist but this was an excellent growth opportunity. We recommended a specific scope of work that the onsite representatives did not want to approve. As most know, this would involve removing the affected flooring and cutting the walls up two feet so that we could decontaminate the structure. We made sure to thoroughly explain and document our recommendations as well as their refusal of service.

The next day, the right-hand person for the high-level representative that had blacklisted our company called us rather mad. Greg could have said, I would, but...I am not qualified to talk to this person. It was very rewarding to hear Greg confidently say, "We would love to forward you the signed documentation that your onsite representatives refused the services that you are now demanding. We can also forward you the follow-up emails to the maintenance person and the property manager recalling our recommendation that these services should be provided."

The person on the other line said, "I will call you right back." Within minutes we had a call from the maintenance person humbly requesting that we return to the property and perform the work that we had originally recommended. From this point forward we were able to say in this, and similar situations, "Our understanding is that person X has stated this protocol is to be followed for this type of scenario."

This situation proves that with the right mindset and habits you can begin to develop professional relationships and build a positive reputation in the market, even if you are a new project manager and have very little experience in the industry. Embrace your suck by challenging yourself to face your fears rather than succumb to the fear of failure. Don't make things more complicated than they are, learn to do it right, do it efficiently, and find ways to do it excellently.

As an important side note, I am not saying that you should lie about what you do or don't know by making something up. Fake it until you make it should be understood as a means of self-confidence, not an operational procedure. Being confident in yourself and your ability to learn something is VERY different from being confident in your ignorance and pretending you know what to do. In the event that you are in a situation where you don't know what to do, there is a way to approach your lack of knowledge while maintaining confidence.

As Greg did in the example above, you will do yourself a lot of good by being honest with what you don't know. I think you can build more trust with a customer and your team by being honest. That said, we should NEVER tell someone, "I don't know." This is a pet peeve of mine. I would make sure that anyone we hired knew my position on this statement. Whether it was a new hire or a temporary worker, I NEVER wanted to hear someone say those three words. This does not mean that we lie, that is actually worse.

When confronted with a question that you don't know the answer to, simply respond, "That is an excellent question, let me get back to you on that," or, "Let me get my supervisor engaged in this discussion so that we can better source a solution." It's ok to not know the answer to something but you do not want to feed the fires of doubt with clients or team members. Rather, you want to be honest while acknowledging that the answer can be found.

Give them a timeline, for example, "I will have an answer for you by tomorrow." Making this simple change in your approach will help you maintain trust in your competency while not pretending to be something that you aren't. Progress comes through failure, not by avoiding it. Your current status, or your prior shortcomings, should not cause you to believe less in yourself. Don't think of yourself more lowly than you ought.

When I was a write-and-run project manager with a national brand in Oregon, we had an amazing experience working with the Eugene Mission. Write-and-run refers to someone who writes (estimates) their own estimates and scopes of work and subsequently runs (project manages) their own jobs. While I was the project manager/estimator I had a project manager/superintendent. So many of the terms can be interchangeable. My partner, David, and I divided our skill sets to tackle our heavy workload.

With regards to the Mission, I had been working to start up a facilities group in our local market. I reached out to the Mission in a professional capacity, as well as for personal reasons. It just so happened that I had scheduled a walk-through with the director about a week before they had a large fire event in their kitchen. Like many things in my life, being lucky means being in the right place at the right time and having some help from above. If you're never out there hustling, trying to make things happen for yourself and your team, you won't get "lucky" that often.

We received the call to assess their damage and help with the immediate response. There are so many great stories I could tell from this one project, but I remember how proud I was that our team was called. I KNEW these awesome people were in good hands (no insurance pun intended), and how skillfully our team worked in this unique environment to move the project forward while keeping as much of their facility operational as possible.

The story I want to share, that relates to personal growth, comes from a few experiences after hours. I was invited to share during chapel time. Some of these intimate experiences were with my young family, some by myself, and another with a good friend who was brave enough to step way outside of their comfort zone to share their story with a room full of strangers.

One thought we shared came from a letter written by a mentor, a man named Paul, to his friends in Rome, "I say to every one of you: Do not think of yourself more highly than you ought, but rather think of yourself with sober judgment[20]." If you're not a fan of the Bible, I think you can still appreciate the poetry in this statement. Thinking of yourself with sober judgment means being sedate and rational. To grow beyond our circumstances, our ego can hold us back but so can a false sense of humility.

We want to be open-minded and measure ourselves as objectively as possible. It's not what you feel but what you have demonstrated that lays the foundation for your potential. It doesn't help you to achieve your goals if you think too highly of yourself. But, this does not mean that we respond with the other extreme by thinking of ourselves too lowly. Whether you think you have messed up in the past, or even if you have the track record to prove it, today can be the first step forward to a new mindset and new habits. I would gladly discuss the faith elements in a private setting, but if it helps, I think this tells us that the big guy is rooting for you.

---

[20] Romans 12:3 NIV

The point of adding this story is not to convince you of anything other than to encourage you to understand, as we tried to do with a room full of our friends, is that being humble doesn't mean you tear yourself down. Each day you wake up and you do your best to move onward and upward.

- If your past performance has been less than satisfactory, today is a new day.
- If people want to point to former errors, you will have to work that much harder to prove to yourself and demonstrate to others that you are ready to help row the ship in the right direction.

As you make progress, use sober, or objective measures to track your progress. Don't let your past or fear of failure cause you to say, I would but…

Be Proactive

One job listing for project management contained this description of the type of person that their company was looking for, "A proactive individual who will work directly with sales staff and homeowners to move restoration projects from start to finish." What stands out to you? Being proactive. A proactive person is not an I would, but… person and if you are going to be a strong project manager, you will have to constantly battle feelings of inadequacy and self-doubt. So, it would be to your benefit to continue to master what you are doing now and learn as much as you can about the roles and responsibilities of the position that you are pursuing so that you can be proactive in preparing to win.

I can remember early on, a teammate of mine expressed, "When they pay me more, I will do more." I told that person, "I think you have it backward. First, you show them that you can do more and then the increased opportunities and pay will follow." They didn't like that but guess who was promoted shortly after and who remained where they were? It should be noted that this comes with the qualification that if your supervisor keeps adding and adding to your responsibilities and isn't providing you with opportunities for advancement, you are getting taken advantage of and it may be time to have a conversation and/or look elsewhere.

Go as far as you can, by learning all that you can, in your current organization. Don't be afraid to ask, "What would I need to do in order to prove that I can take on a next-level role in this company?" Proactive means that you take the initiative to identify the education, knowledge, skills, and qualification necessary to empower yourself to take the next step. Most of the advancements in my career have come after I have taken on more responsibilities to demonstrate that I am capable of being successful with an advanced role.

I was able to ask some of these questions of a large employer in the Phoenix market. Josh Zolin and I were able to share some nuggets from our career origin stories, first on his podcast, *Blue is the New White*[21], and then on my podcast[22]. Josh started working in his father's company and learned the business from the ground up. I asked him what were some of the habits that helped him to grow as a repair technician, a project manager, and now the owner and architect of the growth of Windy City Restaurant Equipment Repair.

Josh would tell you, as an aspiring project manager, "First and foremost is consistency. Consistency is the basis of all growth and can be applied to any area of your life." He builds upon this perspective by outlining a few additional habits that he has found helpful in his journey and will help put you in a position to make and seize upon your opportunities:

- Always trying to be at least 1% better tomorrow. Lift a little bit more, learn a little bit more, help a little bit more, etc.
- Have a vision of where you want to be. Not how you're going to get there, but do your best to envision what it will look like when you've mastered that task, gotten that job, built that company, etc. The

---

[21] Blue is the New White, Episode 87

[22] The DYOJO Podcast, Episode 61

vision will change, and that's fine, but it should always be in the back of your mind.

- Do what is right, not what's easy. It's probably a little cliché by now, but not any less true. The hardest decisions are often the most impactful.
- Also, never stop looking for opportunities. Never be complacent. Never let yourself believe that you've failed or succeeded 100% because neither is true until you speak the words. So, if you choose to speak to them, you better be ready for what they bring with them.

As you pursue project management, do you know what you are getting yourself into?

633

Bridging the Gap between Old School Restorers and The Next Generation

Jon Isaacson

iaqradio⁺

A personal and professional highlight for me was being invited to be a guest on IAQ Radio with the OG's of restoration podcasting, Cliff "The Z Man" Zlotnik and Radio Joe Hughes.

CHAPTER 3

So, You Want to be a Project Manager?

*The first and greatest victory is to conquer
yourself;
to be conquered by yourself is of all things most
shameful and vile.*
Plato

The advantages of being a project manager are typically viewed in relation to getting a professional out of the field, physically performing the work, and into the office, supervising the work. While an office role is not as physically demanding as a hands-on labor position, there are plenty of additional stresses and responsibilities that you will need to prepare for if you want to thrive in this role.

If you are a technician or a carpenter who takes orders from a project manager, you may be tempted to believe that the position comes with some level of autonomy and authority. What you will find as you *climb the ladder*[23] in any organization is that you always have at least one boss. No matter how far you climb, there is still one ass at least one run higher than you. As you advance in an organization you should understand that no role is more important than another, but each piece plays its part to keep the boat rowing forward.

---

[23] Isaacson, J. (2020, November 12) *Climbing With (Not Over) Each Other.* R&R Magazine. https://www.randrmagonline.com/articles/89178-climbing-with-not-over-each-other

You may see financial advancement as a reason to pursue project management. As of the time of this writing, salary.com notes that the average base salary[24] for a project manager in property restoration is estimated at $69,000 with a range between
$55,000 to $75,000. I have heard of project managers being compensated hourly, which has the advantage of ensuring that at least as long as you are logging your hours accurately, you are being compensated for your time. I have heard of project managers making as low as $40,000 annually.

I can tell you that there is not enough money to make you feel compensated enough for what you will do as a project manager if you are in a bad culture or on your worst days. The roles and responsibilities of project management are not consistently defined across the property restoration industry (or the skilled trades). Many restorers report feeling that they are utilized as project managers without the position or compensation of one. I have worked for organizations that titled this role as a superintendent and others that used PM interchangeably with their estimator position (aka write-and-run).

Definition: For purposes of this book, when we say project manager (PM) we are describing someone who manages the project. Often the PM is not directly responsible for producing an estimate but is expected to understand it and be able to execute the work based upon the details outlined in the agreed-upon scope (estimate).

In the big picture, project management is a customer service role in which a degree of technical skill is helpful to supervise production. Your industry acumen is important, your client engagement, and interpersonal skills with the teams you supervise are at least as important, if not more so. In property restoration, in particular, I am consistently surprised by how many organizations I work with have the same modus operandi when it comes to recruiting project managers -- they consistently place

---

[24] Salary.com (2021, August 27) *Restoration Project Manager Salary.* https://www.salary.com/research/salary/recruiting/restoration-project-manager-salary

high technical skills blindingly over interpersonal and customer service skills (more on this topic in Chapter 13).

Expectations and/or key performance indicators (KPIs) for project managers include:

- Work closely with estimators to ensure project scopes and estimates are accurate and in compliance with industry standards
- Set realistic expectations with homeowners in regard to schedule, construction process, and completed product
- Understand each project's budget and find a way to stay under it for the defined scope of work
- Organize project schedules and details in such a way that allows for quality management of maximum workload
- Maintain a high level of safety by observing and communicating all OSHA, EPA, and local regulations
- Consistently and professionally communicate day-to-day activity with customers, subcontractors, and insurance representatives
- Intelligently and resourcefully manage and solve problems

Before we break out these seven categories for project managers and try to help develop skills and abilities, let's talk more broadly about the role of project management. The reason project management is so difficult is that it is both project management as well as people management as a mid-level manager with highly visible benchmarks for success. You may be looking at project management as getting you out of the field but do you know what you are getting into?

I shared some of my feelings related to being in mid-level management in Chapter 1. I will share more on this topic, later in this book, for project managers who are in the role and need some help in developing the right mindset and habits to navigate their roles. We will also talk about the dichotomy of leadership in this position between technical and people skills.

It is helpful for you to understand at this point that success as a project manager requires a unique blend of these two disciplines.

If you are a carpenter, you may be tempted to think that because you know how to put a home back together (technical skill) you know how to be a better project manager than the knuckleheads that you are working for. While you may be right, if you set your bar low, you will always beat it. I would hope that if you are reading this, you have your benchmarks for growth and success set much higher than the worst-performing PM that you can think of. If you have become proficient in carpentry and leading yourself, you will need to develop the ability to lead multiple people, completing multiple projects, usually spread across a large geographical area.

Your technical skill will help you to operate from a place of knowledge but you will need to develop the ability to help other people understand and execute on the agreed-upon scope of work. I am currently working with a talented carpenter that has learned to be a great project manager. As we prepare this person to become a manager of project managers, they are understanding that when you transition from the cowboy (PM) to the rancher (manager), you move from directly herding the cattle (projects), to leading the cowboys (other PM's) who are doing the herding.

If you are a carpenter becoming a project manager, you will have to battle your urges to put your tool belts back on and do the work yourself. Whether you think you are helping by picking up the slack or you want to show these people how it should be done, doing so does not help you achieve your ultimate goal of leading others. You have to develop your ability to lead others to improve their skills and achieve the needs of the project. Your success will now be tied to the success of others.

One job listing for project management described success this way, "Will ensure that each project's scope is completed in an efficient manner, that workmanship meets our quality standards, and budgets are maintained." As a project manager, you have to master the customer experience while consistently delivering on company goals for profitability. While this can feel like competing realities, they have to be achieved in sync with each other. Make a note of this as these two elements are the foundation of a successful business: happy customers and profitable jobs.

Before you can advance, ensure you have the foundation of being able to master your current role and that you have the ability to communicate to others how to do things the right way. If you are currently working as a technician, you can demonstrate your ability to perform the functions outlined in the prior paragraph. Can you comprehend a project's scope and complete it in an efficient manner? If you cannot then you must be honest with yourself and start there.

You may not have access to the budgets for a project but you can be proactive in learning more about the financial aspects of the business by asking your supervisor to explain the budget to you. Initially, they may not be comfortable sharing the numbers with you but they should be able to show you the allotted hours and material list/allowance. We dive deeper into how budgets are formed later in the book; you can use this to help you speak more intelligently as you pursue this information.

If you can demonstrate an ability to lead yourself, and others, to achieve these goals, your managers will likely be more than happy to share more of the picture with you. It's one thing to ask for an opportunity, it's another thing to prove your value in achieving the objectives noted above. If for some reason your manager is unwilling to share any of the project information with you, take the initiative (be proactive) to create your own figures. I will share a simple acronym that will help you understand how to set your own goals and track them.

The Need for SPEeD

Project management is all about managing the project to completion, according to scope, on time, and on budget. The scope is based upon estimated time and material costs to complete the work. We will break this down more in the next chapter. You can begin to master these basics, even as a technician or carpenter, by simply setting daily objectives for yourself. If you know what you will be doing tomorrow, you can set out your materials the night before, have a plan for how you will be efficient throughout the day, and document for your supervisor that you have met or exceeded the benchmarks that you set for yourself.

For example, when you arrive on a project you can use the following acronym to develop your work SPEeD; this stands for:

Scan
Plan
Execute
Document

Use this sequence to set your own goals with your team and see if you can meet them. This is reverse engineering your production rates and will help you to better understand over time what you should be capable of on a regular basis. If you document your goals and how consistently you have met or beat them, this data will be helpful in showing value to your supervisors as well as for your own point of reference when you become a project manager.

We will discuss the keys to team SPEeD in more detail in Chapter 4 as it relates to project management. I wanted to introduce it here as I believe it is a helpful tool in preparing yourself to master your current role so that you can advance from where you are.

SCAN your worksite to understand what needs to be done, how to do it safely, and how you can develop a PLAN that optimizes your resources. As a technician, if you have a detailed work order that your supervisor provides you with the night before so that you can prepare for the following day, you can create the framework for your PLAN before you ever set foot on the worksite.

As a project manager, the PLAN becomes a key benchmark in setting your team up for success. Communicate clearly and consistently so that everyone is accountable for their roles and responsibilities on a given project. Your ability to execute will be contingent upon your ability to communicate your PLAN with your team and get them to buy into your ideas. As a person in a position of leadership, it is important to be able to adapt when you are faced with new challenges and/or information, as well as recognize when someone on your team has good insight and even a better idea/plan to help you EXECUTE.

As you develop as a person in a position of leadership, remember that being a leader is not about always being right. No manager is infallible. Doing it right is always the right thing (integrity). EXECUTION starts with communicating the PLAN to everyone on your team. When people know the PLAN and their role in achieving it, they are empowered to help you EXECUTE.

Communication of the plan is critical to seeing the plan through. Chris Farrell from Philadelphia, PA shared these tips for project managers, "Take care of the work being done. Attention to detail. Don't always micromanage, rather always follow up and check on the work being done." Whether you are a project manager or you want to be, these are great insights for developing your framework of onsite leadership.

Chris shared this key to success, "Find more efficient ways to complete the tasks at hand." This sentiment can be applied in your current position, whether that is a technician in the field, someone learning to be a project manager, or a manager helping your employees develop. The idea of not micromanaging and yet innovating reminds me of a classic story about Charles Schwab who needed to increase steel production in his factory.

After many frustrating attempts to get the team-inspired Charles finally noticed a simple piece of chalk. With this utensil in hand, he asked the nearest worker how many "heats" their shifts usually make. The employee answered, "Six," so Schwab wrote a "6" on the floor. When the next shift came to work, they saw the number, discovered what it meant, and set out to beat their peers.

When Charles and the day shift arrived, there was a "7" on the floor. The competition continued to elevate the team performance, driving this once underperforming mill to surpass all others in the plant. A piece of chalk was all that was needed to innovate a new means of communicating, executing, improving, and even documenting the plan.

In property restoration, we get paid for what we DOCUMENT. If you don't have it written down with an accompanying photo, it will be that much easier for a customer and/or an insurance representative to dispute your charges. If you can master SPEeD from where you are, you will be proactive in pursuing your goals, and you will also have a solid foundation for leading your teams as a project manager.

You will need the will, the skill, and the chill. Practice hones your skill, so the higher you want to climb the more you have to test yourself. It is only as you try, fail, get up, and try again that your chill increases. Chill is the learned ability to understand that you can survive any scenario. I can tell you that I have failed several times when I thought, "This is it. This is the end of the road for me." Yet, I am still here.

As I said in the prior chapter, you cannot allow the fear of failure to hold you in stasis. The saying goes, "Success comes from experience and experience comes from failure." If this is true, fear is part of the process. If we can fail forward we can continue to move forward even when we suffer mistakes and mishaps (something we will discuss further in Chapter 11).

Failure and bouncing back do more to elevate your mindset and habits than success ever will. Growing your chill in the face of adversity empowers you to push through obstacles, redirect your path, and bring quality people to assist your efforts. As you network with project managers and professionals in our industry, you will learn that you are not alone in this quest.

In 2021 the Restoration Industry Association (RIA) celebrated its 75th anniversary as well as the momentum of the Advocacy and Government Affairs Committee (AGA). At this event, Katie Smith[25] so eloquently characterized the common plight of restorers as she received the 2021 Women in Restoration Award, "There are thousands of contractors, but we don't have thousands of problems. We all have the same major headaches."

As a second-generation restorer from Raleigh, North Carolina, and the incoming president of the RIA, she has spent years building her business and contributing to the industry. Connecting with mission-minded restorers will help you shorten your learning curve by sharing creative solutions to "the same major headaches."

---

[25] Clip from The DYOJO Podcast,
https://www.youtube.com/watch?v=C8JPXTVAHUg&t=2s

As I have already done, I will incorporate insights on project management from everyday restorers throughout this book. One such restorer is David Watts, who was involved in the intricate 2019 fire restoration for The Cathedral of St. John the Divine[26] in Manhattan. When I asked him about some of the mindsets that have helped him to be successful in project management. He replied,

- A can-do attitude and the determination to figure out difficult situations.
- Knowing that I have limitations.
- Knowing that I do not know it all.
- Maintaining the desire to learn more about our industry and network with professionals smarter than me to pull me up to the next level in the restoration field.

David mentions networking, and in Chapter 1 I shared a quote from former RIA president Cliff Zlotnik who said, "The shortcut to growth is community." Coming together, aka unity, in the industry, does not mean that we adopt a hive mindset but that we find enough common ground, despite our differences, in order to achieve our shared goals. This spirit of connecting over shared values and collaborating to conquer our obstacles is one that we must carry forward if our industry is going to continue to thrive.

Your network and the voices you choose to listen to are an important elements of your preparation to win. Project management in our industry can be very stressful and demanding (both physically and mentally). David says, "As the trained professionals in the scenarios that we respond to, we have to develop the knowledge and confidence, as well as bring the calm [the chill] to an otherwise disastrous situation." You develop your chill by working your way through problems. There is no such thing as a project without complications. By building relationships with others you can broaden your access to information, creative solutions, and shorten your DANG learning curve.

[26] Blevins, M. (2020, October 26) *Challenging New Heights: Fire Damage Restoration.* Restoration & Remediation Magazine
https://www.randrmagonline.com/articles/89147-challenging-new-heights-fire-damage-restoration-in-a-new-york-city-cathedral

Applying for Project Management Opportunities

In my experience, you cannot wait for advancement. You have to find a way to prove your abilities and seize upon a need so that you can fill it. If you want to grow, you will have to get uncomfortable. If you want to grow your career and see project management as an important next step, keep reading. You need to understand that the role you are pursuing contains a host of challenges that you may not be seeing. If you have the desire to pursue project management, you owe it to yourself to prepare to win and not let your big buts get in the way.

One exercise that is useful in fighting the fear of failure, especially when taking risks, is to think through the worst-case scenario. If I pursue this, what is the worst that could happen? If the nightmare scenario were to happen, could you survive? For example, if you want to apply for an opportunity, what is the worst that can happen? Likely the worst that will happen is that you may have to take some time off for interviews and the company you are applying to may say no. In marketing, I like to remind people that if the customer isn't calling, they are already saying no. The only difference if you take the risk of visiting offices, is that they could say no to your face.

Can you survive someone saying no to your face? Yes, you can and will have to survive multiple interviews that result in a no. An unlikely worst-case scenario is that word gets back to your current employer and you may have an uncomfortable conversation. But, even that could turn into something positive. Either they fire you and you lose a job in a company where your growth was limited or you have an earnest conversation. This conversation could lead to a clearer pathway to internal growth opportunities.

One way that you can get a good sense of both what you need to do in order to acquire a position as well as how close you are to being considered is to apply for the role(s) that you are interested in. This is being proactive and will also expose you to some honest feedback that will help you better prepare to win. Even if you think you are not quite ready to be a project manager, what does it hurt to apply for some open positions and listen to what companies are looking for?

You may not like what you hear or the results but this exposure will also give you a better sense of whether the teams and options are greener in other pastures or if you have a better shot at making something happen where you are (your own pasture). If you start getting some real offers, you may be able to use that leverage to encourage your supervisor to think more seriously about internal advancement.

It is important to create some FOMO (fear of missing out) with your current employers as well as your future career suitors. Be conscious of your leverage. With your current employer, if they ask something silly like, "You'll never leave us, right?" Don't relieve that pressure. They need to understand that you will stay as long as you are cared for, properly compensated, and given opportunities for growth.

This same perspective can help you to answer difficult questions when you interview. You are going to be asked, "Why do you want to leave?" Your answer should be similar to the response to your current employer, "I am looking for the opportunity to continue my career growth and contribute to the vision and mission of a growth-minded organization." Speaking poorly of your current employer makes you less appealing and marks you as an easy candidate for elimination. If you hate where you work or are perceived as desperate to leave, even if they give you an offer of employment it will likely be a lowball offer because you hand-delivered that information to them.

If you are still developing your career, you need to learn more about the expectations of the generations of those who have come before you. Asking questions in an interview demonstrates that you have thought about the role and the organization. Ask questions about their company, their values, and the pathways to advancement within their organization.

Most job openings come with a description of how Company X defines the position you are applying for. Write these down, look them up, try to find articles about the company that demonstrate their values, community involvement, and achievements. Be proactive. To prepare you can have a friend or family member create a mock interview for you. Use the verbiage in the job description as an imaginary interview and discuss how you would answer questions related to those items.

Michael Stein, who we will hear more from in the Afterword, credits perseverance for playing a vital role in his career and leadership development. Mike is a pilot, who also manages and consults in the aviation industry. He says that in his profession, "Governmental agencies frequently post jobs with very specific knowledge, skills, and abilities (KSAs)." He suggests that career seekers, "Find the job descriptions that interest you for which you hold at least half of the KSAs, and work to acquire the missing pieces."

If you want to be a project manager, you will need the perseverance to face rejection and continue to build your knowledge, skills, and abilities. As you do so, you will never find time to work on personal or professional development, you have to make time. Set some goals and do what you need to do in order to expand your mindset and improve your habits, including:

- Wake up early and get someplace quiet
- Use your drive time to listen to books on tape or podcasts
- Sell your supervisor on the value of joining a local professional group
- Schedule a quarterly day trip with high-drive people
- Attend industry events that bring you in contact with growth-minded professionals
- Start your own local networking group

If you have young children, I feel for you. I would strongly suggest that you do your best to balance the timeline of your career goals with the limited time that you have with your kids. It may not feel like it right now, but you can always find ways to make more money but you can NEVER buy back time. I've shared some of my stories about rebuilding my career after the crash of 2008/2009. During this period in our lives, I was so grateful that we were able to eke by with my wife staying at home with our four young children, while I did my best to make things happen at work.

Make the time to build the skills to do more than just pay the bills. David Watts states, "As a project manager you have to develop skills for time management, empathy, communication skills, and organization as these are key elements for a strong foundation when building your career as a project manager."

Time management and organization are tools you must develop to increase your ability to lead yourself. Empathy and communication are critical abilities for success in leading others. If we tie this list to the habits I outlined above for making time, you have your first search queries for personal development resources.

When I asked David about some of the habits that have helped him to be successful in his roles, he shared the importance of the PLAN. The PM must create a process for clear and consistent communication. The PLAN includes customer expectations, resource allocation, budget, problem-solving, and transparency. David says that once the project is assessed (SCAN) the following needs to be communicated early and often to keep EXECUTION on track:

- Set the expectations and goals with the client. You should verbally walk them through the life cycle of the project and follow that up with a written recap.
- As you assemble the resources that will be utilized for the project, you will continue to track and coordinate your resources throughout the duration of the project.
- Set a reserve so that you understand your budget in a manner that you can communicate with your client and your production team.
- It is important to establish regular communication. I recommend daily communication on the progress of the project. If there are any complications or changes to the scope, it is important to communicate these before the customer discovers them. The key is to communicate so that you are ahead of the distribution of the information, even if

something negative or unexpected has occurred. No one likes surprises.

- Open the lines of communications with all parties to keep everything transparent. This process should be consistent with all clients including homeowners, building managers, property managers, resident managers, brokers, adjusters, consultants, and anyone else tied to the project.

We opened this chapter with a quote from the philosopher Plato. I believe James Hellwig, aka The Ultimate Warrior, eloquently transfers these thoughts to the modern vernacular in stating, "Greatness is not given, it is beaten out of oneself." You know that in order to progress you will have to regularly take yourself to areas beyond your comfort zone. Professional development will stretch (1) your will, (2) your skill, and (3) your chill as you drive towards your goals.

You can say that you have the will to succeed, but how consistently are you moving in step with your vision?

A project manager has the role and responsibility of seeing the bigger picture and breaking that down so that everyone can play their part in achieving the goal. You will have to do this with each project but also with your own development as a person in a position of leadership. You will develop your skills as long as you maintain a hunger to improve (be intentional).

Many of the lessons that stick around come through failing, finding a way to pick yourself up, and moving forward.

Fail, learn, and repeat.

Part 2.

A Few of the Nuts,

Some of the Bolts.

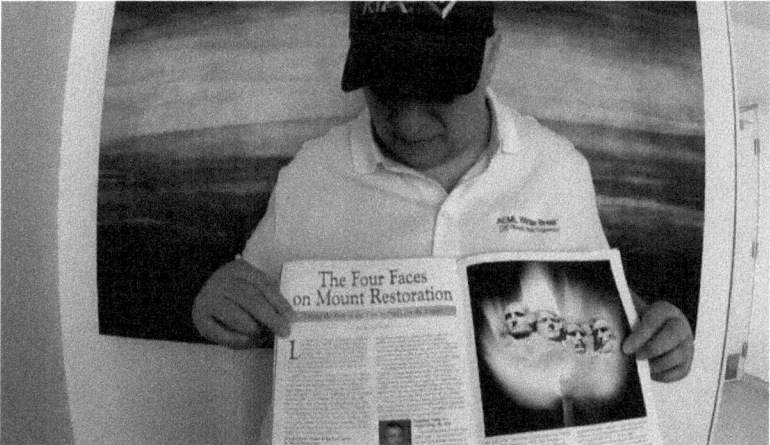

Pete Consigli with his article *The Four Faces on Mount Restoration*

CHAPTER 4

The Standard

Even if you are on the right track,
you will get run over if you just sit there.
Will Rogers

I am sure you have heard of the acronym K.I.S.S.? It stands for Keep It Simple Stupid. Applying KISS to everything that you do will eliminate unnecessary complications. For some reason, we are attracted, like flies to the neon lights of a bug zapper, to convoluting things to the nth degree. Are you a technician who wants to become a project manager? KISS. Are you a project manager trying your best to learn your role? KISS. Are you a manager developing your leadership skills? KISS.

Every company needs two foundational elements in order to be and remain competitive, do you know what they are? Hint, they are in the center of The DYOJO Chart. If you and your organization are going to be successful, you will need to have happy customers and profitable projects (KISS). Your role as a project manager will place you in a role that is judged by your ability to curate the customer experience and to regularly deliver on your company's goals.

Everyone in the organization should understand that profitable jobs start with well-written scopes. My first book, Be Intentional: Estimating addresses the mindset and habits that lead to better outcomes with creating and working from insurance claims estimates. The estimating process should be the start of clarifying the agreed-upon scope of work so that we can set our production team up for success as they execute the plan.

Scope clarity is core to being able to achieve a profitable job. Scope clarity is also core to set the right expectation with your client which is essential to initiating and executing a plan that will lead to a five-star customer experience. Scope clarity is the foundation of production consistency. If we want to produce consistently positive outcomes, we need to focus our efforts on creating clear scopes.

Your roles and responsibilities as a project manager may not include writing estimates but they will definitely include operating from them. I would say that the most common division of responsibilities between estimators and project managers that I see include:

- **Estimators** deal with the money, which primarily includes writing the estimate, negotiating scope with the carriers, and addressing any financial changes to the project.
- **Project managers** deal with the project, which primarily includes understanding the scope and budget, relaying that into work orders for subcontractors and in-house labor, and seeing that the project gets completed on time, on budget, and to the satisfaction of the customer.

If the estimator is doing their job, they will have communicated *The Standard*[27] to all parties to the claim. I believe that when we properly implement this simple narrative into our process we can help steer the process to a successful outcome. Setting the expectations at this point in the process sets the team up to execute realistic expectations during production; something we will explore in the next chapter.

[27] Isaacson, J. (2021, May 5) *The Mindset and Habits for Claims Estimating Success as a New Independent Adjuster.* Claims Pages. https://www.claimspages.com/editorials/2021/05/05/the-mindset-and-habits-for-claims-estimating-success-as-a-new-independent-adjuster

The Standard: Restoring the property to resemble pre-loss conditions, with materials of like kind and quality; no more and no less.

The agreed-upon scope with the insurance company forms the basis for the contracted work, cost, and timeline for project completion. There are three key phases in the scoping process which we outline in The DYOJO Scoping Diagrams. These phases include estimating, negotiating, and producing the work. Producing the work is still part of the scoping process as it is the execution of the work in the prior phases. Also, most projects have either change orders or supplements, which are revisions to the agreed-upon scope.

Keeping it simple, means narrowing your focus. Keeping it simple means doing your best to ensure that all parties are in agreement on the key elements of success. The contractor plays a pivotal role in the development of the scope. Writing for *Claims Journal*[28], attorney Gary Wickert clarifies the importance of a site visit and estimate from a qualified local contractor:

> *The policy should pay for the cost of an experienced contractor to perform the required work to repair or replace the building and put it back to its pre-loss condition. Insurance companies use guideline pricing and "Xactimate" (computerized home replacement cost estimating software) to predict how much materials and labor should cost. However, the estimate prepared by a qualified local, licensed, and bonded contractor who has visited the loss site and reviewed information about the pre-loss structure is generally the most accurate cost for a claim settlement.*

While many contractors would utter a hearty amen to these sentiments, they also outline the high calling of the restoration contractor in the insurance claims process.

Developing the Agreed-Upon Scope

Estimating is a process of establishing the agreed-upon scope. As restoration contractors, we should complete thorough data capture so that we can perform accurate data input. The quality of the data input (composed estimate) is in direct correlation to the quality of the data capture.

> **Thorough Data Capture**
> **+ Accurate Data Input**
> **= Defensible Estimate**

Data Capture

At the data capture phase, it is important to do your team, your client, and the carrier a favor by making the above-mentioned

---

[28] Wickert, G (2019, October 31) *Paying Overhead and Profit in First-Party Claims*. Claims Journal. https://www.claimsjournal.com/columns/road-to-recovery/2019/10/31/293871.htm

standard clear at the outset of every claim. Your introduction could be something to the effect of, "My job is to perform thorough data capture of the site conditions so that I can accurately data input to generate an estimate for an agreed-upon scope (most likely through Xactimate) to restore your property to pre-loss conditions."

Most likely, as the project manager, you are not directly engaged in the project until the producing phase. If it is possible, especially for complex projects, it is helpful to regularly communicate projects that are coming down the pipeline so that project managers can prepare for them. Project managers can add a lot of value to the estimators at this phase by discussing the scope and sequence of work necessary to accomplish restoration.

Keeping it simple includes clarifying the roles of all team members and building consistency into your communication process between these interwoven roles. Common integration approaches between estimating and project management include:

1. Estimator creates the scope of work and composes an estimate for how they perceive the project will be executed. Once the estimator has negotiated with the carrier and the client, the file is handed over to project management to execute.
    a. Pros: This is a common approach and can help to expedite the claims estimating and negotiation process on the front end. You don't bog your project managers down with the project details until the scope is confirmed and the contract is signed.
    b. Cons: This is a common approach and can lead to communication issues as the execution relies on the efficacy of the transmission of details between the estimator and project manager(s). Anytime the project manager, the person who will be hands-on with the

project for the longest period of time, doesn't know about the scope or the client until the scope has been agreed upon, they often are coming in blind to the situation.

2. A write-and-run estimator creates the scope of work and composes an estimate for how they perceive the project will be executed. Once the estimator has negotiated with the carrier and the client, they continue with the project to execute the work.

   a. Pros: This is a common approach that reduces communication gaps between estimator and project manager as it is the same person.

   b. Cons: This is a common approach and can place a high burden on the individual to juggle multiple aspects of the work which can create pressure for the professional to prioritize one aspect of their work over the other. Estimates may lag when project management is prioritized and vice versa. When an organization does not properly balance the workload both responsibilities can suffer. This potentially can be offset with administrative assistants assigned to the write and run project manager/estimator and/or hiring higher competency carpenters who operate as the onsite foreperson.

3. Project managers create the scope of work and hand those details over to an estimator who then translates this into an estimate. Companies like Just Right Construction and Cleaning in Moses Lake, Washington have been developing this type of approach. Once the estimator has negotiated with the carrier, the estimate is handed back to project management to execute.

   a. Pros: This reduces communication gaps between estimator and project manager as well as expedites the speed of trust with the client as the project manager is the initial point of contact as well as the one who executes the project on through completion.

      b. Cons: Communication gaps can exist between the scope communicated by the project manager and the estimator as well as some key details that may assist the estimator to better negotiating the project with the carrier. Whenever information is passing from one entity to another, it is critical that there is a consistent process to optimize clarity so that details are not missed.

No process is perfect, but it is important for an intentional restoration organization to continue to evaluate the strengths, weaknesses, and outcomes of their approach so that they can improve efficacy. As the project manager, you need to understand how the estimates are composed. In 2018 I wrote some thoughts regarding *The Ten Commandments of Xactimate Estimating Success*[29]. The first two commandments of estimating success for intentional estimators (this includes adjusters) cover two of the most important elements of estimating any project:

1.   The sketch is key to enabling the estimator to efficiently utilize their chosen estimating platform and for quantifying materials.

2.   Photos are essential to justifying your line items and communicating scope, especially where unique or complex elements are involved.

The higher the value and the more complex the process, the more photos need to be taken to support the inevitable questions and/or objections to estimating items that are outside of the norms. When the loss you are working on has elements that do not fit in the mold of a "standardized" project, this is when you have to earn your modest salary as

---

[29] Isaacson, J. (2018, September 27) *The 10 Commandments of Xactimate Estimating Success.* Restoration & Remediation Magazine. https://www.randrmagonline.com/articles/88186-the-10-commandments-of-xactimate-estimating-success

an estimator/project manager. All parties are responsible to gather and present accurate information that helps to define, as well as clarify, an accurate representation of the source and extent of the damages.

Sidenote: While your company may not pay for tools such as DocuSketch, MagicPlan or Matterport, these three-dimensional data capture tools can be incredibly valuable for helping with the efficiency of your claims. I have experience using Docusketch which is affordable and expedient[30]. In short, this is a tool that will capture the full 360-degree view of each room, including photos of items ("comments"), and can be utilized to produce an accurate sketch of the property that you can download as an ESX for Xactimate. Many are familiar with Matterport but there are also some great alternatives. Tools like Magicplan are much simpler to use for start-up companies as well as teams that want to have their technicians provide an initial sketch.

Often the communication, with regards to the agreed-upon scope, comes down from the estimator based upon their conversations with the insurance adjuster and the client. By the time the estimator has navigated all of these steps to produce an estimate, there are too many conversations and nuances to be able to recap effectively to the project manager. It's like a game of telephone.

As proposed in this book, one way to offset the communication gap that inevitably happens with this system is to have whoever will be producing the work, and thereby the person who will be hands-on with the project the longest, to either drive the conversation related to the scope or be involved at this critical phase.

At a minimum, you must develop a process for downloading the information between phases. Communication flows first from the estimator to the project manager, and then from the project manager to the production team (internal staff and subcontractors). Whatever process you use, there will be pros and cons, but if you take some time to analyze where the majority of your issues stem from, you may find there are some simple solutions that will help you make progress on your goals. Don't overthink or overcomplicate the process.

---

[30] The DYOJO Podcast, Episode 40

Data Input

While many consumers focus on the price, in the world of insurance, claims property restoration the scope is the foundational element. If we can agree on the scope of the work, which often requires us to identify both the source as well as the extent of damages, then we can begin to construct the cost of mitigation and repairs.

As most in property restoration are aware, the common estimating tool for insurance claims is called Xactimate which helps create a common language between contractors and carriers. Mark Whatley of Actionable Insights recalls in his article covering the history and future of Xactimate, "Starting in 1989, Xactware pioneered a scientific approach to providing building cost data for the restoration ecosystem. From the outset, Xactware's primary function has been to report market prices based upon industry surveys and recent transactions that have occurred[31]."

Xactimate estimates are presented in a format that is different from most formats within the skilled trades. They are based upon quantities aggregated from an accurate diagram (aka sketch) and the scope of work is composed (laboriously) line by line and room by room. Xactimate is often over-utilized as a pricing guide for the insurance claims repair process, but as a project manager, you should be aware of these issues. Whatever program you utilize to draft your estimates, you need to understand and appropriately charge for your total costs as you develop an agreed-upon scope of work.

Common Estimating Approaches

As a project manager, you may or may not have involvement with estimating. It is important to understand some of the common formats for estimating so that you are aware of the factors,

[31] Whatley, M. (2018, April) *Xactimate: The History & The Future*. Actionable Insights. https://www.getinsights.org/resources/insighter-report/xact

assumptions, and potential shortfalls in each format. These estimating structures include:

- Shooting from the hip
- Time and materials
- Cost-plus
- Unit pricing
- Standardized pricing
- Production rates

Shooting from the hip as an estimator

If you are a tradesperson who is starting a business, you may be tempted to think that you can eyeball a project and put a good number on it. Your background in the field should educate your efforts, but you should also understand that you will need to develop new skills in estimating and running a business unless you are comfortable with having bought your job[32] rather than building something sustainable. To improve your estimating skills you will want to learn the differences between these common estimating approaches.

Many of the contractors that we consult with come to us because their estimate was rejected for not being formatted in Xactimate. I usually advise them that we can assist with this process but that I first want them to get an email from the adjuster stating they will pay the Xactimate pricing once we submit the scope in their requested format. Inevitably the costs are 25-30%, if they provide details that are sufficient to justify the scope. This is NOT because Xactimate has that much cream built into the program but because many contractors do not understand how to properly price their services. For many new entrepreneurs Xactimate, or other standardized pricing programs, can be an excellent way to double-check and develop your own pricing metrics.

---

[32] Isaacson, J. (2020, September 11) *Skilled at Trades, Struggling with Business.* Restoration & Remediation Magazine.
https://www.randrmagonline.com/articles/89097-skilled-at-trades-struggling-with-business

Time and materials estimating

The key here is estimating. An estimate is an approximation, typically given to a customer so that they can understand their cost for an agreed scope of work. Before you can estimate, you need to clarify the scope. What does the customer want to be done, what are the options and/or factors that will impact cost and timelines, and what needs to happen in order for you to assist them with achieving satisfaction in the process? Time and materials can be a good way of presenting cost agreements.

From an estimating standpoint, you will break down the scopes of work and pencil out what you believe the time involved will be, then you multiply that by your labor rates. While we won't go into true labor costs at this time, you need to understand what your total labor cost is, which includes your labor burden. *Construction Business Owner*[33] notes, "All costs associated with paying employees, including FICA, unemployment and Social Security should be calculated as part of labor. The lengthy and varied list of indirect contract costs continues with vacation time, holidays, sick days, drivers, warehouse personnel, training, safety, and clothing." Your labor sheet should include all non-direct job-related labor and how these rates are factored for the project.

Clarity is essential. Often time and materials are utilized on large projects, but many clients will request an estimated final figure or a weekly "burn rate" so that they can plan accordingly. Waiting until the end of a project to provide any figures could lead to issues with collecting payment. If you agree to a time and materials estimate, I would suggest providing regular (weekly) updates of the accumulated costs and making provisions for draws based upon percentages of performance.

---

[33] Ganley, J. (2021, April, 2) *Establish Your Labor Burden Rate for Your Construction Company*. Construction Business Owner. https://www.constructionbusinessowner.com/topics/accounting/accounting-finance/establish-your-labor-burden-rate-your-construction-company

- Breakdown of time to perform the work x labor rates
- Materials + equipment + resources + applicable sales tax
- Sub-total x overhead and profit (markup)

While you may not present your final estimate as time and material, I think it is a good means to check your figures against the unit or standardized pricing. Whether you double estimate every project or do this periodically, you should check your estimates against your hard costs for completed projects to update your pricing and understand industry pricing norms, even if you don't follow them.

Cost-plus estimating

This is similar to time and materials in the sense that you are agreeing to cost items and markups and facilitating the work. As a general contractor who primarily sub-contracts work to third-party vendors, this may make sense to ensure your costs are covered. I see many contractors who spend so much time working with a client on the design and acquiring bids from specialty vendors only to be cut out of the project when it comes time to sign the contract and collect an initial deposit.

I would suggest that all contractors use some form of time and material or cost-plus arrangement if they are developing a plan of action with a client. Your time will never be valued by the public until you value it yourself. It is common in my field, property restoration, to hear that the standard 10 & 10 (10% overhead plus 10% profit) covers a broad range of items including planning, supervisory time, and any unaccounted-for incidentals. Before you get too invested in a project, make sure you understand who is paying for your indirect costs.

If you are going to use cost-plus estimating, make sure you understand your overhead costs and your profit goals. If you are doing a few large projects a year, or those projects carry over several years, you have to factor the variables in your overhead so that you don't finish a project with an empty bag.

Unit price estimating

For a long time, RS Means has been an industry standard for construction pricing. Contractors would purchase these books at the local hardware store and could find pricing by trade with factors for their area of operations. As technology has advanced, these tools are more readily available and updated much quicker than the 12-month publishing cycle. One way to estimate drywall is by the sheet or by the square foot, but reliance on these pricing structures can be detrimental as there are many factors that impact completing the work in the real world.

Estimators should spend time in the field with their production teams, even if they are not skilled in the work, it is good to get your hands dirty from time to time. Not only will being in the field help you have a better understanding of the scopes of work that you are bidding on, but it can also be a great way to reduce the "us vs. them" mentality that plagues many construction organizations. As we discussed with Brian Austin, Director of Instructional Design at Verisk, on *The Xactimate Sessions File 002*[34], if you have an Xactware license there are many resources included in that cost. One such resource is the ILX Construction Training, fifty courses that take students through the complete building process, from selecting a building lot all the way to the final inspection.

Standardized price estimating

This is similar to unit price estimating, in many instances they are interchangeable. In property restoration, a common estimating tool is a program called Xactimate. Most of the prices in this software are based upon square footage (SF) or linear footage (LF). I have heard that RS Means, and other providers, have similar platforms that help estimators in the construction field to create estimates in this fashion. As stated before, you should double-check your estimating means to compare real-world costs with whatever system you are utilizing. Estimators should ask their production team members to review their estimates as well as discuss

---

[34] The DYOJO Podcast, Episode 66

approaches to unique scopes of work with trusted industry professionals.

Estimators and installers should not be strangers to each other. If the goal is to create an accurate scope that can be executed effectively in the field, all parties should be involved in the bidding process. Working with insurance claims for over 20 years, it still amazes me how many organizations put so much time into the estimating process, but don't utilize all of the tools readily available in the programs that they have invested in.

For example, an estimate written in Xactimate can produce a scope sheet that breaks out the work to be performed line by line, room by room, but many production teams don't utilize this aspect of the program. Not to sound like I am advocating for Xactimate, but it also provides a components list, estimated hours based upon the figures provided (not always accurate), and breakdowns by category that lend themselves to efficient project budgets.

This is a great time to remind everyone of the good work that the Restoration Industry Association (RIA) has been doing to help level the playing field for restorers. With regards to standardized pricing, the Advocacy and Government Affairs (AGA) committee released the Restoration Pricing Position Statement # 1 which includes this language from the Xactware licensing agreement, "Price data are intended to be a representation of historical information to be used as a baseline or place to begin the creation of an estimate."

The RIA reminds all parties that standardized prices, such as those found in Xactimate, should be understood as reference points. The current pricing list is not the final authority. The position statement continues, "Those data are gathered from contractors, insurance company representatives, and other industry professionals. Since the data are purely historical, standardized price lists lag in time behind actual market prices, particularly when surveys are not conducted as frequently as market conditions necessitate."

Production rate estimating

Production rate refers to the amount of time needed per worker to accomplish a specified quantity of the overall scope.
Xactimate uses square, linear, and cubic footage calculations for most of its pricing, but embedded in this are certain assumptions regarding production rates. You can locate and adapt these assumptions in Xactimate through the yield when the efficiency of a task is impacted by other factors. In the right conditions, how many square feet of wall demolition could your team members accomplish in an eight-hour workday?

> **Basic formula:** 1 technician x 8 hours = _____ SF of Task A. Therefore your company would charge $____ / SF for Task A. You would have to determine if your Task A cost includes basic materials and equipment or if you account for those elsewhere in the bid.

Tom McGuire, the creator of The Edge estimating tool, has been hard at work reminding restoration contractors that Xactimate is not the only way to price a job, especially if they need to produce quick and accurate numbers for a large loss scenario. Writing for *Property Casualty 360*[35], Tom says, "The first factor (F1) is the area to be cleaned. This should be a straightforward calculation — but has to be conducted accurately and verified with the client.

The next consideration (F2) is the number of calendar days you have to complete the job. This may be determined by the client or by an external event, but is often non-negotiable." These factors are essential in commercial large loss where the biggest exposure is loss of business, but they are critical elements of a successful residential project, regardless of size, as well.

The third and final variable (F3) according to Tom is your production rate. He says, "This is arguably the most crucial and

---

[35] McGuire, T. (2019, May 2) *Large Loss Cost Estimating: What's Needed.* Property Casualty 360.
https://www.propertycasualty360.com/2019/05/02/large-loss-cost-estimating-whats-needed

requires a great deal of thought; however, it is also the variable most firmly within your control. If you have a realisti understanding of the capabilities of your people and equipment as well as a clear view of the type of structure and damage you are dealing with, you can estimate precisely what it will take to complete a recovery project under significant time pressure."

Mr. McGuire says that the foundation of successful project management is, "Communicate. Communicate. Communicate." Followed by "Documentation," because, "If you don't document, it didn't happen." Communication is the key to safe, effective, and consistent operations. When Tom and I spoke about this topic he said that he sees too many people getting into trouble because their heads aren't in the right place.

Management of the project starts long before the project manager starts the production process. Simplicity is a means of reducing friction and chaos. Communication is the best tool that you have for keeping everyone on the project working together to focus on the right things.

One company stated the role of the project manager as, "Working closely with estimators to ensure project scopes and estimates are accurate and in compliance with industry standards." If you are a project manager it is important to be able to read and comprehend the agreed-upon scope of work. You need to understand the production rate assumptions of the estimate in order to create your production plan.

In Xactimate you would derive this information from the Components List whereas in a production rate bid you should have access to the factors the estimator utilized for their figures. Every estimating platform has certain shortfalls and pickups which should be downloaded between the team members who created the scope and those who will be responsible to execute it.

A lackluster estimate stemming from an insufficient scope will result in production complications leading to:

- Production frustration
- Lack of efficiency
- Unhappy customers
- Inconsistent outcomes
- Lower profitability

If you regularly experience the four items above, you will want to STOP what you are currently doing and determine what you can START doing to improve your performance. We often focus on the financial outcomes, but these should be data points that open our perspectives to broader issues within our estimating and production processes.

Keep it simple. We distinguish the Process (internal) from Production (external) in *The Four Pillars of Success*[36]. If you want to have consistent outcomes (external) you need to be clear and consistent with your internal processes. The agreed-upon scope should be based upon thorough data capture and accurate data input. The production process should start with thorough data transfer and accurate production planning.

Everyone has to play their part in starting off on the right track and keeping things moving in the right direction.

---

[36] https://www.thedyojo.com/pillars.html

The DYOJO Scope Diagram, Page 1

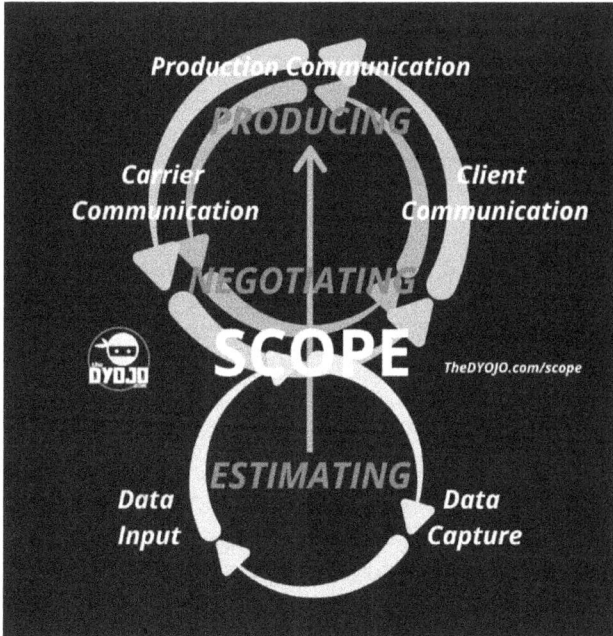

The DYOJO Scope Diagram, Page 2

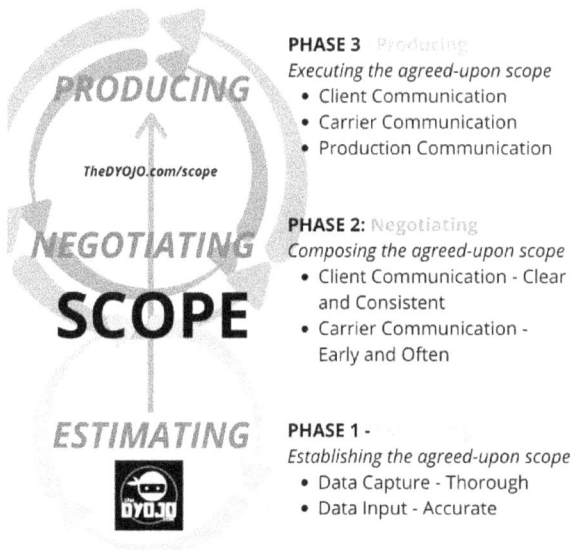

PHASE 3 Producing
Executing the agreed-upon scope
- Client Communication
- Carrier Communication
- Production Communication

PHASE 2: Negotiating
Composing the agreed-upon scope
- Client Communication - Clear and Consistent
- Carrier Communication - Early and Often

PHASE 1 -
Establishing the agreed-upon scope
- Data Capture - Thorough
- Data Input - Accurate

CHAPTER 5

Setting Expectations

*Why do so many professionals say they are
project managing when what they are actually
doing is fire fighting?*
Colin Bentley

At a time when I was struggling to stay on top of all of my duties and feeling negatively about my ability to dig my way out, a co-worker shared a helpful analogy. They said, "Project management is like juggling multiple spinning plates. You're not in trouble until you start dropping the glass ones." Tough decisions and creative solutions are part of the job. If it were easy, everyone would be doing it.

It takes a lot of energy to keep all of the responsibilities of project management in motion. When you are at capacity, or like many managers feel, endlessly over capacity, you have to prioritize which plates you will keep spinning and which ones can fall. There are many days when you have to decide who you will piss off the least.

Comedian Jim Gaffigan has a funny segment where he talks about what it's like to have a fifth child. He says, "Imagine you're drowning. And someone hands you a baby[37]." There are so many times when this is what project management feels like. You will have a workload that exceeds your ability to keep every plate spinning, and someone hands you another plate to juggle.

---

[37] Gaffigan, J. (2106, November 11) *5 Kids*. Youtube.
https://www.youtube.com/watch?v=FbX_dQhHw98

Keeping the plates assigned to you spinning will be your direct role but not breaking plates is a team effort. Broken plates definitely have a team impact. Organizations should be discussing all of these items including how many plates they take on and how to add resources to meet the needs. It's important to remember that everyone on your team has their own spinning plates that they are juggling as well.

If you want to be successful in keeping plates spinning as a project manager, you need to set up a plan to clear your plates as efficiently as possible. If you execute things right, you can get a project going and completed before you have to exert unnecessary energy to spin it again. When you have to make tough choices, it is important to organize and prioritize your workload effectively.

The process isn't easy, but the framework is simple. Scan the agreed-upon scope, set up a clear production plan, set your resources up to execute the work, and document completion. Use this formula to start and finish jobs strongly so that they don't have time to linger in your workload.

Expectations and/or key performance indicators (KPIs) for project managers include: Set realistic expectations with customers in regard to schedule, construction process, and completed product. Understanding what you will need to keep a customer's plate (project) spinning starts with understanding their expectations. Customer expectations and production success start with clarifying and executing the agreed-upon scope.

The standard that we outlined in the previous chapter should guide the process from estimating to negotiation and on through setting expectations for production. Negotiation requires the restoration contractor to be clear and consistent in their client (aka policyholder) communication. Everything should be in writing. Negotiation also requires the restoration contractor to communicate early and often with the insurance carrier. Everything should be in writing.

If you are not communicating and you are not documenting, you will struggle to execute effectively. It is important to clarify the roles and responsibilities of all parties and to continue to follow through on these as you work through the project. Let's take a peek back into restoration history that will help you to take leaps forward in the process of setting clear expectations.

The Restoration Triangle

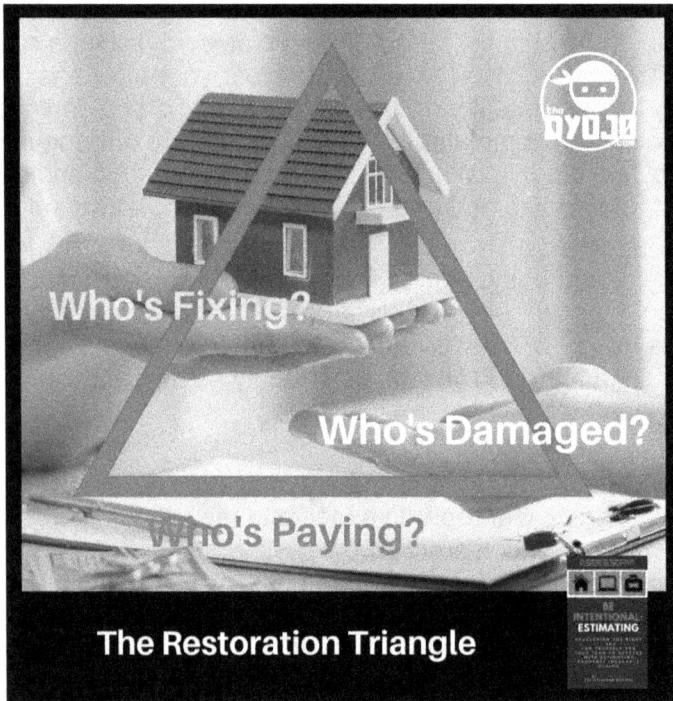

When I started in property restoration, one of my favorite publications was *IE Connections*. Their monthly publication was printed like a newspaper and was packed with great content. In October of 2000, Pete Consigli wrote an excellent article for IE Connections where he advised,

> *"It is critical following a loss that a process starts to have a meeting of the minds among the three parties that are central to a disaster restoration project. These are the property owner, their insurance company, and the restoration contractor of record."*

We introduced Pete in the *Foreword*. He is referred to as The Restoration Global Watchdog because of his encyclopedic knowledge of the history of our industry as well as his active presence in industry associations, involvement in educational developments, and collaboration with efforts such as the Disaster Restoration Reconstruction Management (DRRM) program at Purdue University.

In the article, Pete shares a term that serves as an excellent framework for the claims negotiation process, The Restoration Triangle. I was fortunate enough to be bestowed with a physical copy of this publication while on a road trip with Pete in 2021. Pete humorously summarizes the tripartite as:

- **Who's Damaged**
- **Who's Fixin' it**
- **and Who's Payin' for it**

Damage (scope) assessment

The process starts with damage assessment (aka thorough data capture). Pete states, "Damage assessment is a complex process that entails training and experience. It is important that the experts provide an explanation for their recommendations to either do or not to do something." Adjusters and contractors should be able to communicate so that laymen can understand the why of their approach to observed damages. When there is a disagreement the insured should be able to understand how a particular proposal does or does not comply with the standard.

The details collected should translate from the site visit, via photographs and/or 360-degree capture resources, to an agreed-upon scope with an agreed-upon cost estimate. Thorough data capture leads to accurate data input for an understandable and defensible agreed-upon scope. Depending on the severity of the loss, third-party evaluators may be necessary to first determine the site risks as well as to provide post-project verification of safe conditions. Best practices for the inclusion of a third-party evaluator, according to Mr. Consigli, include

1. Clearly define the third-party evaluator's roles to prevent potential conflicts of interest.
2. Who does the third-party evaluator work for (e.g., who signs their authorization/contract)?
3. What parties in the Restoration Triangle are in the communication loop to receive specifications, reports, lab results, and interpretations, etc.?

Each party presents their information as accurately as they are able, with a clear understanding of the standard. Each party brings something unique to the table that should be heard and referenced as the agreed-upon scope is established.

- The insured (**who's damaged**) has a unique perspective on the pre-loss conditions and the extent of the loss.
- The carrier representative (**who's payin' for it**) has a unique perspective regarding the details of the policy and the responsibility of the carrier with regards to the source and extent of damages as well as any relevant exclusions.
- The contractor (**who's fixin' it**) has a unique perspective on the means, methods, and materials cost that will be relevant to establishing an agreed-upon scope of work to restore the structure.

Damage (scope) declaration

Pete reminds claims stakeholders, "If one of these parties is left out of the process of determining and agreeing on the extent of damage, scope of repair, cost of restoration to a pre-loss condition, timelines, and criteria for satisfactory completion, then there will be problems[38]." A claim should not follow the narrative of

---

[38] Consigli, P. (2000, October) *Disaster Strikes! What ya gonna do...Who ya gonna call? Preventing IEQ Problems after Floods, Fires, and Catastrophes.* IE Connections.

a T.V. drama or a strategy session for *Survivor*, whereby two members of the triangle team up to push their narrative through. For example,

- The contractor and the client should not be in cahoots to figure out a way to "maximize the claim" without justification. *This would be fraud.*
- Nor should the contractor and the carrier be working hand-in-hand to "dwindle" the scope. *This would be short-changing.*

Communication is key to successfully navigating the claims process. Whoever is responsible for the estimate should complete the data capture and data input that will lead to creating a clear scope. Communication is a shared responsibility of the stakeholders in the claims process. The core parties to a claim are the client, the contractor of record, and the carrier must work together to clarify the agreed-upon scope of work.

Damage (scope) negotiation

While negotiation typically falls under the role of the estimator, if the project manager is responsible for change orders then you may have to exercise this skill. It is important that we educate our clients, as an educated insured is an empowered insured. The policyholder has a responsibility to select the coverage that best suits their needs as well as advocate for themselves to see that what they purchased does what it is supposed to do. Namely, restore them to resemble pre-loss conditions.

We should be careful to stay in our own lane but be a helpful resource to our clients, the home, and business owners impacted by damages. One such resource that will help educate and empower the insured includes these ten insurance claims tips from **United Policyholders**[39]. These also help to clarify the roles and responsibilities of the insured:

---

[39] United Policyholders. Top 10 Insurance Claims Tips. https://uphelp.org/claim-guidance-publications/top-10-insurance-claim-tips

1. Be proactive in the claim process and keep good notes. Make sure you maintain a paper trail.
2. Focus on calculating the total value of your damaged or destroyed property and understanding the maximum insurance benefits that are available to you.
3. Think of your insurance claim as a business negotiation—you're dealing with a profit-oriented company and your goal is to restore your assets.
4. Give your insurance company a chance to do the right thing, but don't mistake a friendly representative for a friend and don't be a pushover.
5. Document and support your claim with proof, details and estimates.
6. Present clear requests in writing that explain what you need, when you need it, and why you're entitled to it.
7. Don't pad or exaggerate your claim.
8. Don't sign legal documents without consulting with a qualified attorney.
9. Try to resolve problems informally but complain in writing. Go up the chain of command and/or use government agency help when necessary.
10. Get specialized professional help when you need it.

Damage (scope) expectations

You will notice that tip number one includes, "Make sure you maintain a paper trail." We already know that documentation of the project is essential and yet we do not always apply this record keeping to our communications with the clients and the carriers. A good rule of thumb is to remember that a conversation did not happen unless you can prove it.

Always get, and/or follow up, everything in writing. If you have a conversation with anyone related to the claim, follow that up with an email recapping what you discussed and any agreements you made that affect the scope, cost, or schedule.

- If you have a conversation with the adjuster, **follow up with an email**.
- If you have a conversation with the customer, **follow up with an email**.

I would suggest having a running communication notes (Comm Notes) document (see the sample Communication SOP in Chapter 5). If you have a team involved with the production process, this can be in your customer resource management software (CRM). There are free tools such as Slack, or even something as simple as Google Docs, that will help you create an ongoing record that is accessible to your team. Keep track of the dates, names, and conversations that you had for every project.

There is a helpful saying, which uses some underlying humor, to help set the right expectation for a client: *"You can have it good, fast, or cheap, but you can only choose two."*

We know what cheap and fast looks like; that's obviously what all of our competitors provide, right? This is sarcasm. This simple statement covers the key factors in project success, quality of materials and workmanship + timeline to completion + cost. Clarifying your client's expectations is essential to understanding whether they are a good fit for your team and whether you are on the same page regarding what a happy outcome will be.

If someone else isn't responsible for this statement, I would like to claim it, "The best time to fire a bad client is before the project starts." By this, I mean that when your spider senses are tingling it will not be worth it to take on that customer. Do not ignore the red flags.

Of course, your customer wants their project to be good, fast, and cheap. If you know that these are their expectations, you can work to develop strategies to either redefine them or meet them head-on. In the simplest terms, have the conversation with your customer at the outset of the project, ask them, "What will it take to achieve a five-star customer experience at the end of this job?" Listen to what your customer says, as well as what they don't say.

Dealing With Conflict

Often, there are micro issues within the customer expectations that can either help you arrive at a positive outcome or they can be landmines in the project that set off an explosive chain of negative reactions. Do your best to identify and navigate through these items. Do not ignore them. Get them in writing so that you are clear with your client and your team as to how you are going to achieve the shared goal. Too often we take on all of the burdens rather than making the roles and responsibilities of the client clear.

A project manager is responsible for intelligently and resourcefully managing and solving problems. Any course or training you take helps you to develop the foundation for the mindset and habits that will enable you to succeed. Those principles always have to be applied in less than ideal situations. You have to be able to adjust on the fly, intelligently and resourcefully, without causing further issues.

Emily Weiss (Sumner, WA) is a professional that I had the pleasure of working with directly and saw her rapidly learn the mindset and demonstrate the effective habits necessary for project management in the skilled trades. She shared her thoughts on what it takes to be effective as a PM, "Communication is, by far, the most important and the most difficult skill to master. There is a balance between being Johnny-On-The-Spot with too much responsiveness, and not enough communication."

When we worked together, I was recovering from high-volume program work and it was interesting to observe what some people in different trades and with different backgrounds see as emergencies. In property restoration, we respond to calls for emergency service, but that does not mean that our operations should be chaotic. Developing your chill under pressure is as important as developing your will to learn as well as your skills and abilities. Emily continues, "You need to learn to utilize the right kind of communication, based on your audience. Calm and collected communication is critical when things get difficult. Remove the emotion and just present the facts."

I quoted Kelly Burns, whom I worked with in Seattle, Washington, in Be Intentional Culture. She always had a helpful saying, "We never tell them (client) no, we tell them this is what we can do." Issues arise and you can either help diffuse them with calm and factual communication (telling them what you can do) rather than escalating with the panicked or upset client.

In his in-depth book *Leadership in Restorative Drying*, Ken Larsen covers six steps that can help resolve conflict. Ken states, "A conflict is a problem or issue on a project. They do not just go away. In fact, if the restorer does not address them, they will probably escalate[40]." I know this has been true in my career. It is always better to address something, personally or professionally, early while it is still a small issue. Time does not make issues better, it generally feeds their growth into much larger issues. When a customer does not feel heard, the issues escalate.

When confronted with conflict, Ken advises

1. Listen carefully
2. Do not interrupt
3. Try to gain their perspective
4. Do not make excuses
5. What do they really want?
   (Moreover is it reasonable?)
6. Make it happen.

---

[40] Larsen, K. (2014) *Leadership in Restorative Drying*. Restoration Leadership Institute

Emily cautions that you should not engage an upset customer with elevated emotions. In property restoration, we have to remember that while we may have done this type of work hundreds of times, and it may seem like a small issue to us; to your client, it likely is the first time and it seems like a mountain. As Ken says, "Take ownership of the problem and assure them there is a solution." If it wasn't done right, make it right. Address the issue expediently, and restore the project to excellence.

Your professional success has as much (if not more) to do with how you make clients feel as with what you do. When you can make a frustrated customer feel heard, that you are in control of the situation, and give them confidence that your team is making it right, you will be able to move forward. Anyone can manage a good project with a happy customer, the skill comes in getting what has gone off track, back on the rails, and steaming towards its destination.

The agreed-upon scope leads to the contract and terms. The estimated assumptions create the basis for the cost and duration of the work. If everyone in the sequence of damage (scope) assessment, declaration, negotiation, and expectation has done their job, the project manager should be aware and able to carry the baton across the finish line. Remember that in insurance work, the agreed-upon scope of work is a foundational element.

It is important to remember in all negotiations and professional relationships that you need to be professional, be polite but don't get played.

Four simple claims relationship optimizers for intentional restorers:

1. For us to have a professional "relationship" it must be **mutually beneficial**. If negotiations are being made, they should be made in a manner that is fair to all parties. I see many new contractors caught in situations where they have given too much, thinking the future volume will offset the temporary losses, but find they have little left to give when additional concessions are requested. They think they are playing the game but they are being played.

2. Think of **concessions** in the mindset of a courtroom where **precedence** is being established. An adjuster or consultant may ask for a concession that seems reasonable, but by making this deal are you setting a precedent that you can maintain with future losses and/or in other areas of your estimate? As Lisa Lavender and I shared in a recent article, you must be mindful of **scope creep**[41]. Keep an eye out for those costly losses of time, resources, and profits that pop up as "simple requests" from carriers, clients and our own production teams.

3. As humans, we are loathe to blame our issues on all parties but ourselves, but if we are not making the effort to communicate early and often with the carrier and their representatives, we cannot cry bear at the end of the process when they sit in your chair, rip your invoice to shreds and eat all your porridge. Mutually beneficial relationships and precedence are both enhanced by clear, consistent, and **proactive communication**.

4. We have shared that it is helpful to have an **internal review** prior to sending your estimate to a carrier or third-party administrator. It is also helpful to have a good sounding board before you respond, and possibly overreact, to a customer when you are frustrated. Playing devil's advocate for each other can help team members steer clear of unnecessarily escalating interpersonal issues on a project.

Setting expectations is a critical skill for project managers. The ability to scan your workload and plan the overlapping schedules will help you to keep your current projects on their path to completion while you prepare to onboard new plates.

---

41 Lavender, L. & Isaacson, J. *Nothing is Scarier than Scope Creep.* Restoration and Remediation Magazine. https://www.randrmagonline.com/articles/89124-nothing-is-scarier-than-scope-creep

Have you demonstrated an ability to set realistic expectations with homeowners in regard to schedule, construction process, and completed product? If the answer is no, look for opportunities to learn and exercise those skills. If you think that you have done so, as your supervisor what do you need to do in order to be a viable candidate for a PM role?

David Watts (New York, NY) believes that project management style is an art, and to be a good project manager you have to first define what project management is.

- According to Webster's dictionary online, project management is *the process of planning, organising, staffing, directing, and controlling the production of a system*. Herein is a universal list of skills and key performance indicators if you want to be a strong project manager.
- David shares that the Restoration Industry Association (RIA) training materials define project management as the discipline of planning, organizing, securing, and managing resources to bring about the successful completion of specific project goals and objectives.

Both definitions speak to the importance of clarity and consistency. Various companies have various names or titles for project managers such as estimators, associates, project superintendents, project directors, and the list is endless as the specific job description also varies by organization. David states, "For argument's sake, I will define what I feel makes a successful 'project manager' in the restoration field. First, listen to the needs of your client and build rapport."

At the project outset, I like to set a precedence for how we are going to communicate, how frequently we are going to communicate, and who all needs to be included in the communication cycle.

Residential Project

On a residential project, if you have two partners, it is critical that you follow every conversation up with an email that carbon copies (cc) both parties. You do not want Partner B feeling like they are out of the loop and get yourself caught in a domestic tug-of-war.

This is also where signed selection forms come into play. Partner A can't come back and say, "We didn't authorize that." You will be able to pull up your email to show that, actually, Partner B signed this form and I emailed a copy to both of you on X date. Please understand this isn't a silver bullet that will put the vampire of discontent to rest, but it provides you much better standing than having no signed form and no follow-up email.

Speaking to the residential setting, Mr. Watts states that the customer is typically a homeowner and the project manager must have empathy for this event that has happened to their client. "Listen and understand what their pain is," admonishes David, "Source means to address those needs (mitigate the loss physically and metaphorically). When you listen to your client, let them tell the story, if they need to (empathy), before you start discussing the process (nuts and bolts) of the project." There will always be pressure to push the pace or even to rush.

As we discussed in a prior chapter, build the discipline to stay away from doing things faster, focus on building efficiency as a team (work on SPEeD). David continues, "While we all know we need to get started, sometimes rushing in too fast can be a negative thing. Discuss the bad news with them honestly, let them know that this process will be a stressful, disruptive, and frustrating time for them. It is a process and there will be an end, set everyone up for success by setting realistic expectations." The residential process is often linear.

Commercial Project

On a commercial project, there is typically less of a direct emotional tie to the process and the emphasis is on getting the work completed in a timely manner. For a business owner, the greatest loss of exposure is loss of business. The carrier is typically acutely aware of this reality as well. For many project managers, this can create opportunities for creative problem solving to meet critical objectives.

Communication with all parties is essential. Let's briefly discuss a scenario where our team is responding to an event in an apartment building. The process is normally more fast-paced than the residential situation outlined above. The client, typically a building owner or their property manager, wants you to solve the problem as soon as possible. Time is of the essence.

David Watts advises, "You handle this by outlining what the client priorities are in that building. Their pain may not be as personal as the homeowner, but you still need to understand what their pain is and the source means to address those needs."

Parties to the claim may include the onsite property manager, the maintenance staff, site security, building owner, adjuster, third party consultant, etc. There may be multiple representatives from each category. Typically on large projects, you will want to set a weekly or bi-weekly meeting to discuss priorities, progress, duration, and cost.

As a project manager, it is a good practice to establish your burn rate. In simple terms, this is your projected weekly and/or daily costs of production. Your cost may vary from day to day or week to week depending on how much labor, materials, and equipment you have on-site, but with a simple formula, you can calculate averages that will help all parties be on the same page with general costs.

_____ **quantity x** _____ **rate =** _____ **daily costs for item**

With "item" above you will input labor, equipment, and materials to achieve your calculations. We discuss this principle in greater detail in the prior chapter on estimating in the section on production rate. If you have multiple shifts the rates may change so you will have to create additional columns. Typically a burn rate does not have to be precise but it is helpful in regularly communicating with all parties that we are at X cost to date. You can also project that by X date our costs will be X so that cost reserves can be established.

When damage occurs in an apartment or office building, the unit residents are upset and often direct their frustrations toward their management team. By having empathy and a sense of urgency, David says that our goal as restorers is to get the complaints to stop. In a commercial or retail setting, the most pressing need is to resume business as quickly as possible with the least amount of operational interruption. Because of these unique factors, the commercial loss may not be as linear in the execution, it is important to communicate and document what your team does, as well as why and who authorized deviations from the norm in the service the client needs.

As David said, "Listen to the needs of your client and build rapport." Find out what their pain point or concerns are and source solutions to reduce both. Bring the Restoration Triangle together through consistent communication and keep everyone on the same page as to the scope, cost, and duration of the project. By doing so you can give your client the confidence that Mr. Watts speaks of, "It is a process and there will be an end, set everyone up for success by setting realistic expectations."

Expectations should be clearly understood and documented by everyone at every stage of the process. We tell our technicians that if they didn't document it then it didn't happen. This truth applies to project management. Everything should be in writing to track expectations and agreements. As you continue to juggle spinning plates, make progress on your workload by clearing projects as efficiently as possible.

If you want to manage projects rather than always feel like you are putting out fires, build a process that helps you start strong and finish strong.

CHAPTER 6

Crafting the Customer Experience

*No matter how good the team or how efficient
the methodology if we're not solving the
right problem, the project fails.*
Woody Williams

Life is about opportunity, not convenience. Whenever you are in the phase of proving yourself, you are not going to get the best assignments. If you want a shot at a project management opportunity, most likely this will come in covering for someone or filling in to take on a project where you have to put out a fire. Your opportunity will be less than ideal (a turd) and it will come at an inopportune time.

This is similar to building or expanding your book of business. When you are trying to earn a new referral partner you have to understand that people hate change. They dislike change so much that they will stick with a service provider that is under-serving them long before they will make a change. As the saying goes, "Better the devil you know."

When you do get your chance, either with a customer or with your manager, it is not going to be an ideal project. The scope and timing will suck. For example, the contractor (the "devil" they know) that the client you are chasing is currently using might miss a call at 5 pm on a Friday and so the client contacts you with the opportunity. Be ready. A similar scenario will likely play out in your first opportunity to take on a project management role; i.e. a PM misses a call or screws a job up.

When you are ready to do what you said you would do, whether it is in your own career advancement or when you are attempting to onboard a new client, you must recognize and seize your opportunity. I will share a story that signifies both.

I was in a position to market our team's services with the long-term upside of bringing in more work for the office so that it would create an advancement opportunity for me. "Go get enough work that I have to make you a project manager," was basically my assignment. Challenge accepted.

I stopped into a client's office and I could tell that this insurance agent was going to be my kind of customer. We shared similar values and we hit it off. This agent told me that they were loyal to their current provider and didn't have any complaints. I told them, "I'd like to be your number two. If they ever get overloaded or don't answer your call, give me a shot."

I believe that if you have to knock someone else down in order to make yourself stand out, you don't have much to stand on. There is plenty of work and bad-mouthing your competition is not a good strategy for success. The billionaire owner of the Dallas Mavericks and gritty entrepreneur Mark Cuban writes in his e-book *How To Win*, "Rather than trying to convince people you are the best, let the quality of your work do the talking[42]."

In order to let the quality of your work do the talking, you need the phone to ring. I know that our first few referrals from a new client are not going to be ideal. I tell my teams, give it three projects. After three assignments we will know whether this customer is just using us for their junk jobs that their regular provider doesn't want, or they are giving us a real shot to earn their business. I use this same logic when onboarding subcontractors. "Give us three projects, and then you will get an idea of the type of work we can partner with you on."

---

[42] Cuban, M. (2013) *How to Win at the Sport of Business*. Diversion Books.

So, the call came. We received an assignment that was going to require a lot of leg work to lock down but I sensed it was a real shot. Without breaking the rules we pushed the boundaries of what we would normally do to go above and beyond for this client and the agent. I gave no hint that anything was wrong other than to clarify what was and was not covered under the policy.

Some of the materials were special order items, so I made sure to update the client and the agent at least weekly and follow everything up with an email with all parties cc'd. Communication is critical at every phase of your career development and will set you apart from your competitors and co-workers. We survived the project. I sat down with the agent and we discussed all of the elements that went into making the customer happy. Only then did I share that we were marginally profitable and I was riding the line of what we would normally do.

Why am I sharing this? If you agree that life is about opportunity, not convenience, you have to keep your eyes and ears open for those chances. Working hard and being willing to learn will put you in positions to see and grab a hold of doors that wouldn't otherwise open if you are waiting for something cool to happen. Be proactive. Go make something happen.

Your pathway to project management will not be wrapped up in a pretty bow. You have to be willing to go above and beyond to make your "luck". Use wisdom to discern whether you are being given a real chance to earn your way upward or if you are getting taken advantage of. The same will be true once you are in the role.

You have to do the dance to get your work done, often in less than ideal circumstances. Project management, especially in property restoration, requires you to constantly be ready to pivot. As described in the prior chapter, you have the great challenge of keeping many plates, over a large territory, spinning, with each plate feeling like they are more important than the other plates.

Maybe you are asking, why should I focus on customer experience when all I want to do is make money? First, making money isn't just making money. We will discuss the difference between revenue and profit in Chapter 7. If you want to make money (revenue) and you want your company to be sustainable, you need to profit from the revenue that you bring in.

That agent shared a story where the prior provider, someone they had referred several hundred thousands of dollars of work to over several years, ultimately broke their plate with the agent over less than five hundred dollars. There was a disagreement with a customer and because the restoration company could not resolve it, the agent had an upset customer in their office complaining about the contractor that the agent had referred.

The agent, who has become a personal and professional friend of mine, said they had hoped to mediate peace between the two parties. When confronted the contractor decided to double down on their unwillingness to budge. This opened the door for my team to move from a distant number two that likely would never get a shot to being the new number one. They were unwilling to budge for a few hundred dollars to keep their pipeline and I was willing to risk some margin to earn an account that I knew would be well worth it.

I wonder if the former contractor looks back on their decision and still believes those few hundred dollars were worth it. The customer experience lays the foundation for customer satisfaction, and customer retention is both less expensive as well as more effective than customer acquisition. Simply stated, it's cheaper and better to keep a client than it is to try to gain a new one.

The Importance of the Customer Experience

If you are a project manager and you want to advance your career, customer satisfaction is key to getting noticed and being profitable. An unhappy customer will wreak havoc on your project scope, duration, and costs because you will be playing from behind to get their completion signature. The best way to ensure that the project ends well is to start and keep it going well (prevention).

A few statistics from *Forbes*[43] magazine on the impact of customer experience:

- 84% of companies that work to improve their customer experience report an increase in their revenue.
- Companies with initiatives to improve their customer experience see employee engagement increase by 20% on average.
- Companies with engaged employees outperform the competition by 147%.

Why should you care about customer service? According to these statistics, the juice is worth the squeeze. When you are intentional with crafting your customer experience, those efforts work and will result in increased revenues. It helps your progress and also is a vision that your team can get behind, leading to better overall engagement.

Assuming that the above figures don't overlap, that's 104% return on investment. Employee engagement is synonymous with buy-in. When your team members understand the vision, want to contribute to achieving the goals, and you are helping them develop their abilities, you will have a fighting chance to be sustainable as an organization.

---

[43] Morgan, B. (2019, September 24) *50 Stats That Prove The Value Of Customer Experience*. Forbes.
https://www.forbes.com/sites/blakemorgan/2019/09/24/50-stats-that-prove-the-value-of-customer-experience

Do you want to beat your competition? It's not about finding better people, as though the grass is greener in some other pasture. I am sure this line is something you've used with your employees, yet it is true for employee retention and team development as well. Marion Wade[44], the founder of restoration brand ServiceMaster, said early in his career, "Don't expect to build a super company with super people. You must build a great company with ordinary people."

You have to develop an engaged team and project managers play a key role in the workplace culture as they have direct interaction with the technicians and sub-contractors who are serving your customers. Owners and managers must ensure that these factors are understood and executed consistently throughout the organization. When an owner or manager makes a public statement but doesn't see it through, there is organizational dissonance.

- Customers switching companies due to poor service costs U.S. companies a total of $1.6 trillion
- Offering a high-quality customer experience can lower the cost of serving customers by up to 33%[45]

What is the cost of poor customer experience? Cumulatively, customer attrition has a high cost. Have you ever broken down your customer acquisition costs? Attracting new clientele requires heavy investments of time and resources in repeated doses. If you aren't tracking your efforts at an individual level then you are cutting yourself short of valuable data that will help you to improve your process.

---

[44] Erisman, A. (2020) *The ServiceMaster Story: Navigating the Tension Between People and Profit.* Christian Book Distributors

[45] Morgan, 2019

If you aren't discussing wins and losses as a team then you are missing opportunities to help each other shorten the learning curve. While you must acquire new clients to grow your business, don't forget to double down on your customer engagement and retention endeavors. Fred Reichheld shared research from Bain & Company that demonstrated, "Increasing customer retention rates by 5% increases profits by 25% to 95%."

Developing simple, yet intentional, client engagement and retention measures can pay significant returns for your team. It's no secret that customer retention is driven by customer satisfaction, but did you know that investing in a consistent customer experience can reduce your costs significantly? Again, starting with the intention to develop happy customers will result in better overall profitability.

- American consumers will pay 17% more to purchase from a company with a reputation for great service.
- Loyal customers are five times more likely to purchase again and four times more likely to refer a friend to the company.
- 87% of customers who say they had a great experience will make another purchase from the company, compared to 18% of customers who had a very poor experience.

All things being equal, your reputation is a significant differentiator, especially in communities where word-of-mouth travels (which means all communities). In property restoration, the repeat customer is often overlooked. While restoration contractors will pay third-party vendor fees or participate in rising plumbing referral costs, how consistently do you invest in cultivating and improving your customer experience so that you reap the referral and repeat potential?

To recap, investing in your customer experience will increase your revenue, increase your employee engagement, reduce your costs, increase your client retention, and open you to greater opportunities for new work through referrals. What else do you need to know to

understand that your people skills as a project manager are critical to your success, the
development of your team, and the growth of your organization?

The Customer Experience is Driven by the Employee Experience

If you want to achieve your profitability goals, you have to communicate clearly and transparently with your team members. You cannot tell your team to hit the target, but:

- Hide the target in an undisclosed location (not sharing any of your numbers)
- Refuse to provide them with the necessary tools (how do you hit a target without a bow or arrows?)
- Never set aside time to train them to utilize their weapons (dangerous).

If the target were the bullseye, our tools were bows and arrows, and we were preparing for an annual tournament, wouldn't we invest in quality tools, regular training, and periodic check-ins to track the effectiveness of our team preparations? Yes. Yet, in business, the status quo in many companies is to hide the numbers, be stingy with resources, and inconsistently invest in training.

Alignment (see The DYOJO Accountability Matrix below) is not complicated, but it also isn't easy. You will constantly be working to clarify your organizational expectations and consistently train to refine organizational norms. Remember, accountability is the result of investing in clarity and consistency. "If you are building a culture where honest expectations are communicated and peer accountability is the norm, then the group will address poor performance and attitudes," says speaker and author of *Necessary Endings*, Dr. Henry Cloud.

The DYOJO Accountability Matrix

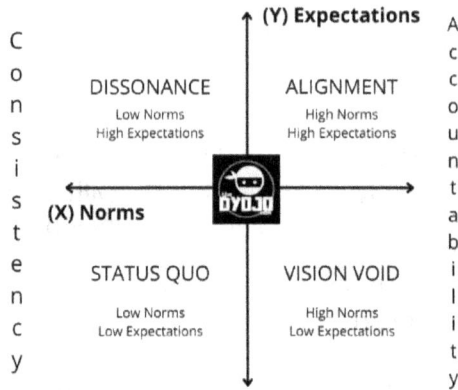

(Y) Expectations

Consistency (vertical left axis)

Accountability (vertical right axis)

DISSONANCE	ALIGNMENT
Low Norms	High Norms
High Expectations	High Expectations

(X) Norms

STATUS QUO	VISION VOID
Low Norms	High Norms
Low Expectations	Low Expectations

There is a progression to accountability, it does not materialize on its own. Accountability for a person and an organization comes from consistency in executing clearly established values. Effective accountability traces itself back to clarity in vision, communication of values, and consistent effort from all levels within the team to live out those principles. A healthy exercise for anyone in a position of leadership is to reflect on their strengths and weaknesses with regards to *the Four Pillars of Success* (aka The 4 P's):

People. How can I help attract, develop and retain good people?
Process. How can I help to clarify our process and build consistency in our systems?
Production. How can I help to improve our output as a team?
Progress. How can I help to inspire our team to build momentum toward our goals?

Your struggle to develop your culture starts with who you let into your team and is exacerbated by acting like the status quo. How do you unlock the secret to recruiting, hiring, and retaining good talent in property restoration?

Property restoration is labor-intensive. As you build your company and scale for growth, you will need good people. Once you have hired all of the friends, family, and referrals from within your inner circles, what are you going to do to attract and retain new recruits? Restorers across the country are having similar issues and hiring is consistently topic number one when professionals meet to discuss their common struggles. Yet, rather than dig deep, look in the mirror, and make some real changes, we often fall into the odd comfort of shared misery.

I will do my best to share some ideas that will help you to shorten your DANG learning curve for recruiting, hiring, and retaining good talent. Before we go any further, I will warn you about what you already know - being intentional is key to success but it is no guarantee of it. You will have to STOP doing certain things that are distracting you from your progress and START doing those things that develop the right mindset and habits for growth.

Before we perpetuate the narrative that younger generations are lazy, let's analyze whether it bears merit[46]. Consider the following, a candidate can work for either:

    A. Your property restoration company where they will be on call 24 hours a day, will have to wade through sewage, work in various climates, and be exposed to unnamed hazards.

    B. Or, they could get the same (or similar pay) at a company with predictable hours, health insurance, free coffee, and college assistance.

---

[46] Isaacson, J. (2017, April 19) *Strong Leaders Always Play The Blame Game.* YFS Magazine. https://yfsmagazine.com/2017/04/19/how-leaders-manage-high-employee-turnover

If you were assessing this scenario without bias to your needs as a restoration company owner or manager, which option would you choose? Would you choose the coffee shop for $_____ (fill-in-the-blank) dollars an hour or the water damage mitigation company that still wants to hire technicians at pay rates from the 1990s? While your blood may boil thinking about how the insurance companies haven't raised their rates to pay you for your services, you would be doubling down on the blame game rather than addressing the issue at hand.

It may feel good to complain, but doing so will net you nothing in the recruitment game nor in the compensation for services argument. Money alone will not attract good candidates, nor will it compel poor performers to transform themselves into quality workers. As you hunt for the magic wand that will solve your recruitment problems, you must not allow that pursuit to cloud your view of the workforce you already have within your organization.

How many of your proven, or above-average, team members have received merit-based, or even cost of living, raises recently? Lisa Lavender shares some powerful perspectives in our book on the impact of saying, "Thank You." For your top performers your "thank you" should show up on their paycheck and/or their opportunities to provide additional value and receive additional compensation.

I recently had a talk with a contractor who thought paying a technician more than a fixed [fill in the blank for your market] dollar figure an hour was getting into deep waters. Believe me, I get it, you cannot squeeze juice from a dried turnip. But, how much money do you throw into recruiting, training, and losing warm bodies without questioning the expense or the return on investment?

Which is a better investment:

- **Option 1** - A few above-average employees who consistently perform at $X/hr higher than the status quo
- **Option 2** - A bunch of below-average employees who are hot and cold in their performance at whatever the going rate is in your market?

If someone can do 1.5x, 2x, or even 3x what a lackluster employee can do, are you adjusting your system to enable you to keep the performers?

I believe that the secret to recruiting the younger generation to work in this labor-intensive industry starts with being clearer with your purpose and vision. Restoration contractors have always struggled to attract employees. The events of 2020 didn't help and there are many factors we could argue about, but it will not do you any good to play the blame game. In short, this is secret number one and it applies to any time in history, to any business, and to any generation. If you blame the people that you are trying to recruit, you are inviting and spreading a losing mindset.

If you continue to do things the way that you've always done them, with regards to recruiting, hiring, and retaining good talent, your failure to adapt is a losing habit. My good friend Gerrett Stier, of GMS Distribution wealth and fame, 2020's breakout beard of the year, and renowned host of The GMS Podcast, recently did a show with organizational psychologist Dr. Jessica Stahl. Their discussion followed a two-part interview with Young Guns in our industry. She summarized culture as the experience your employees have with your organization.

Dr. Stahl shared many helpful insights, including that young people want to be a part of something bigger than themselves, feel like they are part of a family, but also that they trust the people and the processes of the business. While it may be difficult to keep up with the speed in which things change, these core principles are timeless. Resources like this podcast series help intentional leaders to stop chasing their tails and start making real changes.

Blaming the incoming workforce may get you applause from your peers who struggle with the same issues and who also don't want to face the facts that it's your problem (the organization wanting to hire) not their problem (the young recruits who are not applying or staying in your companies). In their excellent book, *Insuring Tomorrow*, Tony Canas and Carly Burnham do a great job dispelling many of the myths about millennials as well as shedding some practical insights into how employers can connect with the current labor pool.

I will warn you, that if you listen to Episode 66 of The GMS Podcast (*The Employee Experience*) and you read *Insuring Tomorrow*, you will have fewer reasons to play the blame game. You will also acquire a deeper understanding of the mindset and habits that will lead your organization to succeed with recruiting, hiring, and retaining good talent.

Not too surprisingly, even as things rapidly change, there are foundational principles that you must continually work on in order to be competitive. Be as intentional with marketing and developing internally (to your people) as you are externally (to your clients). There is no easy road nor is there a shortcut; there is no secret. If you will STOP playing the blame game, you will START to own your way forward.

If you want to pursue your ideal clients, you will need to have people who reflect and deliver on those ideals. If you are unhappy with the clients you have, there may be a direct correlation to the quality of the team you have recruited, hired, and retained. This does not mean that you are hunting for unicorns or ninjas (or whatever current moniker people are using).

Going back to the Marion Wade mindset, STOP searching for the "super" employee and START developing your own "ordinary" talent to be the best that you all can be together. Making this shift mentally will help you form habits that focus your energy on making progress in the process.

As an owner and a manager, you can solve many of your issues by being intentional with your recruiting, onboarding, and training processes. Be clearer about what you need and use that data to drive how and who you hire. Keep and develop the talent that you have. You have spent a lot of time and money to get your staff into the organization, and reap the full investment by seeing the development process through.

Jack Welch, famed leader of General Electric (GE) in its 1990's heyday, had a paradigm for focusing your people's energy as a leader. Jack believed in candor, saying that the best thing you can do for an employee is to tell them where they stand and how they can improve. "Failing to differentiate among employees — and holding on to bottom-tier performers — is actually the cruelest form of management there is." Jack believed in 20-70-10[47]:

- 20% of your employees are top performers, "You should take the top 20 percent of your employees and make them feel loved." Focus your retention energies and resources on keeping these top performers.
- 70% of your employees are middle performers, "Take the middle 70 percent and tell them what they need to do to get into the top 20 percent." These are the ones that you need to coach and determine whether they can progress.
- 10% of your employees are low performers that you need to allow to move out of the organization.

While you would not be alone if you do not agree with this "candid" approach, have you ever stopped to analyze how much time you spend working on issues with your lowest performers? Being clearer with your expectations is an exercise that is beneficial to owners, managers, and team members alike.

How much time do you spend in self-inflicted misery wrestling with clients that you should have fired before the job started and lackluster people you should never have hired?

Too often a lack of clarity is at the root of a lack of consistency in production and performance. Before you can make progress, you must identify roles and responsibilities, with key performance indicators, and regular goals.

---

[47] Welch, J. (2005) *Winning*. HarperCollins.

Programs like Entrepreneurial Operating System (EOS) as outlined in *Traction* by Gino Wickman have helped many leadership teams to get a better handle on this process. When you have issues, you cannot ignore them but you do need to prioritize them. You cannot solve every problem all at once. Your leadership team may not have developed resources for vetting a challenge, so you likely will have opportunities to help model practical approaches.

One resource that Wickman shares is called IDS[48]. This is a three-step process to Identify, Discuss, and Solve an issue. Simple, right? Yet, how often do we overcomplicate issues and allow them to lag in the land of the unresolved? When you are faced with an issue, bring your team in to discuss it, and experiment with solutions.

Like many managers, you are probably asking, "Why can't we find good people?" We all have to take an honest look at how we are perceived as an industry. Then you have to dig even deeper to face how you are perceived as a company in your local market. For many years, property restoration wasn't even a profession that anyone really knew about. Twenty years ago, I knew what construction and carpet cleaning were, but I had no idea that mold remediation, water damage mitigation, or insurance claims were its own industry.

To some degree, this has changed, but in the wider lens of the skilled trades, all organizations are having difficulty attracting and retaining employees. There are outliers, and it will do you good to research similar companies in similar markets that have a good reputation or creative measures companies like Merit Construction have taken to focus their efforts to become "an employer of choice."

You may be tempted to think that must mean a company like Merit has no standards or doesn't discipline its team members. But when you discuss these measures with intentional owners

[48] Wickman, G. *How Can Your Team Solve Issues in Half the Time?* Entrepreneurial Operating System.
https://www.eosworldwide.com/clarity-break/how-can-your-team-solve-issues-in-half-the-time

like Tammy Birklid, you uncover creative ways that modern leaders are building accountability.

If the customer experience starts with the employee experience, how does this change your approach? What would it look like to build a company where people were coming to you looking for a job, not just because they needed one, but because they heard your organization is such a great place to work?

You might say, "I'd love to be an employer of choice, but NO ONE is applying right now." I understand. To borrow the IDS process mentioned earlier: (1) You have identified an issue, (2) Have you discussed with your team what you are going to do differently? (3) Recruiting, hiring, and retaining good talent are not challenges that are going to disappear or be "solved" in the near future. BUT (and it's a big but), you must adapt.

Shouldn't this reality be all the more encouragement to invest in the people you have? Double down on caring for your top ten percent and invest in training your middle seventy percent to elevate their engagement and performance. Create opportunities for team members to thrive in their area of expertise rather than pigeonhole them to promote into an area of incompetence (Peter Principle).

Elevating your customer experience will help you more consistently achieve and expand your profitability goals. A happy customer is much more likely to sign off on a project completion form and issue a final payment than an upset customer. A happy customer is much more likely to refer you to their friends and family, which should create additional access to ideal clients. Customer satisfaction has as much to do with how you make the client feel about the project as the actual work itself.

The client experience is directly tied to the employee experience as your team members are the embodiment of your brand with your customers. Our simple formula from *Be Intentional: Culture* will help you to keep your priorities where they are most effective:

- Taking care of your culture is critical to taking care of your people.
- Taking care of your people is critical to taking care of your customers.
- Taking care of your customers is the foundation of a sustainable business.
- **Therefore, developing, adapting, and caring for your culture is essential to your vitality as an organization.**

CHAPTER 7

The B Word

Alright, stop. Collaborate and listen.
If there was a problem, yo I'll solve it.
Rob Van Winkle, aka Vanilla Ice

If you want to be a project manager, you have to first understand the project(s) that you are managing. The project is defined by the agreed-upon scope of work. This includes the resulting cost and timeframe to complete the defined scope. Insurance is unique in that the scope is often negotiated between the contractor and the insurance carrier. Once agreed upon, this scope becomes the reference for the contract between the customer and the contractor.

Expectations and/or key performance indicators (KPIs) for project managers include: understanding each project's budget and finding a way to stay under it for the defined scope of work. Project management should not be over complicated by the property restoration professional. The role and responsibility of the project manager is to manage the project - per the scope, on time, and on budget.

I think it is important to note that no project should start without a clear contract. We will not go deep into these details but many project managers are responsible for securing the contract so it is important to mention aspects of this portion of the pre-production process. The contract is a key part of setting expectations by clarifying the roles and responsibilities of the parties of the claim as well as confirming the financial agreement.

If you need help understanding the elements of a sound agreement and strategies to better secure your receivables, I would encourage you to refer to *The Book On Restoration Collections*[49] by Edward H. Cross. Ed is known as The Restoration Lawyer for his many years of volunteer service, lending his expertise to core restoration organizations such as the Institute of Inspection Cleaning and Restoration Certification (IICRC) and Restoration Industry Association (RIA). He has dedicated his practice to advocating for the legal and financial interests of the property restoration industry and has successfully resolved over 1,000 claims.

Ed joined me to discuss his unique journey into the restoration industry and his advice for contractors on the precursor to The DYOJO Podcast, something I initially called *Three Questions With A Pro*[50]. Ed advises that all contractors should STOP using "archaic" work authorizations and invest in a clear lump sum contract. In discussing the best practices for lump-sum agreements, he says,

"Despite the name, the original 'fixed' price need not be permanent. It is a basis of understanding to begin the project. The contract should state that the price is an estimate offered in good faith and is based on presently available information gathered during an initial visual observation...the price is subject to reasonable change as further information is gathered[51]."

The estimate that was utilized to negotiate the agreed-upon scope then becomes the reference document for the subsequent contract. Your scope, cost, and duration are subject to reasonable change as further information is gathered. The customer and the production team need to understand what is

---

[49] Available through his website, https://edcross.com/product/the-book-on-restoration-collections/

[50] The DYOJO Podcast, Episode 3

[51] Cross, E. (2008, September 24) *Will Your Contracts Be Used Against You? Gosh I Hope Not.* Restoration & Remediation Magazine. https://www.randrmagonline.com/articles/83627-will-your-contracts-be-used-against-you-gosh-i-hope-not

and what is not in the agreed-upon scope of work. The expectation needs to be set with the customer and as best we are able, the scope should have been written in such a way that it is readily adapted into a functioning production plan.

In this Chapter, we will dive further into the details that go into the production plan. Your job as the project manager is to empower your team to execute the agreed-upon scope in a manner that is on time and within budget. In doing so you have a key role in bringing the expectations of the customer and the details of the scope together. Seven factors that go into a solid production plan include

- Job Costs
- Labor
- Materials
- Equipment
- Subcontractors
- Overhead
- Profit

Job Costs

So often we hear, "That's just the cost of doing business," when working in insurance claims; especially as it applies to charging for overhead and profit (O&P). We will go into the topic of O&P in more detail in just a moment, but remember, this book is a primer on the topic of project management. Your costs as a business owner, manager, estimator, project manager, and so forth, fall into two primary categories: direct (aka job) costs and indirect costs.

Project managers are typically responsible for creating a budget and tracking their direct job costs, which include materials, equipment, and labor. In some companies, they track their project management time (or most of it) as a direct cost, so you will need to incorporate that into your plan. Other companies consider project managers to be exclusively overhead.

In their article, *The What, When & How of General Conditions (Overhead) and Markup (Profit)*[52], authors Jonathon C. Held, Lisa A. Enloe, and Granger Stuck go into helpful detail regarding overhead and profit. These third-party consultants, from the firm J.S. Held, outline some of the many items that should be considered with regards to the overall cost of doing business and therefore should be appropriately charged for:

- **General Conditions** or Overhead, and Markup (Fee or Profit), which are the costs associated with the job site management of the project, including items such as project management staff, job site trailers, telephones, administrative as well as temporary roads, temporary utilities, permits, fees, general hoisting, safety, and cleaning, not specifically associated with individual elements being erected.
- **Indirect costs** can be referred to as General Conditions, General Requirements, or Field Office Overhead, and can also include costs associated with and delineated in the General and Supplemental Conditions of the Contract, and (typically) Division 1 of the Specifications. These documents outline the work rules and obligations set forth and required by the Contract.
- **Markup, Fee or Profit** is intended to cover a portion of General and Administrative (G&A or Home Office Overhead) costs and provide profit for the contractor or construction manager. G&A are costs not associated with a specific project but account for the contractor's business operating expenses including estimating and preconstruction services, accounting, marketing, etc.

From the project outset, the estimator and project manager should be working together to formulate a scope of work that can be executed according to the standard. How often do you hear that something should not be in your estimate because it is

---

[52] Held, J. Enloe, L., & Stuck, G. *The What, When, & How Much of General Conditions (Overhead) and Markup (Profit)*. JS Held. https://jsheld.com/insights/articles/the-what-when-how-much-of-general-conditions-overhead-and-markup-profit

"**the cost of doing business**?" Ben Justesen wrote on this topic in Restoration and Remediation Magazine advising,

> *"Contractors should be making their own prices and charging for all of their costs, whether it be in line items or included in their margin, and the software the contractor uses is inconsequential. It can be a lump sum, time and material plus a percentage, or unit line items. Any way this is done, the retail labor rate must be determined."*

Labor rates are unique to regions, states, and local markets, but beyond this they are unique to your company structure and pricing model. It is unfortunate that many contractors don't fully understand and therefore do not completely charge for all of their costs, direct and indirect alike. Mr. Justesen continues,

> *"One takes their worker's wage, plus the labor burden (payroll taxes), and then a contractor must determine the margin to make on top of that from their financials. A budgeted gross profit can be determined by knowing your overhead and indirect costs plus the targeted net profit as a percentage. This margin will be put into the labor overhead. If one puts a markup percentage at the end of their estimate (O&P), then they would not include that percentage in the labor overhead[53]."*

Whatever you do, your team must identify the metrics to understand your real costs. Ben is a big proponent of reclaiming ground that has been conceded too frequently over the last decades of the industry, he says, "Contractors everywhere determine their own pricing; it is time for our industry to do the same." He as been working closely with the Restoration Industry Association and the Advocacy and Government Affairs Committee (AGA) which has produced a series of position papers[54] to help restoration contractors understand these initiatives and implement them consistently.

---

[53] Justesen, B. (2019, August 7) *The Cost of Doing Business: Determining Your Own Pricing.* Restoration & Remediation Magazine. https://www.randrmagonline.com/articles/88567-the-cost-of-doing-business-determining-your-own-pricing

[54] Cleaning & Restoration Editor (2020, October 23) *The Restoration Industry Association Announces a Release of Position Statements.* Restoration Industry Association. https://www.restorationindustry.org/cleaning-and-

Labor

One area of consideration for your team is whether estimating and project management time is categorized as overhead or direct job cost. While the only way to have a true cost analysis of a project is to track every direct and indirect cost associated with producing the work, a lot of this depends on how you capture your financial data.

If you are starting a company, I would suggest doing your best to track direct costs accurately. If you are the owner and you spend 2 hours on the initial inspection and another 3 hours writing the estimate and discussing the claim with the carrier, it is helpful to track that time as a direct cost to the job. On paper, you will be in the negative 5 hours already, but you will be building the data you need to make decisions based upon objective information versus the subjective measure of how you feel your organization is doing.

As discussed above, if the estimator creates the scope and creates the budget, a common approach is to include hours for project management as part of this process. This may not lead to an accurate capture of project management time, but it can be useful for ensuring financial goals are reached in how the project costs are captured.

If the project manager is creating the scope then they can input how many hours they anticipate for the project as well as reasons for consideration when requesting additional time from the carrier and/or client. This is another area where communication of the organization's goals and approaches to cost accounting are critical to developing your estimating and project management strategies. Everything is connected.

restoration/restoration-industry-association-announces-release-position-statements

In August of 2019, *the Restoration Advocate*, Ed Cross, announced the Restoration Advocacy Report #3. This update from the RIA AGA Committee made this declaration about labor rates in Xactimate,

"Based on our review and comparison with the Bureau of Labor Statistics pricing models, Xactimate utilizes the lowest costs available to measure hourly trade rates. Trade rates for restoration workers should rank among the highest-paid due to the physical work environment (unstable building conditions, hazards, environmental issues), the time-sensitive nature of the work, the investments employers must make in certifications insurers require for technicians, the unique risk exposure entailed with this type of work and many other factors."

Before you can get too hot and bothered about the shortfalls within Xactimate, first you must get a firm grip on the real costs of your labor and overhead, something many companies lack, and second, you must understand that Xactimate updates pricing based on feedback through their upload channels.

Ben Justesen built his restoration company in the "desert oasis" of Moses Lake. You probably have never heard of this small town in Eastern Washington, but Ben is proof that being intentional with your goals can lead to changes that improve your local market, especially **if you work with your competitors as allies to elevate the playing field for all**.

When you are getting started in business, a standardized tool such as Xactimate can be incredibly helpful in creating numbers based on objective measures rather than just shooting from the hip. Whatever estimating approach or software that you utilize, you need to understand where your shortfalls exist and these must be communicated in your production plan so that your production team can create a realistic budget and supplements can be actively pursued.

Materials

Pricing on materials is often in flux. This has especially been true in recent years with a pandemic that has affected multiple points of the supply chain that we often take for granted.

Anthony Nelson, President of Premier Restoration Hawaii, has made a habit of checking material assumptions on Xactimate against common supply stores in his markets.

I don't think any of the readers would be surprised that there are variances, but what is surprising is how deep those variances are on some of the most common items such as drywall corner bead or interior doors, and how some of these materials' prices have not changed in the program in many years. Anthony has been keeping a running spreadsheet with these items and the reference for current pricing.

If the cost of an interior door is off by $50 and you buy 100 doors over the course of the year, that's $5,000.00 of legitimate variance that you should be able to recover versus taking that hit without even knowing it. The Advocacy and Government Affairs committee of the RIA is working to make Xactware aware of these items, but even if they should produce a position paper and training on this topic, it will be up to restoration contractors to present the issue in their market. Rising tides do raise all ships, so this will include educating our peers and even our competitors so that we can collaborate to even out the playing field in a professional manner.

Equipment

If you are a mitigation contractor, you likely have a stock of drying equipment. Repairs contractors approach tools and equipment in various ways. It is important to have and maintain the resources that you need to execute your work. Some equipment is costly, but if it contributes to greater efficiency, while also making the work safer, you will want to take a serious look at pulling the trigger on the investment.

I tend to be a conservative investor in the sense that if I can live without it I almost see it as a challenge to do so just to prove a point. Yet, if my team comes to me with a well-thought-out case for why something should be added to our arsenal, I will do my part to set aside the resources or advocate with the powers that be to pursue the purchase.

This can be a productive process, when the crew wants a shiny new object, have them make the case and use it as a teaching moment to discuss how important profitability is to your organization for making these purchases. Too many owners and managers are hesitant to open up the books, but transparency is a building block to ownership and buy-in from your team.

As mentioned in the prior section on material, Anthony Nelson has also found that many of the assumptions in Xactimate regarding rental equipment also contain variances. While the majority of equipment for reconstruction contractors is "embedded in the line items" or "the cost of doing business" it is important to read the line item descriptions to confirm what is and is not included in the pricing. Items such as scaffolding and boom lifts may be necessary on projects and you want to ensure you are charging appropriately for those costs.

Overhead and profit (O&P)

Ben Justesen notes, "If a business wanted to have a 10 percent net profit while covering a 30 percent overhead, then it would have to make a 40 percent margin on top of covering the aforementioned costs. There is 'overhead and profit', which is a 20 percent markup, which translates to a 16.67 percent margin." As he helpfully broke it down in a class he invited me to at his facility in my hometown of Moses Lake, Washington:

- If your estimate is $1,000.00
- You add 10% overhead (O) and 10% profit (P), total of 20% or $200.00
- Your bill (not including sales tax, where applicable) would be $1,200.00
- If your true costs were $1,000.00 then your actual gross margin at $200.00 is only 16.67%
- $1,000.00 x 20% = $200.00 markup
- $1,200.00 - $1,000.00 (cost) = $200.00 margin
- $200.00 / $1,200.00 = 16.67% overhead and profit
- Therefore, 20% markup leads to 16.67% margin

Markup Infographic

A 20% markup results in a 16.67% margin

$100.00	Estimated Costs
$20.00	**Markup** ($100 × 1.2)
$120.00	Sales price
$100.00	COGS
$20.00	Gross Profit
16.67%	Gross Profit **Margin** ($20 / $120)

Mr. Justesen elaborates, *"One also needs to consider that there is no markup on materials besides the 'overhead and profit.' So the Labor Overhead needs to be a blend of what is needed on top of both the labor and material costs. Both the profit and the budget can be determined this way. Once you determine your base wage and your final retail labor rate for each trade, then you can submit those as feedback. This feedback tool seems to work slowly but it eventually worked[55]."* At the time of his article in Cleaning and Restoration (C&R) Magazine, in Ben's markets, as Just Right Cleaning and Construction is multi-site in Eastern Washington, he saw labor rates increase by as little as $0.50 and as high as $15.00.

Subcontractors

A lot of restoration contractors who have been in the business for some time feel like doing program or third-party administrator (TPA) work is akin to making a deal with the devil. In this mindset, the contractor uploads lackluster estimates get reviewed, then cut, and now they have to execute on an agreed-upon scope that they believe has been stripped of all profitability. What options does the contractor have if they want to make money? Go find a subcontractor that they can pass the low-margin work to and beat them up on their pricing.

[55] Justesen, B. (2018, February 14) *2018 Patricia L. Harman Gold Quill Award: Ben Justesen.* Restoration Industry Association. https://www.restorationindustry.org/cleaning-and-restoration/2018-patricia-l-harman-golden-quill-award-ben-justesen

This may be a simplified version but it happens every day. Does this subcontractor habit make sense? If you believe in the golden rule, this approach is both illogical and the opposite of that basic principle of human decency.

You made your deal, you get beat up and complain about your deal, so you go find someone for whom you can now be the devil and beat them into a deal where you can dish out the beatings. The article I previously referenced from Ben Justesen received the prestigious Golden Quill Award in 2018. Ben discusses this twisted thinking about profit and subcontractors,

"I innocently and naively perceived revenue that produced more than the 20 percent markup of the 'Overhead & Profit' to be 'bonus revenue.' As a result, the only way we could generate the revenue necessary to remain a viable business was to pre-negotiate deep sub-contractor discounts for services and products, while our service sheets were comprehensively composed with each service line item indicated. After much-needed discussions with my father and others in the industry, I learned that a 20 percent markup on a contractor's charges fails to pay both the bills and produce the profit necessary to remain a viable business."

While 20% markup may be common in the restoration industry, as we showed previously this only grosses a 16.67% margin. Many of the contractors we speak to are aiming for something closer to a 40% gross margin to cover their overhead expenses and profitability goals. In order to achieve a 40% margin, your markup on the costs of goods sold (COGS) would look like this:

Margin Infographic

If your goal is a 40% margin

$100.00	Estimated Costs
$66.67	**Markup** ($100 / .60)
$166.67	Sales price
$100.00	COGS
$66.67	Gross Profit
40%	Gross Profit **Margin** ($66.67 / $166.67)

If you want to be intentional with your process and have integrity with your industry partners, what are your options?

- Know the deals you are making
- Structure your team to master those unique relationships
- Be honest with your partners

If you are doing program work, how often do you call and network with the team members within the TPA that you are working with? There are still relationships that can be made. It has been to see what the RIA AGA committee has been able to do in bringing high-level decision-makers in many of these organizations "on the other side" to the table to discuss the concerns and frustrations of everyday restorers.

How often do you reach out to adjusters to discuss unique projects and confirm authorization to perform tasks that may be outside of the norms of the program so that you can document approval? You will not win every battle but you can learn a lot about how to fight competitively and play the game the right way.

For a new company, or one pivoting into insurance claims, program work can be a good strategy for priming the pump for your revenue. It can be difficult to do both TPA and non-program work, but if you structure your systems around the TPA requirements, particularly timelines and documentation (aka Service Level Agreements or SLAs), that workflow can guide all of your processes.

Program work gets a lot of bad press, but many of the successful businesses in our industry have a significant portion of their workflow originating from this resource. If you have been struggling to achieve within the compliance metrics of programs like Contractor Connection or Alacrity, you may find Episode 58 of The DYOJO Podcast to be helpful as we talked about how you play to "win" the TPA game.

Our guests on this episode included, Tye Panzone (Sumner, Washington), who has over 20 years of experience in the restoration field as both a private and a program repairs contractor; and David Smith (Eugene, Oregon) who spent more than a decade managing and writing primarily mitigation but also some "small" repairs with various TPA programs.

The consensus from our discussion was that in order for your business to be successful and profitable while performing program work comes down to structuring your processes to master the system. Approach this issue the same way you approach all others, as a Doctor of Disaster. Some of the advice we aggregated from these practitioners included:

- Be honest and thorough in your estimating (Xactimate comes into play here)
- Establish clear communication with your vendors
- Give consistency and you'll get consistency
- Build out, and constantly refresh, your vendor list
- Find someone who knows the ropes and adapt to the challenges of the market

Preferred vendor programs boast a constant stream of work opportunities (quantity). In order to swim in the shark-infested TPA pool, you'll need to invest in items such as continual training, expedient sharing of job information (real-time transfer), continual honing of your craft, and preparation for a laundry list of compliance items that seem to be constantly changing.

I addressed some of the common issues and some remedies in an article I published in Restoration & Remediation Magazine titled *Help! Claims Review Shredded My Estimate*[56] which was also accompanied by a cringy video that I shot on my iPhone in my garage. The soil in which the seeds of The DYOJO Podcast were planted.

---

[56] Isaacson, J. (2019, December 12) *Help! Claims Review Shredded My Estimate.* Restoration & Remediation Magazine.
https://www.randrmagonline.com/articles/88728-help-claims-review-shredded-my-estimate-the-intentional-restorer-vol-2-with-video

Time Management

Before you can manage a project, or multiple projects for that matter, you need to develop your skills in personal time management. Time management is critical for every professional in every industry. In property restoration, where our best intentions to create a schedule is constantly interrupted by emergency calls for service and production delays, you must have what my father in law calls, "Rigid flexibility."

Don't over complicate things. Get a pad and paper and outline what you must do for the day. Your list of must do's should be short. I find it rewarding to be able to scratch out or check off what I accomplished for the day, in rare circumstances a must do can carry over, otherwise the day isn't over until those items are complete. Scheduling yourself is a great way to discipline yourself to plan ahead.

Thankfully simple tools like Google calendar make sharing your schedule easy so that you are communicating with your team. These items are also easy to duplicate and/or change if something needs to be moved. Don't make the mistake of scheduling yourself too tight. Build in breaks. People from outside the property restoration industry often don't understand the rare combination of workload, interruptions, large territories, working with multiple parties, program updates, nuances of insurance, etc.

You likely will reach points in your year where you could stay after hours seven days a week and still not be caught up. You must set aside time for yourself and your family. If you are proactive through scheduling and communication, you can often head off interruptions or have a good sense of whether something is truly an emergency that you need to respond to with urgency.

My good friend and prior partner in restoration, David Smith, shared a quote from Jim Rohn that has helped him in project management, "Either you run the day or the day runs you." David, like many project managers, became aware of the cycle of juggling a number of responsibilities in an unhealthy and unproductive way. If you only work in property restoration, you may be surprised to find out what is normal when you are outside of the bubble.

The mindset in the quote from Rohn helped David to develop a sense of daily awareness. David recognized that he may not be in complete control of what assignment his organization handed to him but had to take ownership of how he would decide to use his time.

Break your day into increments of time. I have tried everything from writing tasks down on a piece of paper, creating task lists on my phone, and even recently using post-it notes. I still like to physically write things down. I use 1 ⅜" x 1 ⅞" post-it notes and assign either a 1 or 2-hour window of time to each one. If something doesn't get done it has to carry over to the next day, be delegated, or eliminated if it turns out that it wasn't necessary. When you find ways to simplify your life, you can **reduce to produce**[57]. A realistic task list, an organized calendar, or post-it notes can help you be more realistic about what you can accomplish today.

- If you have an 8-hour day, start planning your day with 4 Post-It Notes to represent 2-hour blocks of your time. Set realistic goals for what you will accomplish each day.
- Put a big X through those items you accomplish.
- If something comes up that is more pressing than your prior plan, move that new Post-It Note in and move the prior note to another spot.
- Some items may carry, but you have them on the board and you are prioritizing for yourself as you attack the mountain (as discussed in the prior chapter).

---

[57] WAMOA 2020 Closing Keynote - https://www.youtube.com/watch?v=1LUcihkME1g&t=64s

Budget

If the estimate was written in Xactimate, printouts such as Recap by Category, the Components List, and Scope are incredibly helpful to a project manager. Recap by Category provides you with an overview of the master list of work categories with a labor and materials budget on a macro scale. The Components List provides you with details down to the number of screws or nails estimated based upon the data input into the program. You can get very detailed or utilize key items such as how many sheets of drywall or gallons of paint you will need. The Scope printout is helpful for your production team as you can tape the pages in each room/work area to keep track of scope and work progress.

If you want to be successful as a project manager, Erick Hernandez (Spring, TX) believes that the most important skill you can develop is, "Knowing how to create, read, and adjust your budgets." This comes from knowing what data feeds the reports that you are receiving. Erick comes from the skilled trades and recently pivoted his business to focus on property restoration (with a little help from The DYOJO). For many project managers, it is helpful to understand the basics of Xactimate[58], or the estimating software that your organization utilizes.

With regards to the financials, you want to understand what items are reported and what factors they are affected by. How often do accounts receivable update their costs, which affects how quickly your budget and reconciliation information is reflected? Erick reminds project managers to keep the total budget in mind as well as how much has been spent. This informs your average daily burn rate for labor and materials (engineering your budget) as well as being able to factor in how many days you have left by dividing your remaining budget by your burn rate (reverse engineer). Key questions that Erick asks when he receives a contract:

- How are change orders adjusted to the budget? At what points in the project life cycle do they need to be accounted for in order to reconcile your budget? As a

---

[58] For an introduction to Xactimate and estimating principles, you will find value in my first book, *Be Intentional: Estimating.*

project manager, you want to track your supplements and change orders in real-time so that you know how these affect the scope, cost, and duration. You also want to understand when to share this information so that it can be accurately reflected in the project budget and company financials, something that should be discussed at least monthly in your team production meetings.

- You want to understand who is allowed to charge costs to your project and how those charges are tracked. For example, if the estimator or manager is able to charge costs to a job, how are you notified so that your budget reflects the company's master budget? We are all on the same team, but sometimes team members do things that affect each other without thinking that process through. Make it clear that if you are going to be held accountable for it, you should be included in the cost application.

Erick says, "The lesson I learned here was that you must protect your profit, even from your own team. A smart division manager can bring in profit margins into an annual review and beat you up. As long as you know where they took the extra fat you can justify your performance if need be." A manager or estimator may see some "fat" (available margin) on a project and think that they can "hide" some costs in your project.

Especially if you are new to project management, some members of your team may test the boundaries. Be careful that you aren't lured into bad decisions by deceptively high margin projects. Erick warns, "Even on projects that come in fat, it's easy to cut those margins down by charging extra items to the job."

A Brief Discussion of the Financials

This work is intended to be about project management so we won't go much deeper into organizational finance. All people in a position of leadership MUST understand that you cannot hold your team to a higher standard than you hold yourself. For example, if the company or you as the owner/manager do not share your financials or train your team to understand why they are important, you cannot expect your estimators and project managers to track their numbers more than you.

Your revenue goals, real hard costs, and overhead create the basis for your marketing efforts, sales tracking, and work-in-progress metrics. How can your estimators compose a sheet that reflects the accurate costs for your business if they don't know your labor burden, overhead commitments, and profit goals? For example, if your goal was to reach one million ($1M) dollars in revenue at thirty percent (30%) gross margin over the course of the next year, what would you need to make in the next month to be on track?

- $1,000,000.00 per year
- $83,333.33 per month (divide $1M by 12 months)
- $19,230.77 per week (divide $1M by 52 weeks)
- $3,846.15 per day (divide $19,230.77 by 5 working days)
- $480.77 per hour (divide $19,230.77 by 40 hours for the work week)

These are rough numbers. Revenue is what your company takes in as they bill their customers for work completed. If you were shooting for one million dollars in revenue over the next year with a 30% gross margin, your simple financials would look something like this:

- $1,000,000.00 revenue
- - $700,000.00 cost of goods sold (COGS)
- = $300,000.00 gross margin (30%)

Why is margin important? In simple terms, if you made one million dollars but you spent one million dollars to make that work happen, in labor, equipment, and materials, you would say you, "Broke even," but really you're just broke. You have nothing to show for your effort as a company. In smaller companies, as the CEO/President/Owner/Operator, you may have paid your salary and done well for yourself but your company is running at net zero (or worse).

Cost of goods sold noted above is all of your direct costs applied to the job such as the labor applied, the materials you used, and the equipment you purchased or rented, in order to get the job done. As a project manager, some companies may account for your labor as COGS (costs of goods sold) or you may be considered overhead (indirect cost) or perhaps you split your time in each category.

At the end of the day, your salary is a hard cost, but how your organization accounts for your time may vary from company to company. An organization has overhead costs, which are indirect costs that are not specifically tied to producing the work on an individual job. There are also costs that spread across all jobs. This would include items such as your office rent, vehicle leases, administrative support, etc.

You may be tempted to think that your company is "making too much money." But look at the numbers. If your overhead was twenty five percent then you would have made a net profit (margin) of 5%. This means that the company brought in a million dollars but after everything was paid, they kept fifty thousand dollars. This profit is what the company uses to make decisions regarding raises, equipment purchases, adding staff, etc.

- $1,000,000.00 revenue
- - $700,000.00 cost of goods sold (COGS)
- = $300,000.00 gross margin (30%)
- - $250,000.00 overhead (indirect costs; 25%)
- = $50,000.00 net margin (5%)

Skylar Lewis shared, on the DYOJO Podcast[59], when they conducted a survey to ask their employees what they thought the CEO made, the majority of them answered 50%. Skylar elaborated how it was valuable for their company to make their financials transparent and to assign a line item in the financial report to each employee in the organization.

---

[59] The DYOJO Podcast, Episode 19

The topic of profitability is often discussed in public, but many of those talking about profitability don't know how it works and why it's so important. We say that we want our employees to take ownership and accountability and yet we are hesitant to be transparent with our numbers and provide them with the clarity they would need to take ownership.

Have you demonstrated an ability to understand each project's budget and find a way to stay under it for the defined scope of work? As discussed previously, your manager may not be comfortable sharing numbers right off the bat. You can still discuss the estimated hours and materials allowances for the project. If your boss thinks a particular project should take three days, break down the scope into what you will need to do in order to meet, or beat, that schedule.

If you can find ways to save on time and materials, without cutting corners, you will set yourself apart from your peers. Organize project schedules and details in such a way that allows for quality management of maximum workload.

Scope + Resources → Schedule → Work Orders

You have to know the scope as well as your resources, so that you can outline the work sequence and translate that into a working schedule and work orders. We will discuss this process in the next chapter. Maximum workload is achieved by optimizing rather than overloading your resources.

If there's a problem, will you solve it? The scope is the first link in a sequence of setting your team up for success.

CHAPTER 8

The Nasty Tendrils of Scope Creep

*Face trouble with courage,
disappointment with cheerfulness,
and triumph with humility.*
Thomas S. Monson

I live in the Pacific Northwest (PNW). Our corner of the world is host to nature's beauty on full display. We have the Pacific Ocean, rivers, lakes, trees in abundance, elevation changes, and multiple snow-capped mountain peaks. In Pierce County where I live, the majestic Mount Rainier is omnipresent and always feels like it is just a stone's throw away.

Included in the wonders of Tacoma is the myth of the world's largest octopus, King Octopus, living among the rubble of one of the Grit Cities' greatest engineering failures. The story of this terrible creature wrapping its tendrils into the local lore intersects with a project manager's worst nightmare.

Three years after the opening of The Golden Gate Bridge in San Francisco, which was also built on engineer Leon Moisseiff's designs, Puget Sound prepared to open the third-longest suspension bridge. In the mouth between Canada and the state of Washington, the Pacific Ocean connects to a body of water known as the Salish Sea. Near the Southern portion, The Tacoma Narrows Bridge was constructed to connect the mainland of Tacoma with Gig Harbor.

Designed to be aesthetically pleasing and structurally sound, the bridge opened with much fanfare in July of 1940. Locals were eager to drive across the narrow lanes spanning nearly 6,000 feet over the body of water that separated Tacoma from the Kitsap Peninsula. This beautiful bridge cut the travel time from 2.5 hours to 11 minutes. Some travelers reported feeling seasick as they drove across the bridge.

Issues were brought to light during the construction of the six million dollar bridge as winds as low as 5 mph would cause it to bounce aggressively. In jest, the locals began referring to the landmark as "Galloping Gertie". Some adjustments were made prior to the opening to buffer these stresses but they did not solve the underlying issues.

Four months later, disaster struck as Gertie galloped her last. On November 7, 1940, the following was reported:

"That morning, the center span began swaying between three and five feet in winds of only 35 to 45 mph. The bridge's construction and the effects of the winds upon it created a phenomenon known as harmonic vibration, which caused the center span to roll. It was severe enough to alarm officials, who closed the bridge to traffic at 10 a.m. The violent twisting continued -- a support cable at center span snapped, and the span was now undulating up to 28 feet -- and pieces of the roadbed began breaking off at around 10:30. The center span finally collapsed just after 11 a.m. and plunged into Puget Sound[60].
"

A six hundred-foot section of the bridge plummeting two hundred feet into the waters below. Thankfully no one was seriously injured or died. The only reported casualty was a three-legged dog named Tubby[61].

[60] Long,T. (2007, November 7) *Nov. 7, 1940: 'Galloping Gertie" Plunges Into The Tacoma Narrows*. Wired. https://www.wired.com/2007/11/nov-7-1940-galloping-gertie-plunges-into-the-tacoma-narrows

[61] Foster, L. (2015, September 25) *Giant Octopus Revealed.* https://www.southsoundmag.com/arts-entertainment/giant-octopus-revealed/article_f40fe8c5-7b71-5b39-b9c8-27fa192d0dd1.html

Several investigations were launched to determine the causes for this catastrophic failure. The design and production teams were questioned at length. In the wake of this event, some locals speculate that King Octopus came out of hiding in the Narrows and wrapped its massive tendrils into the demise of Galloping Gertie.

It is true that the Giant Pacific Octopus (Enteroctopus dofleini) is the largest species of octopus in the world. But, the largest Giant Pacific Octopus on record weighed an astonishing 600 pounds and measured 30 feet across in length. These figures put this creepy crawler in a category massive enough to invoke fear but not likely large enough to have played a factor in the collapse of Gertie. Similar to another Northwest legend, Sasquatch, we cannot confirm the existence of a Tacoma Kraken. But, can we really say with certainty that it has been unconfirmed?

According to *Oceana*, the average creature is an impressive 110 pounds and 16 feet across once fully grown[62]. They have been observed in the rapid tides below the Tacoma Narrows strait of the Puget Sound (aka the Narrows). But the likelihood of a PNW mega-octopus is a bit far-fetched, even though the rubble from Gertie makes for a popular eight-limbed mollusc hangout.

The original Narrows Bridge was supposed to be engineered as the most modern and advanced suspension structure to date. The mystery of how it could fail so miserably and so quickly is still argued in the engineering community. One issue brought to light was a collective "blind spot" among "leading minds" in this area of specialty.

J. K. Finch, a professor of civil engineering at Columbia University, published an article in Engineering News-Record titled, *Wind Failures of Suspension Bridges or Evolution and Decay of the Stiffening Truss*. Finch declared, "These long-forgotten difficulties with early suspension bridges, clearly show that while to modern engineers, the gyrations of the Tacoma

---

[62] Oceana. *Giant Pacific Octopus.* https://oceana.org/marine-life/cephalopods-crustaceans-other-shellfish/giant-pacific-octopus

bridge constituted something entirely new and strange, they were not new--they had simply been forgotten[63]."

This summary from Finch calls to mind the truth that *those who fail to learn from history are doomed to repeat it*[64]. When you or your team have issues with a project, you may be looking for a King Octopus to blame. Most fingers pointed to Leon Moisseiff but he was also reported to be actively involved in helping the effort to solve the mystery of why the bridge collapsed.

Deflection Theory had been used by Leon in many other suspension bridges that are still standing. The collapse of the original Narrows Bridge affected the engineer greatly. He died three years after the fateful event. According to a report from Engineering News Record, "Mr. Moisseiff was among the most active students of that failure. Sparing neither his energy nor his reputation in supporting attempts to squeeze the last ounce of useful knowledge out of this disaster[65]."

A few issues that should be recognized by Intentional Restorers:

- During construction, workers chewed on lemons to deal with motion sickness. There were indications that the design was flawed. Failure to listen to the crew or address issues while they are still young will compound negative results.
- Developing a blind spot of confidence when the evidence is pointing you to new information that should cause you to change course. Improper application of relevant science combined with a lack of adaptation.

---

[63] *Tacoma Narrows Bridge History - Bridge - Lessons from Failure*. WSDOT. https://wsdot.wa.gov/TNBhistory/bridges-failure.htm

[64] Winston Churchill paraphrasing George Santayana

[65] Nunnally, D. (2015, October 31) *The Man Blamed for the Fall of Tacoma's Galloping Gertie*. The Olympian. https://www.theolympian.com/news/local/article42065382.html

In property restoration, the estimate is the bridge between clear expectations and a successful project outcome. This document clarifies what is and is not in the agreed-upon scope. As we have discussed in the prior chapters, it is important for everyone on the team to understand the underlying principles that have been factored into the scope so that the scope can be executed effectively.

- A thoroughly written estimate will not guarantee happy customers or profitable projects but it should be a clear passage between the project needs and customer expectations.
- A well thought out production plan will prevent "torsional flutter" (aka twisting and turning) leading to catastrophic failure.

The estimate is the product of thorough data capture and accurate data input. This documentation fuels the negotiation process. The best gift an estimator can give their organization is a clearly written scope of work that is:

1. Understood and accepted by The Restoration Triangle
2. Sets the expectation for the client and the carrier
3. Is readily adapted into an actionable plan for the production team

Executing the agreed-upon scope will require ongoing communication with the client, the carrier, and the production team.

In most property restoration organizations the project manager is responsible for communicating deviations from the agreed-upon scope, i.e. change orders and supplements. Some organizations have the project manager compose their own change orders and supplements, while others divide responsibilities between producing the work and assigning the work to the estimator.

Definition. I define supplements as those claim-related scope items we plan to submit to the insurance company for additional consideration. Whereas change orders are those non-claim-related scope items that we have agreed upon with the customer.

In the course of most claims, there will be some element of discovery or scope revision potentially leading to supplements. If your team did a good job of establishing the standard, you should have laid the groundwork for how change orders and/or supplements will be handled as well.

For example, material costs are currently experiencing large fluctuations in relation to supply and demand. A wise contractor will want to recover their variance (delta) in costs between the estimated material costs assumed by Xactimate at the time of the data input and the real costs (data capture) once the project goes into production.

The supplement process runs back through the prior processes. The question will be whether the contractor and/or client can produce the thorough data capture that supports the accurate data input reflecting the changes being requested.

- For materials-only revisions (supplements), a clear receipt and updates to the components with an F9 note should resolve the materials cost delta in a manner that all parties can review and approve.
- Additional quantities or scope upon discovery will cause a brief cycle back through the estimating process to accurately reflect the increased scope of work and cost in a manner that all parties can understand and review.

The more complex the revision should result in the more details provided to support those changes. Perhaps there were certain assumptions at the time of composing the estimate but new conditions were uncovered and/or new information has altered the plan.

The change order process goes through a similar process without the inclusion of the insurance process. If a customer had X type of flooring and would like to purchase Y type of flooring, your team will have to clarify how change orders are documented and agreed upon. I like to tell customers that we can do anything that they want as long as they have the time and the money. It is important to clarify how changes affect the scope, cost, and duration of the project.

Scope communication is essential to preventing scope creep in many ways.

- **Good intentions**. Often your team members or subcontractors may do something with the best intentions, such as taking care of the customer and doing what is right but may not communicate the additional work that is being done so that it can be documented and billed for.

- **Self-harm.** Many consumers are concerned about being overcharged by contractors, but the reality is that plenty of contractors harm themselves by not capturing these supplements or change order details internally.

When the customer and the contractor are not on the same page with regards to the scope of work, the timeline to completion, and the final cost, it is inevitable that unpleasant conversations will follow.

Contractors put a lot of effort into the initial agreed-upon scope (the estimate), yet lack the clarity and consistency in collecting on these legitimate ongoing changes.

- If you consistently have happy customers but are struggling with your profitability, you may have an issue with lackluster estimates, scope creep, or both.
- If you have unhappy customers and low margins, you have much bigger issues.
- If estimators are able to wash their hands of any responsibility once the estimate is completed, you will struggle to develop collaboration between phases.

- If project managers have a greater workload than they can properly manage, they will struggle to consistently produce well-executed projects.

This realm of add-on work is one where organizations and project managers consistently invite the tendrils of scope creep. Every change impacts the project scope, cost, and duration. As Lisa Lavender shared in our series, *Benchmarks in Growth*[66], "More is not always more." If you do not communicate clear expectations and document your agreements, you invite chaos. Expanding the scope could lead to losing control, profits, and customer satisfaction.

Contractors rail against the insurance carriers for always saying, **"It's a cost of doing business,"** or "That's included in the O&P." Yet, these same contractors give away their time when a customer wants to make changes. As a business owner, manager, estimator, or project manager, you should be as protective of your time with your customer as you claim you are when you bash the carriers on your favorite social media platform.

The agreed-upon scope with the carrier should translate to an executed contract with the client, a deposit, and the scheduling of work.

- If the client decides they want to make changes, should you only be charging for the material variances or should you also be charging for your estimating time? Is estimating time, "Just a cost of doing business?"
- If you create designs, chase down selections, and call subs to visit the site for work that is not under a design-build arrangement, is this, "Included in your O&P?"

For example, I had an estimator that I managed who was so proud that they had quadrupled the value of a kitchen project by designing their client's dream kitchen. It finally clicked in my

---

[66] The DYOJO Podcast, Episode 55

brain. As the estimator was basking in their glory, I snapped, "On paper!" They were a bit shocked. I asked, "Who is paying for all this time we are wasting with this customer who hasn't even signed a contract yet?"

We had a heated discussion about how they hadn't sold anything. They had an imaginary project with a non-committal customer. The estimator had been to the project several times, making several changes to the design, scope, and selections. I told them not to go again until the customer had signed a contract either to move forward with the job or for $X.XX an hour for our design work.

Furthermore, we were doing a higher volume of program work that we were not keeping up with. I had to discuss with the team that in our current corporate structure we need to focus on being restorers, not remodelers. The lost time on projects like this fantasy kitchen was affecting our profits, our production, and our sanity.

Unfortunately the "free estimate" has become a norm that we aren't willing to break away from. As soon as you are out of survival mode as a company, work towards at least increasingly being more definitive in identifying your ideal clients. As a team, you should do some digging into how much time you waste in chasing work that you aren't winning, as well as what actions are compounding rather than reducing your waste.

You can become more profitable quickly when you STOP wasting time, money, and resources and START being more selective. You can't blame the insurance company as the sole perpetrator of wasting your money when you are doing a bang-up job of wasting it yourself. Fix the design flaws rather than look for a monster to blame

Fighting Against Scope Creep

While a project manager may not be responsible for thoroughly capturing the initial site data or composing the accurate claim scope, they are responsible for the execution of the agreed-upon scope. The risk of scope creep is always lurking at every phase of the project life cycle.

Without going too far into the weeds, before we can define scope creep we must understand what scope is. The Project Management Institute (PMI) has provided a working definition of scope[67] as:

- The extent of what a project will produce (product scope)
- And the work needed to produce it (project scope)

In property restoration, the agreed-upon scope often is negotiated between the contractor and the insurance carrier with input from the client. When the scope of work is compiled in an estimating software like Xactimate there are reports that can be useful for all parties. Estimators and adjusters can use a line-by-line review of bid items in the final draft. The production team can benefit from the room-by-room scope report.

If the estimator followed the mindset and habits such as those outlined in Be Intentional: Estimating to provide headers, line item (F9) notes, and detailed photographs, the production team will have a clearer understanding of the agreed-upon scope. This effort should be intentionally made to ensure that all members of the team executing the work clearly understand what is and what is not included in the scope of work.

- **Estimator to the Project manager.** In instances where the carrier has excluded items and/or agreed only to pay them "as incurred" it is essential for the project manager and production team to document and relay those items back to the estimator in a manner that they can properly supplement for the work.
- **Project manager to Production.** In the next chapter, we will explore the process of transferring

[67] Larsen, R. & Larsen, E. (2009, October 13) *Top Five Causes of Scope Creep...And What To Do About Them*. Project Management Institute. https://www.pmi.org/learning/library/top-five-causes-scope-creep-6675

the details from the agreed-upon scope into an actionable plan through items such as a schedule and work orders.

- **Production to Project manager to Estimator.** The same applies to the discovery of additional damages. Often carpenters and subcontractors will do the right thing in the field, taking care of the customer and doing the necessary work to restore to pre-loss conditions, but may not be aware or communicate this additional work so that the organization can be compensated for those costs.
- **Company-wide.** While many in a position of leadership are tempted to blame this on the field personnel, they must understand their role and responsibility to develop processes to clearly communicate agreed-upon scope from the top-down (i.e., estimator to production) as well as bottom-up (i.e., carpenter to estimator).

What is scope creep and how do we fight against it? PMI defines scope creep as, "Adding additional features or functions of a new product, requirements, or work that is not authorized (i.e., beyond the agreed-upon scope). Scope creep can occur in a variety of ways, including, but not limited to, the following:

- Incomplete capture or communication of scope necessary to restore the property to pre-loss conditions at the time of estimating
- Incomplete data entry of estimating line items and/or use of supplementary information to build an estimate that accurately reflects effort required to restore the property to pre-loss conditions
- Incomplete internal communication of agreed-upon scope in a manner that establishes what is and is not included in the scope to those who will be responsible for supervising and/or executing the work to restore the property to pre-loss conditions
- Incomplete external communication of agreed-upon scope to the client in a manner that establishes the proper expectation of what is and is not included in the scope of work to restore the property to pre-loss conditions

- Incomplete internal communication of additional work completed to restore the property to pre-loss conditions in a manner that they can be effectively communicated to the carrier for supplemental consideration of compensation
- Incomplete external communication with the client of additional work completed either A) to restore the property to pre-loss condition and will be presented to the carrier for additional compensation or B) to execute an upgraded scope of work at the behest of the client which impacts cost and/or timeline of the project

The nightmare creatures of scope creep crawl out of the crevices of the project when there is a lack of clarity on the scope, expectations, cost, and duration of the project. While emergency response is inherent to insurance claims repairs, chaos should not be accepted. Be intentional about identifying and addressing dysfunction. When a client makes a "small request" for an alteration to their project, they often have no frame of reference for how this new scope affects the existing production plan. Unfortunately, many estimators, project managers, and the production staff don't understand these impacts either.

In his book, *Joy, Inc.*, Richard Sheridan shares a simple process that his software design team uses for project management. This book demonstrates that project management is best executed with some key universal principles and that there are many parallels between scope creep in these two disparate industries. To ensure that clients, team members, and the organization are on the same page, the Menlo team arranges aspects of the work on index cards. An index card associates a scope item with the time and cost budgeted to complete the task.

The design team regularly meets with the client. In these meetings, if a client wants to make a change without affecting the project duration or cost, they must pull index cards from the project board. There has to be an equal reduction of scope/cost/duration to account for new items. This is a simplified account of the process but there is nothing better than making it visible and helping all parties to see the impacts of "just a little change."

Richard and the Menlo team have achieved a high level of success, which combines customer satisfaction with profitability, by using well thought out yet relatively simple habits such as these. Being intentional should not be confused with undue complexity. The only weapon you may need to vanquish the devilish beasts of scope creep may be a three-dollar pack of 3-inch by 5-inch index cards.

As Lisa Lavender shares in her monthly column in Restoration and Remediation Magazine, *Restoring Success,*

"Don't be scared of scope creep; manage it proactively as a team. Although it is in our nature as restorers to go above and beyond to help those we serve through a difficult time, margins are thin, and overhead continues to grow. We cannot afford excessive scope creep even when it is well-intentioned."

The first step in making improvements is admitting that there is a problem. Perhaps as important is recognizing that process enhancement is the responsibility of everyone on the team. So, put your blame fingers away and get into the mud with your team members to make positive change happen. Often over-complication is a factor in system decline, therefore be mindful not to overcomplicate identification of the issues or design your efforts to correct them. Intentional organizations should train their teams with the mindset of:

- **Doing it right** as a company includes ensuring the client, carrier and your production team are clear on what the scope of work is as well as what it isn't.
- **Doing it efficiently** as an organization means that all parties in the process are engaged in being able to read the scope, execute the scope and communicate when there are legitimate deviations.
- **Doing it excellently** as a team requires everyone to be trained to read a scope clearly, communicate consistently and hold each other   accountable to doing the right thing the right way.

Index cards can work well for conversations with clients regarding scope agreements and changes. Similarly, Post-it Notes can be used to adapt the scope from the index cards into production assignments for your team members. The scope is broken down into a project schedule. The schedule is then broken down into work orders. A visible schedule is key to accountability.

Scope → Schedule → Work orders

I have tried many complex programs over the years and still enjoy using free resources such as Google calendar for scheduling myself and our production teams. I first observed this simple tool being very effective for a local plumbing company that we subcontracted with. I was impressed that you could walk into their warehouse and see a color-coded layout for where their resources were scheduled.

As their team grew they did upgrade to a managed software system. I believe that by using the simplest resources available for as long as you can, your team is able to 1) work out the process that best fits your team, and 2) identify the system that will best enhance your operational capacity.

When you are a project manager, please take this responsibility seriously. If you expect your team to be prepared, they need to know what they are doing in advance of when they are doing it. A visible schedule keeps all parties accountable to communicate the plan. When the schedule has to be adjusted for emergencies, cancellations, or complications, the production resources can be appropriately assigned.

Advantages to a visible schedule:

1. The crew can see what they are doing
2. The crew can prepare for the upcoming workday
3. The crew can see when there are changes
4. The crew can adjust to the plan

If you want to manage multiple projects over multiple locations with multiple resources, you need to have a shared calendar to keep everything in order. If you have multiple project managers using shared resources, the shared calendar becomes exponentially more important. You want to avoid having the same carpenter scheduled to separate projects in different locations at the same time. A shared schedule, that is visible to all, helps to initiate conversations about resources before there are conflicts.

Whatever tool you use as your board (aka the schedule), has to be the driver of your production planning. Each team member is responsible to plan and schedule their work in accordance with the availability granted by The Board. Team members have to be accountable to each other by scheduling honestly. Dishonesty will cause the schedule and team trust to collapse.

If you manage project managers, you must empower The Board and hold people accountable to respect the schedule of resources. If PM A misses on a schedule and PM B is depending on the allocated resource based on The Board, PM B should be given the resource. It should be on PM A to monitor their job progress and whether the assigned resources are on track. PM A should communicate with all parties with enough time to potentially alter their prior agreed plans.

Nothing is more frustrating, especially as a project manager, than doing your job and following the process, only to be told that someone else (i.e. PM A), "Needs this more," so you (PM B) are out of luck. This is not respecting the process or empower The Board to play its role in the production system. Had PM A given several days' notice (at least 3), PM B might have been able to make an adjustment to accompany the team.

As someone who wants to be a project manager, learn how to set realistic goals and give yourself some buffer time. Self-management habits will help you build strong project management habits when you are overseeing multiple projects. If you are a project manager, plan your projects out so that you can prepare your teams and adjust as needed. It's much easier to adjust course when you are already in motion.

If you oversee project managers, build a system that is visible and hold people accountable to respect the process. Accountability starts with clear communication. If you want to build trust so that there will be teamwork, you must hold people responsible for their role in the process.

And all the project managers said, "Amen."

On *Blue is the New White* Podcast #87 with Josh Zolin

CHAPTER 9

Ordering The Work

Continuous effort – not strength or intelligence –
is the key to unlocking our potential.
Winston Churchill

You will often feel like you have a high bar to reach if you want to be successful as a project manager. You will help yourself, your team, and your client to have greater confidence in the process when you can take the big picture and break it into action steps. If you expect your team to deliver detailed work documentation, you must lead by example. I believe you set them up for success with clearly written work orders.

Alex Watts, Director of Regional Maintenance for a nationwide property manager based in Seattle, Washington, describes the role and vision for project management as, "Achieving herculean results by breaking end-goals into manageable tasks, ordering them appropriately and completing them successively." Put this quote into your playbook for project management.

Herculean results can be better achieved when:

- End goals are broken into manageable tasks (work orders)
- Tasks are ordered appropriately so that they can be completed successively (schedule)

The project manager needs to be able to see the big picture (or the end goal) and break that into manageable tasks. A written work order communicates the end goal, the daily tasks, as well as the tools and equipment necessary. Seems simple enough, right? Now multiply that by your workload and spread that across your territory.

Managing the big picture is actually managing multiple pictures, and this responsibility often feels like eating an elephant. Do you know what elephant eaters say? There is only one way to eat an elephant and that is one bite at a time. Your job as a project manager is to take the herculean task of elephant eating and sequence that into bites that your team members can take while keeping the process on schedule and on budget.

Once you start thinking in this way (mindset), you will notice that it becomes a habit that is strengthened, like a muscle, by consistency. You can focus on the herculean results that Alex mentions and get discouraged or you can focus on, "Breaking end-goals into manageable tasks." A well-written work order outlines what to do, in what sequence, and to what end (eating instructions).

Chaos and frustration are fires that are fed by a lack of clarity. Whenever you notice the smoke from project tension rising, take a step back and find out where something wasn't as clear as it should have been. Many great feats ("herculean results") of modern science, and construction, have been completed by ordinary people, working with ordinary teams, because someone was able to break the process down into work that everyone on the team could contribute towards.

You may be frustrated as a project manager that you are not getting sufficient details from the estimator but you cannot downstream that frustration to your team. While you work with your organization to improve the transfer of information from estimating to production, you can (and must) lead by example.

Breaking the work down for others starts with prioritizing your own work. Andrew Golkin (Manassas, VA) believes that a good balance for a project manager includes, "Spending 20-40% of your time on focused planning prior to the project starting and 60-80% of your time verifying it is going according to plan and the product is high quality." For the PMs working in his organization, "That means one or two days per week in a focused space and three to four days per week on the job site, getting to know your trades, customers and making sure that you are present."

Before we talk about creating a production process that is clear, consistent, and holds people accountable, I will clarify what I mean by work order. To do so I will use an example that I have used many times. When I heard this illustration, at a youth leaders conference in Sacramento, California of all places, it made a lot of sense to me on a personal and professional level. I hope you will lock this into your developing project management playbook as well.

You are a parent and you give your child a work order to "clean your room." In your mind this means something and there are certain underlying benchmarks that you expect. Yet, by simply saying, "Clean your room," you have not done your best to ensure that the communication of the expectations is clear.

You may think that it should be common sense. But what many people in a position of leadership fail to comprehend is that common sense is relative. There are many factors that go into making sense "common". Rather than lament the ability of the receiver to understand and execute your unclear work order, you should take ownership and work to clarify your directions.

In the room cleaning scenario, does it really take that much more effort to state, "Child, I want your room clean. By this I mean..."

(Sample Work Order)

Project: Johnny's Room
Address: Home
Date: Today

Goal:
Clean 'Johnny's Room' room to parent's satisfaction

Work Sequence (critical path items):

1. Fold and place all clean clothes into assigned locations (i.e. drawers, hangers, shelves, etc.)
2. Place all dirty clothes into the hamper
3. Return all items on the floor neatly to their assigned locations
4. Make your bed
5. Vacuum your floor

*Diagram of the work area with notations attached

Labor:
3 hours x 1 technician

Questions, please call the assigned project manager:

Parent A
(XXX) XXX-XXXX

Why is a clearly written work order so important? If you are a carpenter or technician, you should be well acquainted with the frustration that comes from not having a clear work order. When you don't know what you are doing, what you will need to accomplish the assigned tasks, and what status the project is in, there will be issues. You have not been set up for success.

If you are a project manager, one of the descriptions of your roles and responsibilities includes, will simultaneously oversee multiple projects over a large geographic territory, coordinating work duties with subcontractors and field personnel. You cannot and will not be in every location at the same time. You have to be able to delegate responsibility. If you want to be able to hold people accountable for outcomes, you must communicate clearly and consistently.

To borrow the previous room cleaning analogy, you will be managing multiple "rooms" that need to be "cleaned" and the work will be completed by "children". All of the quotations from the prior sentence signify interchangeable nouns and verbs. The scope, location, and personnel change day to day and project to project but the mechanism and process for communicating scope should be the same, a clearly written work order.

Whoever creates the initial scope can do everyone in the chain of estimating and production a great favor by communicating the scope of work in both written and visual forms. As an estimator, when I perform my project scopes at the data capture phase of the project, I like to color-code my sketch so that I have a quick reference for work sequences. For example, the scope of work for the floor may be outlined in blue, walls in red, trim in green, cabinets in pink, etc.

These written, diagramed, and color-coded details can be shared with everyone. For example, if your scope of work includes only painting certain walls or you need your team to stay out of particular rooms, color coding on the scope diagram can be invaluable. Many people are visual. If everyone has the mindset of setting the next phase up for success, your team will have a better opportunity to achieve more consistent outcomes.

A color-coded diagram can be helpful when clarifying the scope with the client. The habit of getting everything in writing should be incorporated into every phase. We get and follow up all communications with the client and the carrier in writing. We should do the same internally with our production action plan.

If you have a large project and are preparing for dispatch, having a job startup meeting to review photos, 360 degree captures, the written scope, etc. can be extremely helpful in setting everyone up for success. As a project manager, you want to get as many details as you can from the estimator so that you can provide those details to your production teams.

You will be responsible to organize project schedules and details in such a way that allows for quality management of maximum workload.

- Clear and consistent scheduling communication is your organization showing your customers that you value them.
- Clear and consistent work order communication is your organization showing your employees that you value them.

In order to achieve the ever-coveted, rarely-achieved accountability in your organization, you have to communicate clearly and consistently at every level. For a work order to be effective, it needs to be clear enough to provide the details necessary for the receiver to be able to work from the orders. When the person assigned to the work reads the document, they should be able to comprehend:

- What am I going to be doing?
- Where am I going to be doing this work? This includes the location of the job as well as the areas where work is and isn't to be conducted.
- What materials, tools, and/or equipment will I need in order to accomplish the tasks assigned?

- Are there any special or specific items that I need to address?
- How much time do I have budgeted to complete this work?
- What are the safety risks and remedies?

It is important for people in a position of leadership to keep in mind that the goal of a work order is to communicate with the person(s) who will be assigned to complete the work. It is not enough to document what the writer thinks is clear; those composing the work orders must work to ensure the information can be understood and executed by those on the receiving end of the transmission[68].

Whenever information has to be translated from an estimator, to a project manager, to a site supervisor, or carpenter, your scope communication process must be clear and consistent before employees can be held accountable.

A work order is a transfer of critical information so that all parties are clear on the scope of work. It's one thing when management holds people accountable, it's another thing when team members understand the vision and values and are empowered to hold each other accountable. The author of *Necessary Endings*, Dr. Henry Cloud, has said, "If you are building a culture where honest expectations are communicated and peer accountability is the norm, then the group will address poor performance and attitudes."

Many years ago, my beautiful wife went to work with my team on several large school projects. We needed people we could trust to do what they were instructed by the team. My wife was more than capable. She worked well with the team and has some fond memories of her time with people who stand out as some of the best that I have worked with over my career. They weren't the smartest or the most talented; in truth, we

---

[68] I have written at length on the process of developing the right mindset and habits for yourself and your team to succeed with estimating insurance claims in my first book, **Be Intentional: Estimating**. If you have a desire to dig further into these principles, as well as prepare your team to communicate scope more effectively from the estimating stage onward.

assembled a rag-tag group of people who fought for each other and worked hard to do it right for our clients.

One cool story that came out of the experience was my wife seeing more of what went on behind the scenes. Kelsey was sitting with one of our carpenters during a break and enjoying some treats that he made. In addition to being a quality tradesperson, this gentleman was a talented chef. Word came around the site that I would be stopping by to do a quality control check.

Everyone at this location quickly assembled to ensure the job was in order. This may sound like an activity motivated by fear, but this was the team double-checking that the project conditions reflected the hard work that they had been putting in. There was a sense of shared pride in keeping our jobs clean and orderly.

This was encouraging to hear. Kelsey confirmed what I already knew. Our team was committed to our vision and values. Because our process was clear and consistent, the team held each other accountable to the standard that we all believed in. You achieve a unique and beautiful level of accountability when your team members are the ones holding the line with each other.

As a person in a position of leadership, you often have to address issues in your organization (correction). Before you can build or expect accountability in your culture, you must build a foundation of clarity and consistency:

- Be clear and teach your team to do it right.
- Build consistency and help your team to do it efficiently.
- Develop accountability and show your team how to do it excellently.

Many project managers are frustrated by waste when workers make multiple trips in a day to the hardware store. These extra trips lead to losses on so many fronts. You are losing productivity, money, trust, and the list goes on.

In most markets, a trip to the hardware store consumes at least one hour. If you can reduce one trip to the hardware store, you gain at least one hour of productivity. Over the course of a week, that is five hours of productivity either gained or lost. That's almost an entire shift that your worker is either losing or engaging in productive work activity.

Before we can put all of the blame on our workers, people in a position of leadership have to face the music and ask themselves whether they have created a process of communication that is clear, consistent, and thereby facilitates accountability. We are quick to use, "Garbage in, garbage out," as an indictment against our technicians. But, project efficiency starts with the organization, the management team, and the internal processes of the company before it ever reaches the ground floor.

Holding People to a Higher Standard

When you are having issues with performance, you should take a step back and ask as a leadership team, "Are we holding our team members to a higher standard than we are holding ourselves to?" As I shared in *Garbage In, Garbage Out*[69], managers and owners often lament the poor details they receive from technicians in the field and yet they don't see the hypocrisy of an internal system that regularly sends them frantically to jobs with few details.

When the organization is not clear, consistent, and accountable to their own stated values, it will get unclear and inconsistent results. In the Resources section at the end of this book is a sample outline of what we have used in smaller organizations to help set an expectation and sequence for the project life cycle. Many of these items fall into the responsibilities of the project manager, but the overall process should be a regular point of discussion for the entire team.

---

[69] Isaacson, J. (2020, January 9) *Garbage In, Garbage Out (Part 1)*. Restoration & Remediation Magazine. https://www.randrmagonline.com/articles/88755-garbage-in-garbage-out-the-intentional-restorer-vol-3

- Make your workflow process clear but keep it simple.
- Be consistent and regularly adapt to new information.
- Hold people accountable, starting with the leadership team.

The process of clear communication through complete, thorough, and timely paperwork starts with your investment in the process of receiving project information (intake). You cannot control when a lead comes in but you can control how thoroughly you gather information. This is important so that no one on your team is wasting time duplicating efforts to get the information that should have been received when the call came in.

You may not know all the details for an emergency, but if you have enough data we can prepare your team to respond with the appropriate people power, equipment, and materials. You know that there is a big difference between responding to a sink overflow in a laundry room on the main floor with no crawl space and a busted sewer line in the crawl space of a 5,000 square foot home. The technicians who are trained to respond, the equipment and resources that will be needed as well as the ability to estimate how that team being offline for the project will impact your ability to respond to other losses are all important.

When you master the most basic functions of your organization, such as your work intake process, it builds momentum for tackling more complex issues within your process. When you detect negative symptoms in your business, such as a lack of thoroughness in the project documentation from your team members in the field, it should cause you to seek the root sources.

It sounds simple, and yet when these things are not practiced there are negative ripples throughout the organization. When you commit to taking calls with clarity and consistency you demonstrate to your team that you value this process and that everyone is being held to the same standard. You can begin to eliminate chaos in your organization and build positive momentum by intentionally developing your process.

Set your team up for success. When you build clarity and consistency, you establish a purpose for each person in your organization. When you stand up for these principles, as change will always be tested, you prove your commitment to the cause.

If you want consistency from your technicians:

- Stop allowing inconsistency in your organization from others; lead by example.
- Start clarifying your processes and develop consistency at all levels.
- Focus team members on mastering their roles and responsibilities.
- Work together to achieve accountability to the goals.

A quality scope is the product of thorough data capture combined with accurate data input. Documentation at all levels is essential to seeing a project through from intake to final billing and a five-star review. As Gino Wickman shares in his book Traction, "Most companies strive for external growth, but internal growth leads to future greatness. The paradox is that they will actually grow faster externally in the long run if they are focused internally from the outset[70]."

We prepare for external threats when many of the most common issues are generated from within. As an owner or manager, onboarding the right (ideal) clients, being more efficient with existing projects, and developing from within set the foundation for enduring return on your investments. With this in mind, project intake can be a means to screening clients and setting your team up for success.

What would it do for your people, processes, production, and progress to have never worked for your ten worst clients?

---

[70] Wickman, G. (2007) *Traction: Get a Grip on Your Business.* BenBella Books.

Do you track metrics such as your referral sources, carriers, territories, job size, turnaround time, etc? The intake process empowers you to better screen projects before you ever step foot on the premises. A good intake aligns your organization with the clients that are the right fit for your vision and values. When your intake aligns with your vision, you have a better chance of reducing the amount of bad clients that you invite into your organization.

How often have you made the connection between onboarding ill-fitting clients and issues with customer satisfaction, profitability, as well as your people?

We know those bad clients are a costly tax on all of our systems, yet we continue to do the same things over and over again. These habits affect, or infect, all of our processes, including recruiting, hiring, and especially retaining good people. Clarifying your ideal client should force you to also clarify your ideal employee, both of these ideas sound idyllic but they are not impossible.

Tammy Birklid[71] found these principles to be true as she built her company, Merit Construction in Tacoma, Washington. She has crystalized her team focus with the vision of being an employer of choice. She has recognized that if you want to pursue and keep good clients, you must develop an internal process that attracts and trains good people to perform business in your unique way.

What would happen if you took a different approach?

What would happen if your leadership team adapted from complaining about the issues (playing the blame game) and started to embrace them (lead by example)? What would happen if you changed how your intake process worked? Rather than chasing every job, many of which you know you shouldn't take, zero in on those projects that have a higher

---

[71] The DYOJO Podcast, Episode 59

probability of success with regards to customer satisfaction and profitability.

As O.P. Almaraz shared during *Benchmarks of Growth*[72], develop clarity around your ideal client and develop your team to make progress toward those goals. While it takes time to narrow your focus, what would happen if (over time) you were better about screening your clientele so that you could cut out your worst clients and therefore minimize your worst experiences? It may sound impossible but I think it starts with something as simple as your intake process.

One company with an open position for project management described the role this way, "The primary role of the project manager is to run one or more projects simultaneously, in such a manner that both the customer and the company are successful."

If you are a carpenter or technician, and you want to be a project manager, ask yourself whether you have demonstrated whether you can manage yourself for one project.

- Before you can run multiple projects you need to be able to successfully run one project at a time.
- Before you can oversee an entire project you need to be able to successfully oversee one or more specific work sequences, or tasks, on a single job.
- Before your manager will consider you for a promotion, they will be assessing whether you fulfilled your current roles and responsibilities.

If you believe you are ready for the next step, look for ways to take on additional responsibilities. Push yourself out of your comfort zone. Expand your exposure and prove your ability to take on more work. In property restoration, we constantly have technicians who want to get out of the field, but they don't yet

---

[72] The DYOJO Podcast, Episode 63

have mastery of their existing responsibilities. If you are reading this and you have not been clear or consistent with your paperwork and worksite documentation, start there. If you are doing your job competently with consistently positive outcomes, request the opportunity to take the lead on a larger project with supervisory responsibilities. It may not happen right away, but once you can manage multiple people on one project you need an opportunity to test whether you can oversee multiple projects spread across different locations; or elements thereof.

The path to project management is a marathon, not a sprint. Look for means to earn the opportunity for progressive assignments to test your ability to comprehend and execute the agreed-upon scope of work. We will continue to discuss building your skills for producing the work. But you should have current possibilities for breaking projects down into daily action items that will keep yourself and your team on task.

Don't be scared of failure, it will take time to learn all of this well. Communication is key. This doesn't mean that you will be successful right away as you grow in your responsibilities, but you will have the foundational elements that will help you get there. The expectations and KPIs for project managers that we have listed throughout this book will give you some good targets for assessing whether you are ready to present yourself for the position.

As a current project manager, you should understand the importance of a clear written work order. Creating these will force you to think through the work sequence of your projects and break them into achievable tasks for your team. Success is not an accident.

Developing your skills requires continuous (intentional) effort.

CHAPTER 10

Project Management is People Management

*The P in PM is as much about 'people management'
as it is about 'project management'.*
Cornelius Fichtner

Merit Construction, based in Tacoma, Washington, recently posted on LinkedIn,

"What exactly is the role of the Project Manager? Our Project Managers are responsible for making sure everyone working on a given project understands the end goal of the work and their job in achieving that goal. The PM also has to make sure everyone involved has the tools and resources they need to get the job done in the best way possible for the company, and for our clients."

In the prior chapters, we focused on understanding the scope and cost factors as well as setting the right expectation with the client. All of this groundwork sets the stage for communicating the plan of attack with your production teams. As a project manager, you want to clarify the goal so that you can consistently deliver happy customers and profitable projects. Developing as a leader is a continuous cycle of learning to communicate, challenge, and inspire your team members.

What a great way to summarize the essence and value of the project manager role as, "Responsible for making sure everyone working on a given project understands the end goal of the work and their job in achieving that goal." Whether you are an owner, manager, or PM, the importance of helping your team associate value to their work and find means to take ownership of their part in the effort of the team is key to employee engagement and making progress on your vision. While some people get into management for the money and the control, when you invest in training your team to optimize their people skills this effort results in better outcomes for all parties. As a person in a position of leadership, you want to create clarity, i.e. "making sure everyone understands the end goal of the work." This clarity leads to consistency in your efforts and rowing together to get the work done.

When you combine clarity with consistency, you have fertile ground for accountability, i.e. "their job in achieving that goal." As a project manager you have to be constantly asking, what does this customer want? There are foundational service issues, such as cleanliness and communication, as well as customer trends that you want to stay ahead of, every client is unique and you have to listen for what is important to them. For some, the key may be something that seems to be insignificant, but if you cross that threshold it is difficult to regain trust and goodwill with that client.

Craig Powers is the Corporate Director of Restoration for COIT and is the instructor for the Restoration Industry Association (RIA) 2-day Project Management Course. He says, "Listening during the initial walk-through is one of the most important times on the project. You must hear what is important to the client and exceed those objectives." The PM has the role of finding the balance between what the customer wants and needs and measuring that with what the job needs; or how the contractor needs to perform the job.

Remember, the role and responsibility of the project manager is **project + management**. In this chapter, we will focus on the keys to success in becoming a manager as well as a leader. What is management? This is a loaded question.

Many people at the ground level of an organization wonder what those in "higher" levels of leadership value in their management structure. As contractors often complain about engineers, or others who don't do, "What we do," those in the field have these same thoughts about middle-level managers (from time to time). As we discussed in the scope defining process, your system for management should be in alignment with your stated goals and values.

A common confusion in many organizations is to complain about the lack of profitability and to blame it on individual factors. Those in upper management complain that middle management doesn't understand the numbers and that the ground-level employees have no sense of urgency in achieving the goals. As with the scope issues and their relationship to efficiency in production as well as the impacts on profitability, often the root cause is related to communication.

A good deal of this confusion can be traced to unclear or contradictory messages:

- We say we value customer service and experience but we regularly measure, review, and discipline-based upon profitability exclusively.
- We lament low profitability but we rarely share the numbers with the team or train them for financial competency, even in mid to high-level management.
- We come down hard on the team for sagging revenue or profits, the team rallies, but then we act as though it was only survival and the benefits are not tangible.
- We dig deep and swear things will change in the tough times but once the fire is out we move forward without capturing the lessons and therefore soon repeat them.

What we measure gets our attention. What gets our attention has a chance of improving. If you gather relevant financial data, you are ahead of most of your competition. If you have staff that are able to understand these figures, you are pulling away from the middle of the pack. If you train on understanding and strategize on means to achieve your goals, you are above average. If your financial literacy is clear, consistent, and accountable, you have a fighting chance of being sustainable. This is oversimplifying the topic but you should get the picture.

At a minimum, your organization should understand your break-even point. What do you need in sales (revenue) and profitability on a weekly basis to survive as a company? At the earliest stages of business, when the company is small, this is easy to know even if you aren't tracking it, i.e. did we make payroll for our three employees? But you know as a business owner that payroll is only part of your costs. How many businesses do you know who put their taxes in the "optional" envelope and are consistently panicked at the end of the year?

As a project manager, success in your role will often be judged by your competency in these <u>twelve overlapping functions</u>

- Project scope
- Job budget
- Worksite timelines
- Production rates
- Job costing
- Employee development
- Subcontractor acquisition
- Resource management
- Communication
- Quality control
- Customer experience
- Portfolio profitability

People in a position of leadership are judged by bringing money in and making money on that money. We will discuss some of the differences between revenue and profitability later. For now, I want to focus on those factors that lead to profitability, namely the mastery of people skills with project management and customer satisfaction.

Of the twelve items listed above, all of these require building a team to help you achieve these goals. There is so much focus on the numbers, when it's the people, particularly the people directly interacting with your clients, that facilitate profitability through doing things right, doing them efficiently, and putting a touch of excellence on what your company does.

Charles Cassani was the recipient of the distinguished Martin L. King Award for 2020. This award is presented to individuals who are recognized for their exceptional service and dedication to the restoration industry. Charles notes that more emphasis should be placed on the PM process. "I recognized back in the late 1990's that my best project manager needed a coordinator/assistant to record and document his activities."

Charles began adjusting the way his company approached the roles and responsibilities of a project manager. By distributing the load they saw better outcomes. "In our company," continues Mr. Cassani, "We support PMs with project coordinators, billing support administrators who proof and coordinate billings with TPAs, TPCs, and Customer Relations Specialists." With competent help project managers are better able to service the customer and achieve the company goals.

Developing Your Leadership Skills

You may be tempted to ask, "Am I a leader?" My first impulse would be to say, if you have to ask this question, you aren't. But before you dismantle your efforts to become a leader, I would encourage you to STOP asking the wrong question and in-so-doing, get your development on track. Leadership is not something ethereal, mystical, supernatural, or metaphysical. Second, this is a useless question as it creates no value even if it were answered. Leadership is not a position.

- Ethereal - leadership is not delicate. You won't break it if you at first suck at it, nor will you ruin all future chances if you fail.
- Mystical - you should not treat leadership with awe, mystery or fascination other than to note the positive effects of good leadership and harness those tangibles in your own life.
- Supernatural - no spider bites or glowing rocks required. While some people seem to have more of "it" than others, the principles of good leadership can be understood, practiced, and developed by anyone.

- Metaphysical - leadership does not transcend physical matter or the laws of nature, rather it requires a physical presence to encourage purposeful outcomes.

There are those in history that transcend their time and thereby stand out in our distinctions of strong leadership. Leadership is a daily practice. There are no leaders, only people in a position of leadership. No leader arrives without their own journey of trial, failure, and growth. You are a leader. You must be intentional to develop your leadership.

Leadership is often placed on a standard that is only approachable by those worthy to wield its magical powers. This is not true. Do not make leadership more complicated, or prestigious than it is.

- Leadership is leading
- Leaders are those who lead
- Everyone is a leader
- Recognize that you are a person in a position of leadership
- Good leadership should create more leaders

The question is not whether you are a leader. The question is not even if you are a good leader. Good leadership is a subjective measure related to abilities, intention, and outcomes. Good leaders have their bad moments and bad leaders have their positive qualities. This is true of any person in a position of leadership at any level.

Leadership categories that impact your everyday life include your self, your roles, your responsibilities, and your example to others. You are a leader in each of these key areas and you must be intentional to develop your abilities. Everyday leadership categories of significant consequence include:

- Your - self
- Your - roles
- Your - responsibilities
- Your - example

As a leader, if you want to ask an effective question, ask yourself, "Am I on course or off track?" This is important because, in order to answer this basic question, you have to establish some clarity as to what your goals are. If you are clear on your goals, you can develop actions and track whether you are consistently moving towards or away from your goal.

Questions of substance will require you to look in the mirror and assess measurable results using sober judgment. Asking whether you are a leader is not the right question. You are. What you need to ask is whether you are on course or not. If you are brave enough to ask yourself this question, you are on your way towards progress in the process.

There is another tough question a person in a position of leadership must ask, especially if your roles and responsibilities have you overseeing a team of people. "Am I on track due to intention or coincidence?" The prototypical leader enjoys receiving praise for success and shirks responsibility for failures. This is the reverse of servant leadership. As our friend Chad Kerlegan[73] says, "Leaders take the hits and give the credits."

Whether things are going well or they are a dumpster fire, the person in a position of leadership must ask if their outcomes have been the result of being intentional or merely coincidental.

- Is the team winning because you have been intentional in helping them prepare for and achieve success?
- Or, are things going well in spite of your efforts (or lack thereof) as a person in a position of leadership?

STOP asking dumb questions and START doing intentional things. As the process evolves, you will have to adapt, so the development of your leadership skills is never over. If you work through the process of taking ownership of your role as a leader, getting yourself and your team on course and being intentional, it's not as though the game is over. Repeat daily.

---

[73] South Sound Connection 006

When we manage something, our goal is to ensure that it doesn't end up in chaos. As you develop your skills in management, it is important to understand that you are one piece of a much larger puzzle. Often new managers let their title go to their head, thinking somehow that this is good leadership, when the contrary often leads to much better results.

You have probably heard of servant leadership, this perspective of serving those that "serve" you, which should be applied to management as well. It is important to recognize that as a manager your job is no more or no less important than anyone else's. You should have defined roles, responsibilities, and key performance objectives that are interrelated to the people "below" and "above" you on the organizational chart (or ladder).

As a manager, as long as you don't screw things up you will be successful. In many organizations it's a low bar of entry as well as a low standard for retention. Unfortunately, the common logic seems to be that if you were good in one area, typically managing yourself in a role such as sales, that you somehow will be good in a role that requires you to oversee others.

The equation is something like this:

> *Employee A is good at X,*
> *Therefore, they will be good at Y.*

Is this equation true? Employee A is good at sales, therefore Employee A will be good at training and managing others in sales[74]. While Employee A can learn to develop these skills, it isn't as easy as snapping your fingers to make it happen. In my opinion, the role of project management exposes a professional to more of the skills that are necessary to develop into a strong general manager than estimating. But many organizations promote salespeople into upper management roles over project managers.

---

[74] See my video, *Five types of people get promoted to management, do you agree?* On Youtube - https://www.youtube.com/watch?v=fSH9p1Hf5CE

If you are an estimator, help yourself round out your skills by keeping some dirt under your nails by getting your hands into the project management for the estimates you write. This will help you be a better estimator as well as better equipped as a person in a position of leadership. If you are a project manager, help yourself round out your skills by educating yourself on how estimates and the broader finances work.

Self-management is not the same skill set as people management. Self-management is critical to success in people management in the sense that to be effective as a person in a position of leadership, you must first lead yourself. If you have spent the majority of your life being successful self-managing in doing individual tasks, it will take time to learn to manage others and perhaps even longer to learn to lead.

Leadership has less to do with your title and everything to do with how you interact with others. You likely have observed status quo leadership and may not have had the best examples of what it means to be a person in a position of leadership. Every "leader" will teach you something, they will either teach you a positive example of how to lead, or they will teach you a negative example of how not to lead. Both are informative.

I had the pleasure and challenge of co-authoring a book with real-world leaders who discuss how small things make a big impact when being intentional with your effort to develop a strong workplace culture. In this book, I shared four leadership styles that impacted my career. To get the broader context of these people, you will have to read the book, but here is a brief summary[75]:

- **The Talons** of the world, either had no positive examples of leadership, or at some point bought into the perspective that looking out for yourself at any cost was the only way to survive. If you have reached a point where your heart is that hard towards others, you may want to consider finding some help. You have some wounds and scars that need to be dealt

[75] *Be Intentional: Culture*, Chapter 6

with for yourself and for your team. Ill intentions repeated will lead to a dark place in business and in life.

- **The Peters** of the world are the by-product of swearing that they wouldn't be like their worst boss, only to miss that developing positive skills is as important as not repeating those negative traits. Good intentions without guidance or a consistent process lead to the same confusion and demotivation that exist with a Talon-like environment. Peters have been hurt; they are trying to do the right thing but they need to keep their focus on clarity and consistency in order to build real accountability.

- As I said, one of my first managers, Denis, demonstrated that a manager's role is to insulate their team from those things that will distract them from their purpose or suck the wind out of their sails. **The Denis'** of the world are confident in who they are; they know their strengths as well as their weaknesses. As such, they are able to assist their team members to find their strengths and contribute those facets to the growth of the team. Denis' embrace their identity[76] and live their purpose. They know how to scale the right way and will help those around them move upward with them.

- **The Sharons** of the world have built a business from the ground up and continue to have a direct hand in operations. As an owner, whether you feel like things are going well or you're constantly pulling your hair out, take a moment to give yourself credit for daring to follow your instincts and building

[76] Isaacson, J. (2019, February 4) *Clarifying Your Identity as a Leader Will Help You to Build a Thriving Team Culture*. IZ Vents. https://www.izvents.com/words/clarifying-your-identify-as-a-leader-will-help-to-build-a-thriving-team-culture

something. If you need to get things back on course, join the club, you are in good company and we are rooting for you. Keep taking small steps in the right direction and celebrate your progress in the process. Sharon's are confident in their role and happy to help others develop their leadership legs. A Sharon knows how to cheer (encourage) and jeer (challenge) their team members.

If you get into management and your only benchmark for success is to be better than your worst manager, you will be contributing to the problem not the solution. It is important to identify, in your negative examples, what the root causes of their malpractice were and how you are going to actively work against those factors in your own leadership applications. As you learn on the job, you will apply pieces from your past, using both the negative and positive examples to inform your own leadership development.

Developing Your People (Soft) Skills

Understand a scope so that you can create actionable schedules and clear work orders are skills that you will be constantly refining. Improving your technical skills as well as your people skills will help you improve your project outcomes. Can you name a single team that has succeeded without people?

No people = No team = No success

Understanding how to work successfully with people is a skill that every person in a position of leadership has to intentionally develop on a continual basis. In a tight labor market, recruiting, hiring, developing, and retaining good people is essential to success. This is true for your direct reports, or in-house team, as well as your subcontractors, vendors, and customers.

There is no finish line when it comes to working with individuals. Many have come to label people skills as "soft skills" which require "emotional intelligence[77]" (aka EQ). Soft skills are defined as, "Personal attributes that enable someone to interact effectively and harmoniously with other people." Whatever you choose to call them, what manager couldn't use a boost in their ability to interact effectively with other people?

Intentionally developing your people skills is critical to your success as a person in a position of leadership and as an organization. You will win when you continually humanize your process. One way to build a framework around these concepts, is to understand the importance of building emotional credits before you make emotional debits.

Emotional credits before emotional debits

How often do you hear leaders complain about the incoming workforce, "They just don't make them like they used to." We talk over and over about how the fight to be an intentional restorer includes refusing to allow yourself to play the blame game. If you are struggling to connect with the younger generations, is that one hundred percent their fault?

If a young person can get a job at a coffee shop for fifteen dollars an hour versus working with your company where they have to go into sewage filled crawl spaces and respond at all hours of the night for similar pay, are they being lazy or are they being smart by rejecting your offer?

In *Insuring Tomorrow*[78] there is a great story about an interview that could have been a missed opportunity. Of course the applicant showed up late, wasn't dressed for the part, and wasn't prepared for the inquisition; someone most hiring managers

---

[77] Isaacson, J. (2017, November 6) *Lead with Empathy*. IZ Ventures. *https://www.izvents.com/words/lead-with-empathy*

[78] Isaacson, J. (2017, October 19) *Reviewing Insuring Tomorrow by Tony Canas and Carly Burnham*. Restoration & Remediation Magazine. https://www.randrmagonline.com/blogs/14-r-r-blog/post/87695-guest-blog-reviewing-insuring-tomorrow-by-tony-canas-carly-burnham

would readily pass on. Instead, this manager asked the person if they had been to an interview like this one before. They offered the applicant some clear expectations and a second chance to return the next day better prepared to re-apply. Because the interviewer took a few extra minutes to better understand and engage someone who gave a terrible interview, both parties benefited from the addition of new talent to the organization.

People in a position of leadership are encouraged to remember that not all millennials (or any other terms that are created for incoming generations) have received good mentorship. You have to be more discerning and determine whether giving them the benefit of the doubt, with regards to lack of experience. Take some extra time to be clearer in your development process. Your organization may capitalize by finding the diamonds in the rough that your competitors are complaining about and discarding (the status quo).

While there is a labor shortage, if you are refusing to adapt to the market you are expediting your descent into obsolescence. It is important to remember that no one grew up the way you did, had the same work experiences you did, and they don't view the world, in general, the same way you do. You likely felt this when you entered the workforce. Try to tap into those feelings from when you were a newbie.

Managers are unique.
Employees are unique.
We are all human.

As a project manager, developing your people skills is paramount. This relates to your ability to train, discipline, and keep your team members. It is helpful to understand human dynamics within the simple metric of emotional credits and debits. Understand that in many ways people are like banks - you have to make emotional deposits (credits) if you want to effectively make emotional withdrawals (debits). I am not talking about manipulation. I am talking about human interaction.

As a person in a position of leadership, you often have to address issues in your organization (correction). Before you can expect accountability in your workplace, you must build a foundation of clarity and consistency in your culture. If you preach that your team members have to develop their skills in order to succeed with your organization, in the same way, you must develop your soft skills if you want to be successful as a leader.

You are a person and you have been promoted to a position where you now manage other persons. If you have effectively learned to manage yourself, you will have developed some mindsets and habits that should help you to help others to do the same for themselves. It is important to remember that you are a unique person and each of your team members are unique persons. The golden rule is a strong foundation for success as a person in a position of leadership.

The Golden Rule states, **"Do unto others as you would have them do unto you."** The essence of the principle is that we should treat everyone with the same universal respect and goodwill that we want to be extended to ourselves.

Reacting to ill-treatment

In reverse, this does not mean that if someone treats you terribly that they are setting an example of how they would like to be treated. How often have you thought or heard, "If that's how they are going to treat me then they are going to get the same (or worse) right back." When faced with ill-treatment our natural response is to get defensive and even to retaliate. Such reciprocal action drags us away from our values. Taking the higher road is a commitment to operate with high standards regardless of the results.

Being a pushover

This does not mean that we endure or allow abuse. We also want to set a standard of both how we will treat others as well as how we expect them to treat us. The golden rule should not be manipulated by others to enable them to trample over you as a person and a professional. In a business setting, this can be a helpful tool when a team member is being mishandled by a client. "Dear client, our company works hard to follow the golden rule and would request that you do the same. If we cannot treat each other with this universal standard of respect then we will have to rethink our working relationship."

Treating people as individuals

Applying the golden rule requires us to empathize with those we are serving. We should be asking how this person thinks, perceives the relationship and would like to be treated. We want to be considered as individuals as do those we interact with. Taking time to listen, observe and apply the knowledge that we gain enables us to adapt to optimize our personal as well as professional relationships. You would want to be treated as an individual, correct? So treating others as you would want to be treated means developing the ability to understand and interact with them as individuals.

Doing the people-stuff right is never easy. Getting to know your people and being on-point can be exhausting. You will make mistakes. Having emotional or relational "currency" as a manager is important so that you can take draws on the goodwill that you have built up with your team. If you get it right today, you still have to get up tomorrow and do it right again.

Intentional leaders learn to empower the people around them to achieve the project objectives. You can do this at any level so start practicing these skills now.

Part 3.

Mindset & Habits.

Lunch at RIA 2021 with industry legends Claude Blackburn (founder of Dri Eaz), Charles Cassani (RIA MLK 2020 Award Winner), and Pete Consigli (The Global Restoration Watchdog)

CHAPTER 11

Intentional Restorers

Excellence is an art won by training and habituation.
We do not act rightly because we have virtue or
excellence,
but we rather have those because we have acted rightly.
We are what we repeatedly do.
Excellence, then, is not an act but a habit.
Aristotle

Do you ever stop to think about how many countless hours and resources, literally blood, sweat, and tears, have been invested in the formation of our industry? It is beyond quantification. When you dig into property restoration history, you uncover innovators like those that Pete Consigli, dubbed *The Founding Fathers of Restoration*[79] in his penultimate article from March 2007 in Cleaning and Restoration (C&R) Magazine.

Sadly, two of these pillars, Lloyd Weaver and Martin "Marty" L. King, are no longer with us. The other two faces on Mount Restoration, Cliff "The Z Man" Zlotnik and Claude Blackburn are thankfully still with us. Cliff remains involved in the Restoration Industry Association and produces a weekly podcast with "Radio" Joe Hughes. Their weekly podcast, IAQ Radio, is the OG of restoration podcasting as they were doing their show long before podcasting was a thing.

---

[79] Consigli, G. (2007, March) *The Four Faces on Mount Restoration.* Cleaning & Restoration Magazine.
https://www.restorationindustry.org/sites/default/files/docs/Founding_F athers_of_Restorat.pdf

Mr. Blackburn, aka the Pickle Ball Philanthropist[80], as he was dubbed by a local journalist, has been content with his prior role in the industry and is no longer directly involved. If you do a little bit of digging you will find the brand that he built is one of the most recognized in our segment of the skilled trades.

Humble achievers such as Cliff and Claude don't introduce themselves as founders of marquee brands or creators of some of the most successful products and industry-leading processes. Their mark is embedded into the fabric of how dedicated restorers do business. When you dig into our rich history as an industry, you find that many of the issues that we face as "modern" restorers aren't that different from the challenges early restorers were dealing with.

Pete Consigli wrote an article originally published by IE Connections October 2000 issue, titled Disaster Strikes! What ya gonna do...Who you gonna call? Preventing IEQ Problems after Floods, Fires, and Catastrophes. Before we dig into Pete's Dirty Dozen, let's explore what it means to be an Intentional Restorer.

In training team members, I want them to think like Doctors of Disaster. When we think of medical professionals, most are familiar with the phrase, "First, do no harm," which is often misattributed to the Hippocratic Oath[81] and supposed to govern all decisions a doctor makes. According to the National Institutes of Health, the Oath signified the early stages of medical training, calling new physicians to swear to uphold a number of voluntary professional ethical standards. While it appears that the Oath did not include those words we erroneously ascribe to it, many of the elements aptly apply to modern property restoration:

---

[80] Rudolf, J. (2020, October 2) *The Pickleball Philanthropist.* Island Unseen. https://juleerudolfblog.wordpress.com/2020/10/02/the-pickleball-philanthropist

[81] National Institutes of Health (2002, September 16) *Greek Medicine: The Hippocratic Oath.* https://www.nlm.nih.gov/hmd/greek/greek_oath.html

"Into whatever homes I go, I will enter them for the benefit of the sick, avoiding any voluntary act of impropriety or corruption. So long as I maintain this Oath faithfully and without corruption, may it be granted to me to partake of life fully and the practice of my art, gaining the respect of all men for all time."

In 2007, when the Association of Specialists in Cleaning and Restoration (ASCR) rebranded as the RIA and unveiled the first motto of their 60-year history, "We make it better. We promise." In the October 2017 cover story of Cleaning & Restoration Magazine (C&R), Pete Consigli and Cliff Zlotnik cited the late Martin "Marty" L. King who characterized what we all do as "the business and profession of damage repair[82]." The duo expanded on the meaning of the promise of the motto noting, "The business of restoration is finishing projects on time and on budget while satisfying the stakeholders, often under adverse situations while remaining professional and making a profit."

Intentional Restorers have the high calling of "making it better" when it comes to assisting our various clients with disaster response and repair. If we are going to "do no harm," our process must include measures to ensure that we properly identify the extent of the damages, prevent cross-contamination, thoroughly address structural impacts, and restore the property to resemble pre-loss conditions.

Writing for Indoor Environment (IE) Connections in October of 2000, Pete noted twelve common reasons (the Dirty Dozen) for failed restoration projects[83]. As a project manager, if you know what often fails, you can develop your process around preventing these from happening on your jobs. See if these aren't still issues that modern restorers face to this day:

---

[82] Consigli, P. & Zlotnik, C. (2017, October 26) *Connecting Mission With Motto.* Cleaning & Restoration. https://www.restorationindustry.org/cleaning-and-restoration/connecting-mission-motto

[83] Consigli, P. (2000, October) *Disaster Strikes! What ya gonna do...Who ya gonna call? Preventing IEQ Problems after Floods, Fires, and Catastrophes.* IE Connections.

1. The building didn't have a contingency plan. Chaos and confusion ruled.
2. There was either no insurance coverage, insufficient coverage, or an excluded occurrence.
3. An unqualified contractor was called in to perform the work.
4. An incomplete investigation was performed which led to an improper scope of work.
5. The proper procedures or best restoration practices were not followed by the clean-up personnel.
6. Conflict between the insurance company, the building owner, and other parties to the claim led to "gridlock" and nothing happened or the problem worsened.
7. Too many "experts" were involved.
8. Hidden agendas, lack of funds, and shortcuts led to trouble.
9. A pre-existing condition (e.g., chronic leak, construction defect, prior mold) was not identified or was hidden in an attempt to "expedite" the claim.
10. Incomplete assessment of the building's history and occupant health.
11. The project never had a "meeting of the minds" of the involved participants to agree on a scope of work, job cost, completion criteria, and timelines.
12. Attorneys were called in to "help" resolve the problem.

While there is so much good content to dive into, I will remind the reader that we discussed meeting of the minds in Chapter 5. These are principles that we all know as restorers and business people, and yet, so many of the issues that we face in our industry come down to missing a few key details on a project. Clear and consistent communication among all parties to a claim is essential to consistently positive outcomes in disaster response services.

In the original article, Pete countered the Dirty Dozen with the Reliable Dozen which included the admonition to:

1. Be upfront. Be clear on your expectations and be specific on how they will be evaluated if you are the property owner and/or their representative.
2. Follow the "spirit" of recognized industry standards, guidelines, and published best practices when specifying and/or scoping a project.
3. Be honest, ethical, and try to do what's right and fair.

While I have been in this industry for nearly twenty years, there are plenty of people who have been there much longer and who have made significant contributions towards shaping those early formations. Like many modern restorers, I am eager to make a difference, but I am still learning how important it is to listen and observe before jumping in or expecting doors to open. Being an intentional restorer includes learning about our history and implementing those best practices that have been tried and tested over decades.

The Hippocratic Oath included the concept of apprenticeship, whereby the skilled would share the lessons they learned, often by trial and error, with those committed to learning the craft of medicine. For this collaboration to continue in our industry we need modern restorers who innovate solutions for the ever-evolving market as well as those seasoned restorers who remind us that we aren't that different from our predecessors.

As we continue to collaborate, perhaps we can properly quote and implement this sentiment from the Oath, *"So long as I maintain this Oath faithfully and without corruption, may it be granted to me to partake of life fully and the practice of my art, gaining the respect of all men for all time."*

Your company should view training as your internal means of apprenticeship. If you are an owner or manager, nothing should substitute for The _____ (enter your company name) Way of doing things. Those in a position of leadership need to download their technical and practical knowledge so that everyone on the team can practice the art of restoration in harmony with the vision and values of your organization. A leader is not satisfied with followers but works to make more leaders. An Intentional Restorer wants nothing more than to see their team members develop into Doctors of Disaster. This does not happen by accident, it must be an intentional process.

As good as their courses are, it is not enough to ship your technicians off for "certification" from an Institute of Inspection Cleaning and Restoration Certification (IICRC) and call it good. In his book *Leadership in Restorative Drying*, Ken Larsen shares three important distinctions:

- **Standard Practice** is a phrase used to describe practices normally and regularly performed by professionals of a trade. They may or may not reflect competence.
- **Standard of Care** in the structural restorative drying industry has been defined [by the IICRC S500 consensus body standard committee] to be: "practices that are common to reasonably prudent members of the trade who are recognized in the industry as qualified and competent."
- **State of the Art** refers to the highest level of general development, as of a device, technique, or scientific field achieved at a particular time.

Chasing Perfection, Catching Excellence

Like many of you, I've had to build teams with technicians that were cross-trained in water damage mitigation, mold growth removal, contents inventory and pack out, crime scene decontamination, fire damage restoration, and a myriad of skills in between. Early on I found myself getting lost in where to focus my attention.

While it's silly to believe that we can train our people to master anything by holding training once a week for thirty minutes to an hour, it is essential that we do so. If you want your team to perform, you have to regularly train them. The collaboration on team and worksite issues, as well as clarifying your expectations around work scopes, is as important as the training itself.

This chapter opens with a quote from Aristotle, "Excellence is an art won by training and habituation." He states that acting rightly, i.e. doing the small things, leads to excellence. He concludes, "We are what we repeatedly do. Excellence, then, is not an act but a habit." You will not be a Doctor of Disaster because you have taken a certificated course or multiple courses, but because you repeatedly (consistently) do the right thing.

Vince Lombardi stated his perspective this way, "Perfection is not attainable. But if we chase perfection, we can catch excellence." As a project manager, you are a coach. You must lead by example, always developing your own skills, and helping your team members to develop theirs. Excellence is the product of doing the right thing consistently.

Do it right + Do it efficiently + Do it excellently.

Sometimes we don't know where to start. Always start with the question, "Do I know how to do it right?" This can be a loaded question because everyone has their opinion on the right way to do something. Doing it the right way starts with compulsory standards which include Occupational Safety and Health Administration (OSHA) safety regulations as well as the building codes of local jurisdictions.

If your work is illegal, unsafe, or non-compliant, you can objectively say that it does not meet the low threshold of Standard of Practice. Similar to the idea of "do no harm", your customers should at least be restored to resemble pre-loss conditions, NOT be worse off for having interacted with your organization. Doing it right may start with a nice certificate that you hang on the wall, but that should initiate the learning process not conclude it.

The next measure of doing it right would be work that meets industry Standards of Care and best practices. These are voluntary standards that record the consensus norms of our trade. In property restoration, these would include guidelines such as the Institute of Inspection Cleaning and Restoration Certification (IICRC) S500 and S520 documents for water damage mitigation and microbial remediation respectively. Know the law and follow it. Know the standards and, as part of the pursuit of excellence, learn to apply them accurately.

Mastery in any area means we follow the consensus standards as a baseline, but that we continue to learn, innovate, and adapt our practices. The S520 Standard and Reference Guide for Professional Mold Remediation includes this disclaimer on the opening page, "Users of this document should stay updated and informed about developments in the field of mold remediation, implement changes in technology and procedures as appropriate[84]." State of the Art does not have to be complex to be effective.

All professionals are bound by laws and regulations, yet as restorers, "In certain circumstances, common sense, experience and professional judgement may justify a deviation from this Standard and Reference Guide." All our decisions are subject to new data, "Which may invalidate any or all of the information contained herein." On the jobsite, your technical knowledge will have to be combined with practical knowledge if you want to accomplish your goals.

Recently I asked restoration contractors, "What is the frequency of your team training?" Many of the responses were helpful and it was encouraging to hear how many people in a position of leadership are being intentional with this discipline. Some of the answers included:

- Robert More (Boonsboro, MD), "Not frequently enough in my opinion. I think structure is important in any meeting or training, which is why I am a huge fan of Traction by Gino Wickman and the Entrepreneurial Operating System (EOS)."

---

[84] IICRC (2008) *IICRC S520 Standard and Reference Guide for Professional Mold Remediation, Second Edition.* Institute of Inspection, Cleaning and Restoration Certification.

- Nick Sharp (Sharpsburg, GA), "Repetition is needed after certifications are finished to make sure technicians know the processes necessary to mitigate a home. Informal training needs to be daily and formal training really should be weekly."

- Tiffany Baer (La Vernia, TX), "I like to rotate topics and do small focuses for the week. Make it fun, but keep things in focus."

- Jason Turnball (Fayetteville, NC), "We do short morning training videos daily (Morning Tech Meeting). Refreshers on how to behave, what a good attitude looks like, customer service, and so on. Then we talk about any issues from the previous week."

- Stephen Ardeneaux (Conway, AR), "We have a Monday morning training meeting along with brief daily meetings the rest of the week. Our weekly training meeting covers topics - safety, communication, company news and events, current projects, team focus (i.e. one thing or word to focus on as a team), and transparency (open the floor to the staff to talk about anything from the previous week, good or bad)."

- Robb Nimmo (Temecula, CA), "We do bi-monthly technician meetings. I'll assign a technician to select something that they are weak in to train the rest of the team on this topic. This way, that technician will have to research and educate themselves, while the others who may be stronger in that area can help by asking questions which enables the whole team to dig a little deeper."

I appreciate the concept behind Robb's approach in having a team member research and teach something they struggle with. If this is executed well, then it sets the tone that it is positive to talk about where you need help in our company (culture). When I was working for an abatement company in Sumner, Washington, they did an excellent job of empowering team members to have no fear in asking for help. Those in a position of leadership would consistently review projects and numbers in regular meetings.

The process included the habit of having multiple sets of eyes reviewing a project to help identify potential issues at bidding, outset, and job progress. The PM was encouraged to express concerns and reach out to team members for ideas so that problems could be addressed while they were manageable rather than hoping they would solve themselves.

As Robert mentioned, this company was also implementing the EOS system in their business and that led to a greater sense of clarity and accountability as well. While you may feel like a middle manager and that the company as a whole does not embrace this idea of sharing your struggles, you can create this within your own team (direct reports).

If you are an owner or manager, there is great value in candid conversations that maintain accountability for project outcomes but also encourage your team members to share their concerns early, while the problems are small. Doing so helps to build a culture where the organization can work together to source solutions.

We train to be Doctors of Disaster, yet we often fail to bring this same scientific approach to our people skills, leadership development, and cultural improvement. Lex Sisney, our guest for The DYOJO Podcast[85], has a wonderful book and system he titled *Organizational Physics*. If you have a scientific mind, this resource will help you apply these principles to the common and repetitive issues in business.

The reader will note that at several points in this book I have emphasized in sentences an item that you should STOP doing as well as the appropriate replacement action, i.e. something you should START doing. I first heard about this simple framework from Lex. He applies this skillfully to a situation where you are training and/or disciplining a team member.

---

[85] The DYOJO Podcast, Episode 22

The next time you are communicating something that needs to change, help your team to understand and adjust their mindset and habits in a sequence of STOP-START-IDEAL. Mr. Sisney advises, "Begin first by communicating what they need to STOP doing, then communicate what they need to START doing, and then paint a picture to define in unarguable terms what the IDEAL would look like[86]."

As a manager it is important to address issues while they are fresh or poor mindsets will be perceived as acceptable and will become habits. In these coaching moments, you want to cast the broader picture, or as some people call it, discuss "The Why." Being candid with your team is helpful in building clarity and accountability in the growth process, as we discussed in Chapter 6.

Pursuing excellence means we are constantly improving both our production (external) as well as our process (internal). The scientific process of recognizing symptoms so that you can address sources is critical on the ground level with employees as well as at the organizational level with the whole company. If you treat the symptoms, they may eventually go away as the body heals itself, but you will be much more effective if you can get to the root cause that is producing the symptoms.

Apply the same investigative mindset that we teach our teams to use in water damaged homes when you are dealing with interpersonal and organizational challenges. We know the carpet is wet. If we set an air mover on the wet carpet, we may or may not effect a change in the environment. We have to ask, "What is causing this carpet to be wet?"

As we use our moisture meter to further determine the extent of the damages and close in on the potential source(s) of the damage, we are able to better determine what would prevent additional water from affecting the structure. Once we address

[86] Sisney, L. *Communicating for Better, Faster Change Management.* Organizational Physics. https://organizationalphysics.com/2019/09/18/communicating-for-better-faster-change-managemen

and stop the source, we now have to determine and deal with the extent of the damages.

As a person in a position of leadership, this is the same process with regard to conflict resolution and team development. Issues will arise within your team. Don't get hung up on the symptoms, try to dig into the sources and work your way through to the symptoms only after you have identified and begun to treat the causes. The longer you allow an issue to fester the greater the extent of the damages will embed themselves into your team dynamics.

If we want our team to pursue excellence we must be pursuing State of the Art leadership development. This does not mean that we have to be Ph.D.-level psychologists that solve the deepest rooted issues in every employee we hire. But, if you want to be above average as an organization, you have to invest more than the average (status quo) level of care in improving your ability to address the people-stuff.

You will always be a student of the industry, if you want to be an effective manager you also have to be a student of people. Cornelius Fichtner is regarded by many as a leading thinker in the area of project management. With regards to soft skills, Cornelius says, "The P in PM is as much about 'people management' as it is about 'project management."

So, what do you need to STOP doing so that you can replace those ineffective energies into what you should START doing to continue to develop into the leader that your team needs?

Mistakes, Mishaps, and Teaching Moments

Training is often reactionary. Someone messed something up so the boss calls an all-staff meeting. "Everyone get your a$$ in the conference room, NOW!" The team knows what is coming, it's the same speech, just a different week. As we just discussed, there is no science or objectivity applied to this recurring scenario.

Rather than proactively train and eliminate the fear of failure so that the team can collaborate, an endless cycle of frustration is repeated. The crew hates it as does the manager, and yet, we continue to plug the carousel in.

I think it is important to understand the difference between two kinds of mistakes:

1. Doing the wrong thing <u>with</u> a comprehensible reason
2. Doing the wrong thing <u>without</u> a comprehensible reason

Do you believe in honest mistakes? I would define an honest mistake as someone thought they were doing the right thing. If they can articulate why they did what they did, and in some way the logic makes sense, then you can address the errors in their calculations. Through training, you can help them not to repeat those same flaws. Someone doing the wrong thing for the right reason can be a great teaching moment for the whole team.

If we have a culture where our team members feel confident that they can share their concerns, such as questions or weaknesses, then we can help our organization reduce honest mistakes before they happen. By empowering employees to ask questions rather than pushing forward when they aren't confident in a key decision, we allow our team to be collaborative in their approach to work.

I can remember the first meeting I held with a team that I inherited when I took over the restoration division for a national vendor. We had some mishaps on a project and I asked, "Tell me about this," as I pointed to some pictures which showed poor execution of cleanliness. Immediately the fingers were flying, "That wasn't me, that was so-and-so."

I stopped everyone and explained that I didn't know how things went down in the past, but two things were going to be true moving forward,

1. If one of us messes up, we all mess up as poor performance reflects poorly on our whole team;

2. I am not looking to blame anyone, I am looking to identify the issue so that we can discuss ways to fix it moving forward.

It took a while, but eventually, I was able to prove that these two values were true. Our meetings became increasingly productive as we were able to openly discuss when something went haywire. We would put the error up for everyone to understand, discuss, and review approaches for not repeating the same mistakes in the future. I think it is important to distinguish between honest mistakes, laziness, and blatant disregard.

Scenario two is the employee who did the wrong thing and cannot articulate a comprehensible reason for why they did what they did. Gino Wickman has a humorous and helpful acronym for analyzing ability; **GWC**[87]

- Do they Get it?
- Do they Want it?
- Do they have the Capacity to do it?

If they don't get it, want it, or have the capacity to do it, they are in the wrong position. For example, you may have put someone in the lead technician role on a project, when they explain the mishap and their reasoning, you learn that they clearly are not yet ready for this level of responsibility. That doesn't mean they should be fired, they either need more training or will be limited in how far they can advance with the organization.

When someone makes a mistake and can't explain their reasoning, you have to determine whether they need more coaching, are lazy, or express blatant disregard. We go back to the core qualities:

- **Are they honest?** Did they make you aware of the issue or did you have to find out from the customer?

---

[87] Dube, C. *GWC - The Difference Between "Capacity" and "Get It"*. Entrepreneurial Operating System. https://www.eosworldwide.com/blog/gwc-difference-between-capacity-get-it

- **Are they hardworking?** Was this an oversight or lapse in judgement that occurred while they were otherwise trying to do the right thing (an honest mistake) or was it laziness in their operations or disregard for the wellbeing of others?
- **Are they willing to learn?** Did they own their mistake and want to be given the opportunity to show that they can be trusted?

While it may sound odd, I would rather have an employee show blatant disregard than laziness. Blatant disregard shows intention. If we sit down, we probably will find that this employee is upset about something, which may or may not be valid, but they are acting out for a reason.

- If they have <u>a valid concern</u>, you will learn something from the discussion. You will still have to address their failure, but there is hope you can fix the underlying issues and possibly strengthen your relationship.
- If they have <u>an invalid concern</u>, you still may be able to educate them on why their perspective is wrong and why what they did has consequences, but there may still be something to salvage in the employee if you address it expediently.

One of the worst things you can do is ignore or fail to address someone who is acting out. I will say that with the proviso that every situation is different. I have strategically utilized a cooling period or allowed a situation to play out before I addressed it. You must ensure that you aren't avoiding conflict due to fear or an inability to engage. We will discuss discipline in Chapter 14, in this chapter we want to focus on training.

Few things make my blood boil like laziness. That said, don't assume everyone who appears to be lazy is rotten. Have you ever asked anyone, "Why aren't you doing anything," and they responded, "We were done. There wasn't anything to do." This is logical, to a degree. While many of you reading this may have heard, "If you can lean, you can clean," is this part of your on-boarding discussion? I know it was for me.

Whether you were a full time employee or a temporary laborer working with us for one day, you got the speech, "I don't EVER want to see you standing around. If you don't know what to do, grab a broom and sweep until there is no dust left on this earth."

Ok, it probably wasn't that dramatic, but it was consistent. Before you rip into someone for being lazy, be sure that you and your team have been clear about work direction and what to do when you don't know what to do. On the other hand, if someone is outright lazy, you can't help them. I can't make you a hard worker, but if you will work hard, I can teach you anything.

Be as scientific in your approach to developing your team and solving interpersonal issues as you are with doing the work of property restoration. It doesn't get much clearer than what Lombardi, Aristotle, and The Hippocratic Oath shared in this chapter.

- **Vision**: Lombardi gives you the big picture, "Perfection is not attainable. But if we chase perfection, we can catch excellence."
- **Process**: Aristotle gives you the breakdown of how you must operate, "Excellence is an art won by training and habituation. We are what we repeatedly do. Excellence, then, is not an act but a habit."
- **Values**: The Hippocratic Oath delivers the high calling of Doctors of Disaster, "So long as I maintain this Oath faithfully and without corruption, may it be granted to me to partake of life fully and the practice of my art, gaining the respect of all men for all time."

May your company be an assembly line of Intentional Restorers.

CHAPTER 12

A Framework for Success

I trained for years to run nine seconds,
And people give up when they don't see results in
two months.
Usain Bolt

You have heard the phrase, "Jack of all trades, master of none." In property restoration, where we respond to so many disaster scenarios, it is difficult to find means to help our team members master all the skills of our craft. Yet, a doctor is a doctor whether they are general practice or a specialist, such as a brain surgeon or endocrinologist. The DYOJO Chart is what I have used to help keep myself and our training regimens on track as we develop Doctors of Disaster.

While "Jack of all trades" has a negative connotation, as though a Jack isn't as good as a master, there are two things we should consider. First, Jack was and still is, a common name. Way back in the day, a Jack might also be known as a knave. Or a more modern 16th-century adaptation would be a Johnny do-it-all which *The Phrase Finder* translates as *Johannes factotum*[88] (which sounds like a Harry Potter spell).

I love being around Jacks and Johnnys who are honest, hard-working, and willing to learn. This concept of jacks and trades has evolved into careers such as the blue collar lumberjacks who are prominent in the Pacific Northwest. Molding growth-minded individuals into intentional restorers is why the resource in this chapter was created.

---

[88] Martin, G. *The meaning and origin of the expression: Jack of all trades.* The Phrase Finder. https://www.phrases.org.uk/meanings/jack-of-all-trades.html

Second, you should be encouraged to know that this attempt to use Jack-of-all as a slight is an incomplete citation and also would place you in good company with a high achiever. Apparently Robert Greene observed the young William Shakespeare hanging around the theater and penned the words,

"An upstart crow, beautified with our feathers, that supposes he is as well able to bumbast out a blanke verse as the best of you. Beeing an absolute Johannes fac totum, is in his owne conceit the onely Shake-scene in a countrey [sic]".

If anyone looks down on you as an aspiring professional, a new project manager, or a training manager, it appears that at least one person did not have high regard for the now world-famous playwright. The whole quote is reported to be, "A jack of all trades is a master of none, but oftentimes better than a master of one." As you develop these sundry skills for you and your team, the Doctors of Disaster pride themselves in being Johnny do-it-alls.

So that you don't spiral out of control, The DYOJO Chart helps you all to keep the two big picture elements that are critical to success in property restoration at the center of your efforts. You want your team to understand the importance of creating happy customers and producing consistently profitable jobs. We break the contributing factors into four quadrants. Let's discuss these elements in a bit more detail, starting with safety.

Quadrant 1: Safety

Safety stands on its own as it transcends all of these issues. If your people are not safe and/or healthy, they cannot work with you. Do everything in your power to train them properly and keep them whole. You cannot achieve **a culture of safety**[89] without training regularly on how to be safe when performing the work items that are required to complete your projects.

---

[89] Isaacson, J. (2019, February 3) *8 Keys to Building a Culture of Safety*. IZ Vents. https://www.izvents.com/words/8-keys-to-building-a-culture-of-safety

Many companies that excel in safety conduct at least a monthly safety meeting where the team performs a deeper dive into relevant safety topics. Three keys to effective training[90] include:

1. Training should be clear
2. Training should be concise
3. Training should be interactive

These all-staff meetings communicate that safety is the responsibility of the whole organization and the owner as well as high-level management. Everyone should attend and contribute so that the team sees these safety measures are important to and apply to all. The "big" meeting should be supplemented with regular toolbox safety meetings that are conducted daily where regular safety topics are addressed by localized teams.

Every project should start with a safety audit and pre-task plan which is reviewed and signed by anyone coming to that jobsite. As with everything, if you don't document, it didn't happen. Yet, it is not enough to hand out pieces of paper, have your employees sign them, and call it good.

In Maslow's Hierarchy of Needs, he expresses as part of his Theory of Human Motivation that unless the base needs are met, humans will struggle to reach higher states of realization. Safety serves as the second tier of human needs and motivation. As humans, we all require a sense of safety if we are going to operate beyond our physiological needs into a state of belonging. When an employee feels like they are safe, they can begin to feel like they belong, and this dynamic is key to retaining good talent in your organization.

---

[90] Isaacson, J. (2018, February 4) *Three Fundamentals of Effective Training.* LinkedIn. https://www.linkedin.com/pulse/three-fundamentals-effective-training-jon-isaacson

Lisa Lavender, COO of Berks Fire Water Restorations, Inc. (Reading, PA) shares her perspective on the importance of safety[91], which includes but is not limited to:

- We care about our team and want them to be safe and healthy.
- We must strive to meet and/or exceed safety requirements and remain in compliance.
- Due to the nature of our work, our safety-mindedness has a direct impact on the safety of our customers and those we serve.
- Safety has a direct impact on the bottom line of the company.

A culture of safety will save you money by keeping your organization out of trouble and keeping employees working at their job. According to OSHA, "It has been estimated that employers pay almost $1 billion per week for direct worker's compensation costs alone." As a project manager, you fall under the duties of the Occupational Safety and Health Act, Section 5 Duties "General Duty Clause" which states,

> "Every employer (1) SHALL furnish to each of his employees employment and a place of employment which is free from recognized hazards that are causing or are likely to cause death or serious physical harm to his employees; (2) SHALL comply with occupational safety and health standards promulgated under this Act."

You will want to familiarize yourself with the OSHA Standards for General Industry, a helpful way to do this is to take an IICRC Health and Safety Technician (HST) course and/or the OSHA 10 and 30 Hour courses. The objectives of the HST course include,

---

[91] Lavender, L. (2015, November 5) *Restoring Success: Building a Culture of Safety.* Restoration & Remediation Magazine. https://www.randrmagonline.com/articles/86691-restoring-success-building-a-culture-of-safety

"The certification will promote the importance of hazard and risk assessments and how to implement controls on the identified hazards. The hierarchy of hazard controls will be emphasized so that eliminating, reducing, and controlling hazards will become the focus of health and safety instead of just regulatory compliance."

You want to continually elevate your ability to identify hazards and reduce the likelihood that your team will be negatively impacted by their occurrence.

Richard Carpenter of Durango, Colorado, nails it when he says, "Our industry really is all about dealing with controlled chaos." Remember that, controlled chaos. Or bringing control to the chaos. As we have said multiple times, we respond to chaos but we should not be escalating it within our teams.

Richard continues, "Every project is different. A project manager needs to be able to think creatively to color inside the lines (OSHA, safety, S500/520) while knowing when to color outside the lines because at some point you'll probably have to." Some of the resources that Mr. Carpenter suggests that a project manager adds to their tool belt include, "Safety meetings, tailgate talks, being able to get disparate personalities to work together well for a common goal."

We demonstrate that we care for our people and our customers by being intentional and consistent with our safety measures. Project Management Institute states,

"The project manager sets the example for the entire project team. Whatever the project manager focuses on will be viewed by the team as important. The saying, 'Actions speak louder than words' is true. Project managers who place a premium on integrating safety into their projects will ensure better overall project performance[92]."

---

[92] Terrell, M. (2000) *The Project Manager's Role As A Safety Champion.* Project Management Institute. https://www.pmi.org/learning/library/project-managers-role-saftey-champion-8879

There is much more that could and should be said about safety. I contemplated building another chapter on this topic as it is essential to project management and sound business practices. In the end, I believe that what we mention here and throughout the book will help lay the foundation for the right mindset and habits with regard to safety. Constant evaluation of hazards is an important habit for any project manager.

- <u>Benefits of safety to the organization</u>. A safe organization will have healthy team members who feel valued and are able-bodied to contribute to the team goals.
- <u>Benefits of safety to the customer</u>. If the team that was assigned to a project becomes injured, they cannot help the customer or the company complete the project. How traumatic is it for your team member and the client, when someone is injured in their home or business?

Quadrant 2: Proficiency

Technical + Practical = Proficient

Technical knowledge and skills are important, they are the foundation for doing things right. Consistently doing things the right way allows us to make observations and adaptations that will help us be more efficient. In the field, an employee with practical skill will often out-perform one with only technical knowledge. Instead of "street smarts" think of "trade smarts," whereby you may have a team member who has learned and/or has intuition, but may not be the best at explaining what, why, or how they do what they do.

Another employee may be able to pass all the training and certification tests, but when it comes to making things work at the ground level, they struggle. As you advance into leadership roles, you need both, combined with the people skills that we have spent a lot of time discussing. You must develop both sides of your team. Too often employees are left to either figure things out on their own or to learn from their peers, this may produce some positive results but until you add some intention to a process, the results will continue to be inconsistent.

- <u>Benefits of proficiency to the organization</u>. When you invest in training your team members, it helps your leadership team to be more clear about what is important and this clarity is what drives consistency in your processes as well as accountability among your teams.
- <u>Benefits of proficiency to the customer</u>. When your team members know what they are doing and why they are more confident in speaking about and performing their duties. When the organization is clear, the technicians can be clear, and the customer has greater trust in the people, the process, and the brand.

Quadrant 3: Efficiency

Planning + Execution = Efficiency

The last thing you want to tell your team is, "Do it faster." Obviously, project pace is critical to profitability and customer satisfaction, but speed can kill. When a project drags on, the customer satisfaction bottoms out as do your profits. Every stakeholder in an insurance claim is happier when we meet or beat, our target duration. Yet, if we tell our crew to go faster, this only increases stress and leads to further chaos. The law of entropy takes over, speed only drives the train further off the rails.

You don't want people moving faster if this results in lower standards of quality or cutting corners. Have you heard the painful reality, "How come there is never enough time to do it right but always enough to do it over?" Our efficiency goes back, like most things, to training. If a project is really struggling, the best thing you can do may be to hit pause and help the team reset. Clarify the remaining objectives, delegate responsibilities, and follow through on the execution of tasks.

If your project completion timelines are slower than they should be, don't be distracted by the symptom of speed, dig into areas where you can reduce waste, clarify your plan(s) of attack, and increase your ability to execute accurately. If you can take a bit more time on the front end (before the work starts) to plan out the project properly, you can hit the ground running and reduce stoppages until you are complete.

Doing it right the first time, from the start of a project to the finish, is the most efficient, effective, and profitable means of crossing the customer satisfaction finish line. When you step in to help, be aware of the tendency to take over rather than assist your team members in coming to a resolution. Even project managers need to learn how to Scan, Plan, Execute, and Document.

If you want to increase your job completion turnaround time, train your team SPEeD.

- **SCAN.** What are we looking for when we arrive at the project? What is the extent of damages and where is the source? Once we have identified the affected areas and have a mental map of the work that needs to be done, we need to PLAN our approach. Leaders love to talk about "when I used to be in the field." While this nostalgia may be fun banter, use these moments to actually teach your team members what mindset and habits helped you to be successful when you were a technician. Conduct a leadership download and break down how you would approach a scenario from notice of the call to customer satisfaction. What you think should be common sense will never reach that level of shared values unless you spend the time to train your team to accomplish the work in alignment with your values and execute your unique process. The same is true for training project managers, in the traditional division of roles between an estimator and PM, as they often have to learn to SCAN the PLAN created by others and EXECUTE based upon the information they receive.

- **PLAN.** This is especially important for team leads. We must help them develop the ability to communicate clearly and effectively with their team members. When the person in a position of leadership on the job site is not an effective communicator, the job will lag. I am sure you have noticed a common thread throughout this book on the importance of communication. Just because someone doesn't communicate effectively now, doesn't mean that they can't learn to do so. I am sure that you weren't great at it right from the get-go. The same is true here as was said about SCAN, teach your team to utilize the best of what made you successful. Discuss scenarios, train consistently, and walk them through the process on a real job. As a project manager, you have to learn to scan the project, develop your plan of attack, and effectively communicate these elements to your team.

- **EXECUTE.** I tried to teach my up-and-coming team leads that it was not a sign of weakness to allow any team member to share their ideas and if they had a better one. An idea that got the work completed more efficiently so that we all went home sooner, is good for all. So, don't be afraid to go with it. That said, there are also times when it isn't up for discussion, the lead knows what they are doing and they have to develop their ability to get the team moving in the right direction. Leadership is complex and everyone develops their voice in their own way. At the end of the day, everyone on-site should want the same thing, to make the most of our time and achieve our objectives as efficiently as possible by working together. As you develop your voice as a person in a position of leadership, you have to develop your ability to connect with your team, communicate responsibilities clearly, produce consistently, and hold everyone accountable for their roles in achieving the goals.

- **DOCUMENT.** Everyone's favorite task, documentation. In property restoration, we do not get paid for what we do but what we can document that we did. You cannot hold your team to a higher standard than you hold yourself to and your expectations cannot exceed your norms. If you expect thorough documentation in real-time, this standard has to be carried through from the time of the call for a new project and on through every phase of the job. I outline this principle in greater detail in Garbage In, Garbage Out Part 1. You may have it in your head that there is a high bar (expectations), and you probably complain to your peers about the lack of quality from workers these days, yet your norms are inconsistent. Do you train on your perceived standards? Do you hold everyone accountable to the same measure? Do estimators get away with murder while technicians are written up or disciplined for every infraction?

You need to develop your own ability to scan, plan, execute, and document before you can help others to do the same. Rather than panic at every restoration disco, we want to be calm and collected in our decision-making process. This does not mean that as Doctors of Disaster that we don't have a sense of urgency. Rather we respond to chaos with calm, we act intentionally but not erratically.

Your plan will change as the project unfolds. You don't have to have a perfect plan in order to start or finish strong. As we grow our professional careers and our businesses, we understand what Mark Springer[93], president of Dayspring Restoration, shared as one of his favorite quotes, "A good plan today is better than a perfect plan tomorrow[94]."

The right mix of planning prior to execution will help us to reduce dysfunction. With regards to chaos in a company, author Lex Sisney has developed an *Entropy Survey*[95] which helps to identify and address three core organizational challenges:

---

[93] The DYOJO Podcast, Episode 41

[94] Attributed to General George S. Patton. It is argued that this is misquoted and may have actually said, "A good plan, violently executed now, is better than a perfect plan next week."

[95] Sisney, L. *Entropy Survey*. Organizational Physics. https://organizationalphysics.com/entropy-survey

- <u>Effectiveness vs. Activity</u>. Where should we focus our finite time and energy to make the most impact?
- <u>Signal vs. Noise</u>. What is the signal we should pay attention to and what is just the noise?
- <u>Diversity vs. Dissonance</u>. How do we gather diverse perspectives and align them to avoid dissonance?

Entropy is disorder or disorganization. When there is high internal friction there is a greater draw on the limited energy and time already being expended in your organization[96]. As Lex points out, we tend to think that chaos is random when in actuality it is the result of wrong mindsets and habits being repeated within your team functions.

Developing a means to test and address those three core organizational challenges will help your team move in the right direction with common language and a shared process for working through issues. We want to move from activity to effectiveness so that we spend our limited energy towards making progress.

The fourth quadrant on The DYOJO Chart is Service which is made up of cleanliness and communication.

Quadrant 4: Service

Cleanliness + Communication = Service

Cleanliness is godliness in property restoration. A commitment to cleanliness will save you from a lot of headaches. I enjoy watching Gordon Ramsey on *Kitchen Nightmares*. In my opinion, the failing restaurants suffer from a few common

---

[96] Lex Sisney's book, *Organizational Physics* fulfills its sub-title as it outlines *The Science of Growing a Business* by applying principles from the observed world and connecting them to the integrated organism we call a company. I had the pleasure of discussing many of these principles with Lex on The DYOJO Podcast, Episode 22, where we also talked about how intentional entrepreneurs can go about "Growing your business without compromising your values."

issues which include blaming their customers for their terrible sales, obnoxiously defending their terrible food, disgusting conditions in the kitchen, and executing a menu that is too complicated. Chef Ramsey shows up in disguise, orders the items from the menu that the style of restaurant should be mastering, and inevitably reveals himself after nearly throwing up because the food is so bad.

The owner will bow up, telling Gordon that he doesn't know anything about food. The accomplished chef has a particular knack for putting obstinate people in their place before making a bee-line for their kitchen. Cleanliness is no guarantee of success but it is an indication of your values and your efforts.

When a restaurant is failing, Gordon will get to work reshaping the mindset and habits of the team, even investing in remodeling their business, but they all have to roll their sleeves up and start cleaning. Usually, this involves mounds of rotten food stored in the walk-in and grease traps that are on the verge of igniting over the cooking stations.

Cleanliness and Confidence

If your team members are clean in their personal appearance, does this promote confidence in themselves as well as from their clients? Yes. Conversely, if an employee looks disheveled, does this make a poor impression or lower customer confidence? Yes. Personal cleanliness (pride) drives professional cleanliness (order). If an employee has low standards of personal hygiene, this will carry through in how they care for their company vehicle, tools, and equipment, which in turn impacts how they care for the client's home.

I can remember a co-worker who had only one company shirt provided to them. Yet, this brand publicly prided itself on the appearance of its team members. By the time I met this person, the shirt was nearly threadbare. The company policy read a certain way about how many uniforms team members would be provided in a year and yet the manager wanted to save money by reducing that quota. Employees who worked in crawl spaces, hanging drywall, and smoke sealing fire-damaged homes were blamed for getting their uniforms dirty.

It's difficult to tell your team members to have pride in the brand when the brand skimps on providing or maintaining uniforms. Whether you believe in company-provided uniforms or not, the appearance of your team members when they first arrive at a customer's home is important to their perception of your company. If you can only make one first impression, what does the appearance of your team do to aid in building confidence in your ability to assist them in their time of need? Uniforms don't have to be fancy, but having people arrive in clear company apparel helps to identify your team.

Cleanliness and Efficiency

When you know where your supplies, tools, and equipment are, because they are well kept, clean, and stored in the same spot after each use, you do not waste time looking for that one item. Clean employees, clean vehicles, clean warehouse, clean worksites, clean production, and clean billing.

If you have children, you know that simply telling them to clean their room is not enough clarity to lead to an outcome that you both will be satisfied with. In Chapter 9 we discussed the issue with a lack of clarity between perspectives on a "simple" work task such as "Clean your room, I will be back in an hour." We have communicated the broad scope and given a duration, but without further details, this work order is unlikely to achieve the desired outcome.

You need to be clearer in your directions if you want to bridge the gap between what you expect and what you have communicated. You may take it for granted or feel like many of these items should be common sense, but they do not become commonly understood or executed without clear and consistent direction:

- Keeping a tidy uniform or wearing appropriate work attire
- Maintaining an orderly desk or office space
- Cleaning your work vehicle, inside and out, at least once a week

- Ordering your tools in cases, maintaining them, and returning them to the same spot after each use
- Maintaining certain stock of materials and equipment in your vehicle
- Setting up dust control and surface protection at the start of every job
- Cleaning your workspace at the end of each day

Whether you believe it or not, all of these items are subjective. Unless you define what you mean by key items of cleanliness, such as those outlined above, you will struggle to develop a common understanding within your organization. Teach your team members why these items are important, how they contribute to achieving your shared goals, as well as means and methods to accomplish the desired outcome.

If you are pursuing project management, these are some of the work functions that go above and beyond your responsibilities in the field and will help you demonstrate to managers and owners that you can be trusted to take on more. Cleanliness is a transcendent function of the work, it will help you be of service to any company at any level.

- <u>Benefits of cleanliness to the organization.</u> Mastering the "small" things helps you to build momentum for taking on bigger and bigger goals. When everyone, from top-to-bottom, is responsible for cleanliness, there is accountability.
- <u>Benefits of cleanliness to the customer.</u> Building clarity and consistency around your approaches to cleanliness help to demonstrate to the customer that you respect their home and care about their concerns.

Communication

Going back to the nightmare kitchens from Gordon Ramsey, another common function he provides is simplifying the menu. Many of the restaurants that struggle have an incredibly complex menu which leads to issues with controlling costs and delivering a consistent end product to the customer. Narrowing the focus of the team on the areas of highest competence can help create better outcomes. Communication and cleanliness are foundational elements of the customer experience.

Travis Parker Martin, co-founder and VP of Product and Marketing for KnowHow, asks, "What's the biggest difference between a project that succeeds and a project that fails?" The team at KnowHow has analyzed over 1,000 bad reviews of restoration companies in the US, and the answer is, unequivocally, communication.

- 36.8% of all 1-star reviews cited frustrations over a lack of communication between the restoration company and the customer.
- Of those, over 30% were complaints specifically around a business not following up on quotes, requests, phone calls, etc.

What's the lesson according to Travis? "Project Managers can have an outsized influence on the success of a project, simply by communicating well. Running late? Fire a quick text. Anticipate a delay? Pick up the phone. Not sure if insurance will approve your estimate? Reach out to them. Tiny, little gestures that were once basic social etiquette can drastically alter the perception a customer has of the entire restoration process and can give you a leg up in ensuring you consistently deliver five-star experiences to your customers."

Their research confirms that proactive communication is a key factor in setting yourself and your team up for success. Simply using your phone can help you eliminate almost 40% of your common complaints. Travis states, "It feels like a cheat code," but it takes discipline to pick up your phone, even when you don't want to. He continues, "If you feel yourself avoiding a conversation, it's a sure-fire sign that you need to have that conversation as soon as possible - connecting human-to-human, as opposed to letting the customer's imagination run wild on why you aren't returning their calls."

Have the conversation, don't avoid it. Get that burden off your plate by addressing the issue. Answering your phone will give you a massive opportunity to distinguish yourself from those around you. Learn how to have hard conversations respectfully and promptly, and watch the difference it makes with your customers, your team, and your career. Issues only compound when you refuse to address them.

Sample Communication SOP

During the scoping and negotiation phases, the estimator should be keeping a written log, we call it our Comm Notes, of all conversations and agreements with the carrier and the client. We all want to be able to collect for the work that we complete yet many businesses allow their communication to be inconsistent.

Communication is directly tied to your ability to collect. In mitigation, contact the adjuster early and often while ensuring that the client is clear on their responsibilities. In repairs, your contract should outline your billing process, which should include deposit and progress billing. It is important that you set up your habits as a project manager for keeping your communication clear and consistent. At the organizational level, the following may be a good start to creating a standard operating procedure (SOP) around communication for your team.

1. Our goal is to be transparent in our communication, whether the job is program or not, the customer will be included, or at least updated in real-time, on all relevant communication about their claim.
2. Our goal is to practice proactive communication, by this objective we want to attempt to answer our customers' questions

before they ask them. Most customer questions are related to the timeline, scope, and cost of the project. We will provide at least one quality touchpoint per week, preferably on the same day each week to form a strong habit. A quality touch is a phone call or visit, and at least one additional quantity touch, i.e. email or text, throughout the duration of the project. This is important at all phases, even when "nothing" is happening. For example, "I am calling you to remind you the cabinets have been ordered and they are still 10 days out. We anticipate they will arrive at the supplier on X date and will provide you another update next week around this time to confirm everything is on track."

3. Any communication with parties to the claim should be tracked in our communications portal (i.e. Comm Notes, program, and/or CRM) so that this information is updated and available to all members of our team.

One of the best means of ensuring that you have been clear with the customer and to establish consistent communication, thus heading off those random calls at odd hours from the client, is to set the expectation at the project outset and follow through with regularly scheduled proactive communication.

Proactive communication is a process of setting the expectation with the client for how and when communication will occur. We want a clear process that we consistently follow. This includes discussing what is and isn't an emergency so that our team members can maintain normal business hours. The goal of proactive communication is to understand the client's concerns and needs and attempt to answer their questions before they have them. This should not be considered a complex process but rather systematizing what we know about claims so that we can help create as smooth of a process to restoration as possible. Periods of non-communication will create frustration for the client and increase the likelihood that there will be issues with customer satisfaction and therefore profitability at the project conclusion.

Quantity touches are those items that keep us in simple contact with our clients. Being intentional and tracking our efforts is important with our current clients, new client outreach, employees, subcontractors, and anyone that we work with within our network. Set goals around how many quantity-based touches you want to achieve per week, month, quarter, etc. We should ask and learn how our clients like to be communicated with, for example, some really appreciate texts while others don't use technology.

Quality touches in marketing are how we intentionally move client outreach into professional relationships and sales opportunities. Quality touches with our existing clients or those projects in our pipeline is how we create a consistent customer experience. Even if a customer prefers texts to phone calls, they should have at least one verbal or physical interaction each week. If the project is still in estimating then the estimator should reach out, once in production the project manager should discuss and set expectations around how and when to achieve these goals. Because people are our greatest asset, it is important to remember that quality touches apply to our employees and subcontractors as well. Remind people that you care by setting aside time for them.

- Benefits of communication to the organization. Managers like to tell their employees, "Garbage in equals garbage out" when it comes to scolding them for their inconsistent documentation. Yet, the same is true for our processes as a team. Project details must be captured in real time in a format that is updated and accessible by all the members of your team.
- Benefits of communication to the customer. As has been noted multiple times, communication is key to building trust and keeping a project on track. It is rare that a customer complains about too much communication, but lack of communication is among the top complaints.

Train your team to do it right the first time. Embrace the challenge of being a Jack-of-all-trades in restoration. Keep yourself and your team on track by mapping out your training plan to address core competencies and build upon prior sessions.

When I was overseeing a sizeable mitigation department, we typically received projects such as large pack outs or bio-decontamination in groups of threes. In these scenarios we would pause our planned training to re-visit our training on those areas of immediate need. As a project manager, you have to develop rigid-flexibility. Have a plan, but always be prepared to adapt.

If you haven't watched Kitchen Nightmares, you may find some value in seeing how consistently chef Ramsey refers back to basic, universal principles when turning a failing operation around.

The DYOJO Chart

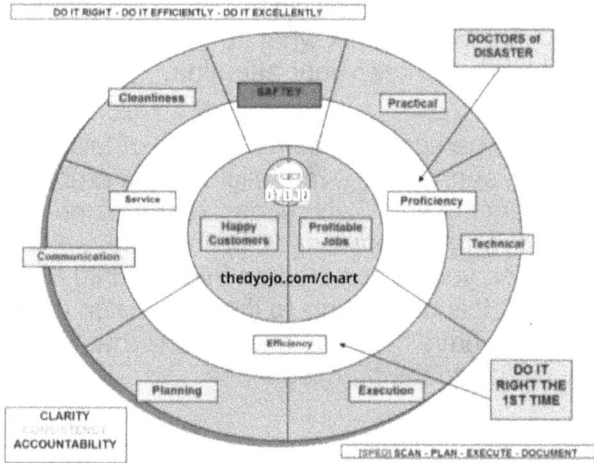

CHAPTER 13

Qualities of a Good Project Manager

*"Confidence comes not from always being right,
but from not fearing to be wrong."*
Peter McIntyre

I think it is quite stupid when I see a job posting with ninjas, superstars, or A-players in the title. The reality of the superstar and their impact on teams in business is a dynamic that I would encourage you to STOP perpetuating. While the concept is much more prevalent in professional sports, it does not always work out as visioneered. If you are not a fan of sports analogies, I think what I am about to share has enough tabloid fodder to keep your attention.

The cult of personality has a long trail of failed ventures in business, sports, and even religion. You probably aren't a soccer fan, but you likely recognize the name David Beckham. *The Beckham Experiment* by Grant Wahl reads as a what-not-to-do when you've acquired an international mega star. The lessons in this book apply to the restoration company that thinks they have hired the missing link that will take their organization to the promised land.

While David was not the first star that American soccer brought into the fold to attempt to elevate the environment, he certainly was the one whom many thought would be the bearer of the awakening of Major League Soccer (MLS). Most readers will recognize the Beckham name but likely share a lack of knowledge for his skill as a player. You probably know, and care, even less for the early history of professional soccer in the United States.

Writer Franklin Foer shared this perspective, "David Beckham is more than a gifted player. He is a multinational conglomerate. And in Grant Wahl's extraordinary telling, his sojourn in Los Angeles makes for a gripping tale about the business of sports and the growth pangs of American soccer." In addition to being a global icon, which was elevated by his marriage to Victoria Adams, aka Posh Spice of British super girl group, The Spice Girls, David was a highly respected athlete. A few of David's accomplishments include:

- Debuted as a professional soccer player at the age of 17 for one of the most historied football (soccer) clubs, as well as one of the most recognized sports brands, in the world - Manchester United (MU). He was captain of the team for six years
- Won the Premier League six times, the FA Cup twice, and the UEFA Champions League once
- Represented England in the FIFA World Cup tournament three times
- When he left MU, he joined an equally storied club, Real Madrid and won their league championship
- Beckham has consistently ranked among the highest earners in football, and in 2013 was listed as the highest-paid player in the world, having earned over $50 million in the previous 12 months[97]
- Beckham has been hailed as one of the greatest and most recognizable midfielders of his generation, as well as one of the best set-piece specialists of all time[98]
- David was awarded the sexiest man alive in 2015 by People magazine

[97] Settimi, C. (2013, April 17) *The World's Best-Paid Soccer Players*. Forbes. https://www.forbes.com/sites/christinasettimi/2013/04/17/the-worlds-best-paid-soccer-players/?sh=61d70efe7b1f

[98] Hughes, Matt (16 May 2013) *David Beckham was one of best and most significant footballers of his generation*. The Times. https://www.thetimes.co.uk/article/david-beckham-was-one-of-best-and-most-significant-footballers-of-his-generation-sj08rbfx9g5

Sports team owners and management groups drool at the potential for positive financial as well as performance enhancements by bringing a celebrity figure to the team. There is a mythical formula in business and professional sports that theorizes the missing component is that one player who will take us over the top – and of course that one player is always somewhere other than from within the current program so that one player is cyclical pursuit by struggling organizations.

For the Los Angeles Galaxy, bringing on David Beckham brought the spotlight for a time. Unfortunately for them it also brought a wide angle view from behind the scenes. This story serves as a modern day Aesop's Fable for any leadership team when working with "stars". Some of the cautionary plot points that will emerge include: rushing an injury, mismanaging personalities, surrendering control, and poor communication.

In soccer, there is an honored tradition of allowing the team to decide who wears the captain's armband. A player who emulates the team values, sets a tone for the group, and serves as a key intermediary between the coaches and players. Alexi Lalas, a former player, American national team star, and general manager states, "In a professional sports environment, you'd be surprised to know the gravity with which it's [captains armband] seen and how important it ends up being." The captain's position matters because it is earned.

Captains being voted on by team members is common in many sports. For some reason, the Galaxy management thought they could jump start or usurp the process. Given Beckham's prestige as a player as well as a star, if David came to camp and played as expected, it would have been a natural progression for him to be named captain voluntarily by the players as well as the standing captain. At the time, that captain was the young Landon Donovan who was an up-and-coming star in his own right.

The suits of the organization, in all their wisdom, decided they would prime the pump for Beckham's reception within the LA Galaxy by awkwardly asking Landon to hand over the captain's armband before the international celebrity had even set foot on the pitch. As the story goes, David was not the leader, or interested in being, what the Galaxy expected. As noted by Wahl:

"It was one thing to take part in team events, but it was another thing to lead, to act like a captain, to rally the players during tough times and represent the greater good of the team— with the coach, with the front office—even when it might not have been in the personal interest of the captain himself."

Beckham was a good teammate who knew how to joke around as well as when to be serious, yet when the team needed a boost or the captain to take the lead, the star did not take the prompts. He had the armband but did not intervene in the manner a captain should. "Captain Galaxy", as some referred to David, was placed in a role that he had not earned nor was the right fit for.

Management had their grand ideas. By trying to mash something together, they put Beckham in a position he was unwilling to fill and ostracized their homegrown talent in Donovan. This interrupted the natural growth of their team. The Beckham Experiment sold a lot of tickets but did little to propel the Galaxy's success.

Did the Los Angeles organization make money on their experiment? Yes. But they could not put a consistent winning effort together in the three seasons that Beckham was associated with the team. An international superstar was not the sole solution. Medal of Honor recipient Woody Williams is attributed with saying, "No matter how good the team or how efficient the methodology, if we're not solving the right problem, the project fails."

If you were a soccer fan, you would know that it would be hard to pass on the opportunity to onboard someone the caliber of David Beckham. Like so many "savior" hires, there are either rose-colored glasses when assessing the fit of the person for the role. When vision and values are not in line, it will be difficult for any hire to help move the mission forward.

If you are an owner or manager, I would love it if this point caused you to take a second look at the people you already have in your organization. *Perhaps the missing piece you need is already on the team*[99]. Who would your team members give the company armband to?

Bad hires and mistakes happen. We are human and we get excited. Being a solid organization or a good project manager is NOT about never making a mistake, but is about working your butt off to prevent the big ones, owning where you messed up, and learning from the process. You prepare and train to do it right the first time, but you stand by your work and you make it right when it isn't.

Those responsible for hiring should place an emphasis on determining a candidate's abilities with regards to interacting with customers, subcontractors, and the employees they will supervise. You want to be intentional about bringing your vision into alignment with your processes. These principles should guide how you recruit, hire, develop, and discipline/reward your team members.

If you agree the project management role is a customer service role, make sure you are prioritizing that reality. This does not mean the technical skills of a candidate are not important in the role. If you hire people who don't like dealing with people and wonder why the process doesn't work, you are going to struggle more than you should with hiring, developing, and retaining project managers.

Insurance claims work is high on customer service and overlapping layers of documentation. So, it would make sense to take someone who can barely use a smartphone and spent the better part of their interview complaining about customers and subcontractors, and hire them for a people-centric, data-driven, technology-heavy role, right? Enough snark. Let's take a look at some of the characteristics of candidates for the role of project management:

---

[99] Read Chapter 11 from *Be Intentional: Culture*

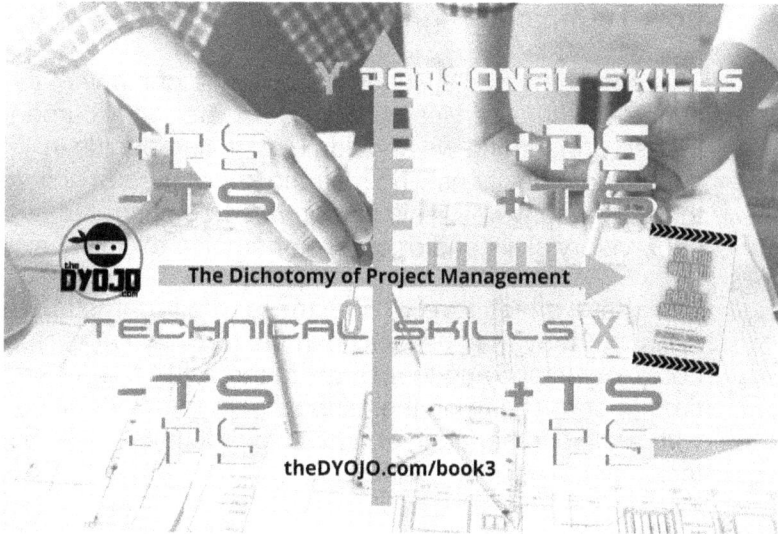
The Dichotomy of Project Management

theDYOJO.com/book3

High Technical, Low Personal

A candidate who has dedicated their life to learning the technical skills of their trade is valuable. This person may be near mastery level in their area of specialty. Someone with the ability to identify, communicate, and execute with a high level of competency is a must for any organization, especially in the skilled trades. It is often said that it takes over 10,000 hours of practice to become competent in anything. Often those who achieve this level in a technical skill do it to the exclusion of other abilities.

Those people who are most adept with technical skills may struggle with the people stuff of the business. There are some people who have rounded themselves out in both areas, but even they likely are stronger in one over the other. This does not mean that this person should not be a part of the team, just that you will need to be aware of what their strengths and weaknesses are and find ways to supplement their gaps as they develop those other attributes. It is important that you do not set them up for failure by putting them in positions where they are responsible for all of the people stuff. If you have a candidate that is honest, hard-working, and willing to learn, you can help them develop their full arsenal of capabilities; it will take some time.

Low Technical, High Personal

This candidate has a working knowledge of many of the aspects of your services but isn't a master-level carpenter. Please understand we shouldn't be putting people in supervisory positions who have no knowledge of how to do things the right way. This person has demonstrated strong supervisory skills and/or customer service excellence.

They have a high level of adeptness with regards to people skills, but they may be lacking in the technical aspects. Options could include having them work in the field for a set period of time prior to taking on their supervisory roles or pairing them up with a project manager who has high technical skills but is lacking in their people skills.

If you do a lot of subcontractor work, where you have good subs you rely on for their technical acumen, pairing them up with a candidate like this can round out the transaction with the client to provide an engaging experience. In this example, your employee handles the people stuff while your subcontractor handles the technical stuff.

This can be effective as long as all parties respect and learn from each other. Your candidate must learn to develop their database of understanding how the trades work. You will also want to find ways in which they can help your technical people to learn to develop their soft skills.

Low Technical, Low Personal

This person is better suited for a role other than project management. Unfortunately, candidates like this slip through the cracks when they do a good job of marketing themselves as being more skilled in either area than they really are. If this person is hard-working, honest, and willing to learn, we want to get them into the organization with an opportunity to advance if they develop their skill sets.

You want to find means of assessing technical and personal skills prior to hiring. It is not a great idea to hire someone you think has potential and immediately shift them into management. Hire them, outline a development strategy, and empower them to earn the opportunity for a leadership role.

High Technical, High Personal

Remember, a high rating is relative. We want to judge based upon objective measures. Often those who excel in one area, their strength or ideal role, are going to have a weakness, which is the area that is less developed or polished. My first response to somebody who comes across as skilled in both is to be cautious that anything too good to be true probably is. But you also don't want to pass on the opportunity to have a high performer in your organization. As with all positions, it is important to set the roles, responsibilities, and expectations early with high performers.

If you have a weak culture, a high performer can steamroll your structure. You want to develop a clear, consistent, and accountable culture so this person can embrace and enhance your vision. Too many owners are looking for silly terms like "ninjas" because they have the false impression that if they could just find a "superstar" they can put something in cruise control. Nothing could be further from the truth.

Setting clear roles and responsibilities enables you to delegate to someone who will own their position so you can be less involved in that area and focus your attention on another problem. When I asked Josh Zolin, author of Blue is the New White, how would you describe the roles and responsibilities to someone seeking this position as a career growth opportunity? He said he would tell aspiring professionals that key disciplines include:

- Leading a team of people to complete a mission-oriented task
- Oversee the process, production, and overall quality of a finished product or structure
- Taking responsibility for the good and the bad of your team
- Instilling confidence in the customer or end-user of your ability to meet deadlines

- Organizing and scheduling people or subcontractors to work in succession with the intent of creating as little downtime as possible

His book is all about changing the narrative around telling young people that they have to go to college in order to be successful. If we are going to change our outcomes, we need to identify means to update our thinking and approach to the current market. We cannot keep doing the same outdated things and expecting to get anything but the same, expiring results.

Daring to Think Differently About Roles and Responsibilities

If you are trying to build your organization around vision and you place a high value on your values, you need to take a second look at how you have been treating the role of project management. Project managers need to be "high touch", meaning they are constantly in contact with the customer and making them feel good and confident about the process. As Josh said above, "Instilling confidence in the customer."

There is so much emphasis in our industry on estimating when this is only one piece of the puzzle and the tools available to outsource, or at least supplement, much of that task is getting increasingly better. Can you outsource your project management? Before you say yes, understand that giving your subcontractor a scope printout and some photos does not qualify as quality outsourcing.

Delegation requires the delegator to provide ownership to the person being delegated to. When you haphazardly pawn off your responsibilities, you may avoid a few initial headaches but your temporary reprieve will be built on quicksand. This isn't delegation, it's withdrawal and it will catch up to you.

A good comedian has a skill for observing elements from our lives and showing us how ridiculously we conduct ourselves. The pop culture favorite TV series *The Office* has some hilarious troupes that cast a humorous light on workplace culture. An episode titled *Health Care* (Season 1, Episode 3) serves as an uncomfortable and yet funny view into delegation gone wrong.

Michael Scott defers his managerial responsibility to choose a health plan for the staff to his right-hand man, Dwight Schrute. Dwight turns the opportunity into a power grab and cloisters himself in the conference room, posting a sign "Dwight Schrute Workspace." Even though Michael is willing to delegate this important decision to Dwight, he will not allow him to call the conference room his office.

Dwight may be perceived as the bad guy, but at his core, he does his best to do what he is asked. He would not have been voted by his peers to wear the Captain's armband but he was given the responsibility. In this instance, he is being asked to put the company first, cut costs, and choose a plan. Mr. Schrute goes to the extreme. When his peers review the plan he has chosen, they are upset, noting that he cut everything. Dwight is proud of his decisiveness,

"What did I do? I did my job. I slashed benefits to the bone. I saved this company money. Was I too harsh? Maybe. I don't believe in coddling people. In the wild, there is no health care. In the wild, health care is, 'Ow, I hurt my leg. I can't run. A lion eats me and I'm dead.' Well, I'm not dead. I'm the lion. You're dead."

People in a position of leadership like to use phrases like, "Delegate and elevate," but as is observed in this episode of The Office, sending your responsibilities downstream will not create a good working environment.

To delegate is defined as appointing another as your representative. Michael Scott, the manager of the office, did act in accordance with the definition. As often happens in real life, he grants the responsibility because he doesn't want accountability. Dwight is set up for failure and it only makes the issue worse for Michael.

Another Dwight, Mr. Dwight D. Eisenhower, who served as a five-star general, commander of Allied Forces in Europe during WWII, and the 34th President of the United States, is credited with a simple system for prioritization. It has been referred to as The Eisenhower Method or Decision Matrix.

- Important + Urgent = Do now
- Important + Not urgent = Do later
- Not Important + Urgent = Delegate
- Important + Not urgent = Eliminate

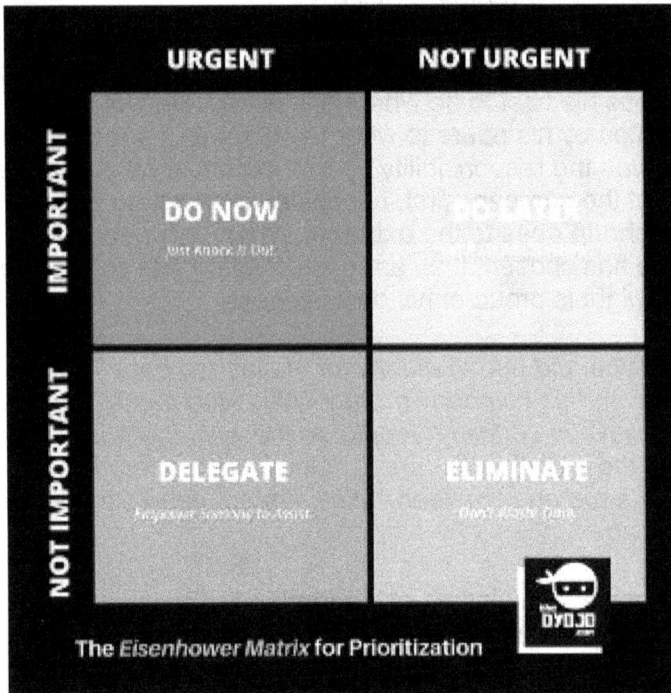

The *Eisenhower Matrix* for Prioritization

This decision matrix is designed to help you decide how best to use your most limited resource: time. Michael Scott's matrix was:

- I don't want to do it + Everyone will hate me = Give it to Dwight.

I am certain General Eisenhower would not approve or define this as quality delegation.

The office staff are upset with Dwight's recommendation. He becomes the villain and yet the origins of this debacle are handed down from a corporate office that wants to cut costs for profits. Michael's boss, Jan, tells him at the opening of the episode, "You know the whole reason that we're doing this is to save money. So you just need to pick a provider and choose the cheapest plan."

Headquarters defers to executives who defer to managers and Michael defers to Dwight. Rather than fix the issue, the big wigs get the masses to fight among themselves. In any workplace, you will find Jans, Michaels, and Dwights. As viewers, we are drawn to Dwight's outrageous antics and yet the issue goes much further upstream than the assistant to the regional manager.

- If you are an owner, you need to model the leadership qualities you want to see in your managers.
- If you are a manager and you want to see your team develop, you need to be intentional with the example of delegation you set.
- If you are a project manager, you need to think through how you assign work to subcontractors and staff.

Author and coach, Lex Sisney adds some valuable insights in his article *Delegation Strategies: When Not to Delegate*. His decision matrix includes the axis between the level of conviction and the degree of consequences. When a situation is of high conviction yet low consequence it is a great opportunity for a leader to delegate for the purpose of developing others.

"If they make a mistake, it's manageable, and you'll both learn and grow from it. But you'll often be pleasantly surprised at their results too, which further builds trust between you and

encourages you to give them high(er) consequence projects in the future[100]."

As you recognize individuals on your team who may be able to take on additional responsibilities, you will need to create opportunities for them to demonstrate their abilities. When someone is honest, hardworking, and willing to learn, they have the foundation for taking on new challenges. *"Whoever can be trusted with very little can also be trusted with much[101]."*

Josh Zolin stated that a core competency is overseeing, "The process, production, and overall quality of a finished product or structure." As we advised aspiring project managers to take an inventory of how well they are executing their current roles and then seek opportunities to take on additional responsibilities. Owners and managers should be looking for the same.

Back to the prior question of whether you can outsource project management, no. Project managers have to be your eyes and ears for the client, the production process, your in-house staff, your subcontractors, and often are the energy center of your organization. This high-touch interaction should be an emphasis for the recruiting and training process.

With the right systems in place, you can recruit, develop, and empower your project managers to manage projects with consistently positive outcomes. Remember, we want happy customers and profitable jobs; neither to the exclusion of the other but working in harmony for the benefit of all. These two core items are definitely of high consequence and should be treated with high conviction.

---

[100] Sisney, L. (2020, March 2) *Delegation Strategies: When NOT to Delegate.* Organizational Physics. https://organizationalphysics.com/2020/03/02/delegation-strategies-when-not-to-delegate

[101] Luke 16:10 NIV

I will share some other personal thoughts on the status quo versus innovation in project management perspectives. To keep myself and the reader on track, one thing every organization needs to do is have a clearer understanding of the roles and responsibilities of the project manager as it relates to your organization. Your vision and values, as well as your unique process, will define what a project manager means on your team.

This book is designed to help you work through those processes. Additionally, thinking through the broader context of leadership and how you develop that in your company is critical. The main thing is not assuming everyone views the position and execution of leadership the same way that you do. Continually expanding your perspective through outside sources and internal conversations is how you will continue to stay ahead of the curve.

The project manager contributes to the leadership of the organization. As such, the organization needs to identify candidates that embrace as well as enhance the company's core values and continue to invest in helping those contributors develop. When organizations partner with their people in a position of leadership, this helps to elevate the engagement and performance of the team. Here is an example of how one company took on this task.

How does a company that was started in 1929, by a former minor league baseball player with an eighth-grade education, as a door-to-door moth-proofing provider, develop into an industry-leading brand? Founder Marion Wade was able to grow his service business from its meager origins in Chicago, Illinois, to an international organization grossing over $2 billion annually in 2019.

Author Albert Erisman masterfully digs into the foundational principles that contributed to the 90+ years of exponential growth as a marquee brand in property restoration. His book, *The ServiceMaster Story*, sets out to demonstrate how early leadership navigated the tension between people and profit as well as the unique role that faith played in those formative years of the organization. Personal and professional development starts with the right mindset and habits, so it was encouraging to read about the leadership distinctives from this industry giant.

Distinctive #1 - The shingles on a roof mindset of leadership

Marion Wade built his company by seizing an opportunity to develop and provide a product, which he called Fumakill, that was better than his moth-proofing competitors. Marion had to perform the awkward dance that so many entrepreneurs are familiar with. He was wearing all of the hats - selling, serving, and adapting his invention. When he was selling, he wasn't producing. When he was producing, he wasn't developing the product. Even though he was losing sales to perform hands-on research and development, he was sure his investment would be worth it.

Mr. Wade also began to notice a value of the work itself, not just how he did the work, which would become a foundational principle as he brought in talent to help him build his company. Servant leadership was a hallmark; the ServiceMaster code was known as shingles on a roof whereby leaders worked together to fully utilize each other's skills.

Marion had definite ideas on the role of his faith in how he treated people as well as how he conducted business. Many proclaim their values; Wade took great care to hold himself and the four proceeding generations of executive leaders to these shared values. Marion was the starter shingle for the leadership dynamic, and those who followed him would be overlapping and complementary shingles.

Coincidentally, his first hire came at a time when his business stumbled into an opportunity to integrate a new service line, fire damage restoration, which would become a capstone division for the emerging brand. When Wade made the key decision of onboarding Ken Hansen, the job description he provided outlined a rough yet vision-forward process: "You start to learn the business by going out on production jobs. Then you can move into sales. This experience will equip you for real leadership. After that, you can start where you are needed most."

Distinctive #2 - The six weeks on the front lines habit of leadership

As ServiceMaster grew, each person in a position of leadership would come to embrace their predecessors as key contributors whom they honored and from whom they sought ongoing counsel. This demonstration of respect for each other and their shared values carried over into how they treated their employees. Even as an owner of a growing company, Mr. Wade regularly participated in the work that his teams provided.

One day, a former colleague came by a job site where Marion was on his knees scrubbing away and offered him a well-paying director of sales training position with his company stating, "You could be making many times more than whatever you're earning now and have a job with some dignity."

Conversely, the experience is further engrained in Marion's resolve that executives should engage in the cleaning work of the company to understand both the work and the response workers often receive when doing manual labor. Wade would say, "A job only has as much dignity as the man gives it."

Throughout the early years and through several layers of leadership, this core value was held in high regard and practiced from top-to-bottom in the organization. All of the four executives at the helm of ServiceMaster participated in at least a six-week field training to acquaint themselves with the work, the workers, and the organization.

Like *Undercover Boss*[102], the executives would perform the work front line employees delivered on a daily basis, only they had no disguises. Wade and his predecessors believed in the value of their people and the work the organization did. Bill Pollard shared his perspective that, "People are the subject of work, not the object of it."

---

[102] See Chapter 11 in *Be Intentional: Culture*

Distinctive #3 - Taking care of your employees as a leader

This book opens with two quotes from Marion Wade that all persons in a position of leadership should acquaint themselves with:

"Don't expect to build a super company with super people. You must build a great company with ordinary people."

It is interesting how many companies are founded by pioneers who then develop their organization to a point that, if they walked through the door, they would not qualify for employment. While procedures and standards are part of the maturation process, these should not be to the exclusion of recognizing the value any individual can bring to the team.

ServiceMaster placed a high emphasis on training and leadership development; what many refer to as soft skills today. Ken Wessner noted, "Training is not so much about what we want people to do, but rather what we want people to be."

Those who wanted to grow their careers in the organization needed to develop their technical skills, but they also had to understand the commitment to servant leadership. Aspiring leaders saw these principles in the examples of their executive leadership team through overlapping shingles and the six weeks on the front lines, whereby they engaged with and recognized the value of their team members:

"If you don't live it, you don't believe it."

Erisman's subtitle is, '*Navigating the Tension Between People and Profit.*' We shared a wonderful opportunity to discuss this topic together in greater detail on The DYOJO

Podcast[103]. Working from Pollard's quote, which we mentioned earlier, Al discussed how ServiceMaster did a good job of rightly viewing profits as an essential means, but not the goal or end. As Don Flow phrases it, "Blood is like profit - necessary to live, but not the reason for living."

While the first five executive leaders were not perfect in every instance of maintaining their shared vision and values, their common mindset and habits helped to keep them accountable. In describing integrity, the author notes that "The best definition is wholeness - that is when a person is the same in any situation." While some readers may not share the faith claims of Marion Wade and the early leaders, those who conduct business intentionally can certainly identify with the struggle to live out their values in all facets of life and business.

As an owner or manager, hiring for the project management position, I hope I have given you some food for thought. I hope the concepts in this book will lead to better outcomes in recruiting, hiring, and retaining good talent. Be mindful of your hires and of your rituals (i.e. the Captain's armband) so that your processes are in alignment with your values.

If you seek to establish high standards (expectations) and to build a culture of high norms, you will constantly be helping your team members improve their leadership skills. No candidate will be perfect, so please don't overlook your internal resources. Developing talent is often more rewarding, in the long run, than chasing superstars.

Build a great company with ordinary people.

---

[103] Episode 49

CHAPTER 14

The Life Cycle of Your First Management Promotion

The only qualification to get better:
being willing to suck when you start.
Rachel Stewart

My kids ask about the olden days, "You know, like back in the 1900s." There are moments as we laugh that we realize there are reference points and resources which they will have no framework to comprehend. One such resource that we used in the Land Before Time was the *Thomas Guide*. You may have to look that up.

Modern travelers take for granted that you now can get instantaneous directions. Your phone contains global positioning system (GPS) technology that will talk you through the intricacies of your journey to any destination. In the days before cell phones, you used to have to sit down at your computer to print your directions from programs like Mapquest.

If you complain about Siri getting lost, at least Siri is able to re-route when a road is closed or doesn't exist. Prior to online directions that you would print out, there were Thomas Guides. Wikipedia describes them as, "Paperback, spiral-bound atlases featuring detailed street maps of various large metropolitan areas." And I am old enough that I used this tool to navigate areas just North of Los Angeles County when I started in the restoration industry.

The Thomas Guide had a reference index. You would look up your street and be provided a page as well as an index from which you could begin to construct your routes. As crazy as it sounds, in metropolitan areas such as Los Angeles, California, with the Thomas Guide you could more readily re-navigate when there were traffic jams because you could focus on the area you were headed to rather than having to mess with the jumbled monstrosity of a large paper map.

The major thoroughfares of California were full of uncharted waters for someone like me that learned to drive in a small Eastern Washington town with only a handful of stoplights. With the Thomas Guide, I felt like I could master the seas, or at least not get so lost that I would be left to die in the vast expanse.

Navigation is an essential component of exploration as it relates to achieving your personal and professional goals. Technology has advanced and you may be able to master the latest and greatest electronic gadgets but that doesn't mean you understand how to navigate your journey, connect with the best resources, or conquer your ambitions.

Mentorship has become synonymous with coaching, and both have become hollow catchphrases in many circles. Connecting the pieces for yourself is complicated when you have so much noise vying for our attention. It's important to identify sound resources while maintaining the pursuit of your vision. Wherever you find help, they should assist you in shortening your DANG learning curve but not hijacking your learning process.

If you are like me, when you receive your first promotion into a management role you will be excited and scared. You will be excited because you feel your hard work is finally being recognized and that you have an opportunity to affect positive changes for the organization you are paired up with. Similar to being a parent, you probably have a list of things that you have pledged you would never do if you ever got the chance to be in charge.

As a human, you likely will also be a bit scared. We have fear of the unknown and this will be the first day that you will step out of the what-if into the what-now of your professional career. It will be time to spread your leadership wings and see what you can do.

You may even struggle with imposter syndrome, worrying that the teams you manage may discover that you don't know what you are talking about or that you don't always have the right answers. The truth is, you don't and you won't. Being a person in a position of leadership is not about always having the right answers, rather knowing how to resource the right answers in a manner that leads your team forward.

Some of the greatest leaders that I have worked with have been very honest about their challenges in the moment and shared openly with our teams: "Here is the challenge, here is what I think we should do, I am open to input..." As we discussed previously, using a framework with your team such as Identify, Discuss, and Solve (from Gino Wickman) can be a powerful tool. **Let's look at some of the challenges that you will face as a new manager.**

Promoting from within:

What you do is more important than what you say. You obviously want both what you say and what you do to be in alignment, but your teams learn more from your example than from your prepared statements.

I can remember my first day as assistant manager for the team that I had worked side-by-side with (an internal promotion). For this particular scenario, my father-in-law advised that rather than have my manager make some special announcement I should just take the reins at the next meeting.

As an internal promotee, my team members knew that I was a hard worker, that I was honest, and that I had earned my spot through being willing to learn. That didn't mean that they weren't going to test me in my new roles and responsibilities. Perhaps it worked in my favor that I was initially resistant to becoming a manager. The position had been offered to me much sooner but I thought I was going another route.

As I shared in my first book, I was planning for a career in law enforcement. My mentor, Denis Beaulieu, and I had the opportunity to reflect on our time together during The DYOJO Podcast[104]. I shared a funny story about one of the assistant managers whom Denis hired. In addition to crapping himself one day on the way to work, he did not respect our team and the pride with which they conducted themselves.

As a new manager, if you are going to lead your team, you have to find ways to connect with them, collaborate on your vision, and find shared means to conquer your goals. If you are a new manager, remember you are a person in a position of leadership. You are still a person.

Being a manager does not make you better than your team. Even if you don't intentionally put out that vibe, it's a dynamic that you have to be aware of. You will learn the art of walking the line of serving your team so that they can serve the customer while holding the line of your organizational standards. This managerial art form is an amalgamation of developing your unique method of leadership while learning from the positive examples you have received from others.

When you promote from within, everything is the same, and yet everything is different. You want to maintain the momentum you built as a team that opened the door of opportunity for you and continue to grow the team so that you can open that door for others. You are not special, but you have a job to do.

---

[104] Episode 15 & 83

You must maintain the work ethic that brought you to this opportunity while learning to help the team in new ways that you couldn't while your sole responsibility was being in the field. The team wants to know that you still value their hard work and aren't trying to become a tyrant.

Many new managers struggle with threats to their authority that only exist in their heads. If you have a misunderstanding, start by asking a question. Asking questions allows you to initiate a conversation without assuming there is an issue. You don't want to fan the flames of drama when the fire can be prevented by simply removing the oxygen from the situation.

We talk more about how to address issues and discipline later in this chapter. Before we get to the topic of discipline, be sure that you are building your leadership foundation on core principles including

- Establish your leadership by leading, not with grand speeches. Lead by example.
- Maintain camaraderie with your team while creating respect for your new role, communicate in terms of the responsibilities everyone has (at every level) to do their best to help the team grow.
- Continue to work hard, even if that is in a different way than what "hard work" used to look like when you were in the field. Your job is different but you still need to bust your butt to make things happen.
- Don't make leadership more complicated than it is. You are a person in a position of leadership. Find examples that help you fine-tune your methods, but most of what you will learn will be by trial and error. Learn with your team, and be honest and humble about the process.

There is a paradox to having a position of leadership where you create a level of separation without being separate. I think the proper mindset for everyone is understanding that my job may be different than yours, but things work better when we all focus on accomplishing our own tasks for the good of the team. If I do my job, and you do your job, things will work out.

Managers and workers alike need to understand the power of what Phil Jackson, who coached Michael Jordan and Kobe Bryant, says, "Good teams become great ones when the members trust each other enough to surrender the me for the we." As an aspiring manager, you want to be the type of leader that inspires trust in your team members, both for your role and for the vision of the team.

Promoting from the outside:

Many of my professional experiences have been with starting up a restoration division within a construction company or completely from scratch. In those situations, you are building a team so you can set the expectations from the start. This is not an easier challenge, it is a different one. In any situation, you have to discover who you are, how you are going to establish your voice, and how you are going to make progress on your goals.

When you take on an existing team, no one knows you, which is both a strength and a weakness in the situation. You will learn that what you were hired for and what the powers-that-be sold you on may not be in alignment with the environment you are walking into as a new manager.

Many organizations and leaders do not have a clear grasp on how wide the gap is between their expectations (perceptions) and the company norms (reality). I have found that it is good to set aside some time to observe the people, process, production, and progress of the organization and understand it before you launch into your change initiatives.

Joyce Gabriel came to property restoration with a customer service background but no direct industry experience. She has grown from a project assistant to lead project manager and now is building a mitigation department for a local contractor. She notes that "Too many changes too quickly will create more resistance than necessary."

Regardless of how poorly the last manager was performing, you will meet people that had a connection with them. You want to navigate the transition of power and the changes to the team dynamics with tact. So let's discuss the four basic scenarios that you will be walking into with regards to how management and the staff felt about the prior manager.

Loved by the people, Hated by management

When a prior manager was loved by the people or had a good connection with them, you are going to have a challenge in winning them over. Staff can be attached to a prior manager for a variety of reasons. These ties are typically related to emotions or performance. The prior manager may have been a people person who gave everyone what they wanted. This makes team members feel good but is not a recipe for success (purely an emotional tie).

You will want to engage your team in a greater purpose which will require a balance between professional boundaries and personal connections. If the team had strong emotional ties to the prior manager because they protected the team from management, there may be a foundation you can build upon. If they liked them because they played favorites, you will have some deconstruction work to do before you can build your foundation.

Whatever the scenario is, you will never know the whole story and I believe that it doesn't benefit you much to spend a lot of time digging into what people think happened. Don't put too much value into what anyone wants to tell you; it's not productive. The hiring of a new manager always brings a sense of uncertainty to the staff.

It is helpful to have a general sense of whether their ties to the prior manager were related to emotional or performance factors so that you can begin to develop your own connections. Determine what remnants of a positive mindset and habits exist in the team so that you can begin the process of leading the team forward.

Listen to what management is looking for and where you need to target your efforts to keep them happy while you set up shop. Often your first 90 days in a new role are a bit of a grace period. My experience is that you want to make the best of this opportunity by finding what things you will need to succeed and get them approved before the honeymoon phase with management expires. This may be a cynical perspective, but it has been true over many assignments.

Loved by the people, Loved by management

You're doomed. The primary scenario where this happens is retirement. If a manager leaves for other reasons, they probably will not be liked by management. Whenever someone leaves, regardless of how well they performed, they often become the scapegoat for issues. Many have said that you never want to be the next person to replace a beloved leader. If you are in this scenario, it can be done, but it will be a challenge.

You want to honor the traits and achievements of the prior manager while making it clear that you are here to continue to raise the bar for the employee and customer experience. If it is possible, you may want to reach out to this former manager and pick their brain. Be careful about bringing them back in, as this can backfire even if they are well-intentioned people.

Honor the past but look to the future. I have had multiple organizations propose something to the effect of dual management for a period of time; don't be fooled, it's a terrible idea.

Hated by the people, Loved by management

This will be a tough situation. If a prior manager was disliked by staff for valid reasons and removed by management expeditiously, there is some hope that you are walking into a positive transition of power. But this is not typically the case in my experience.

When upper management drags out the process of removing a poorly performing or toxic manager, it cultivates an overall dissatisfaction and distrust among the people within the whole organization. You will be mending fences on all fronts as well as establishing your voice within the company, with the people in your office, and upper management.

Perhaps this prior manager was disliked for unclear reasons, i.e. they got results but did not have the best tact in achieving them. It is helpful to get a sense of if the people were at odds with the prior manager because they were a hardass yet pushed the people to be the best they can be. Or maybe they flat-out antagonized their people and drove them beyond their limits. Without bringing up the past too much, you will begin to build a picture of why this prior manager was unpopular with the team.

Really, the only helpful information here is determining for yourself, not based on the opinions of others, whether there were legitimate gripes and what you need to do in order to move forward. Legitimate concerns may include making promises that weren't followed through, which will make your first few months difficult as you work to convince people of your integrity.

Hated by the people, Hated by management

This sounds like it might be the best scenario to come into but it also can be a sign that everything is a mess. The blame game is not productive and corrodes trust. You will need to nip gossip in the bud and work to develop a strong local culture so that your team gets back on track.

If everyone is pointing fingers at each other, the crew with the prior manager, the management with the prior manager, and the prior manager with all of the above, you have to develop means of separating those issues and building a foundation of trust first between yourself and the team. Spend some time observing the four pillars before you make any knee-jerk decisions. You will find that there are some diamonds in the rough as well as people who everyone thinks is a leader but actually is hurting your team.

If you arrive in an office full of emotional craters left behind from the prior wars between the staff and management, the only way to level the field is with one scoop of dirt at a time. You want to dig in without making more holes. Uncover what is useful and build from any mindsets or habits that are positive. Start to develop your plan for addressing what you believe needs to be fixed. Be observant. Watch what people do. Communication is key internally as well as externally, so use your first days to establish how you will clearly and consistently have the discussion as a team.

Finding Your Voice As A Leader

As we have said, finding your way is going to be a unique process. While I believe it is important to adopt elements of servant leadership whereby you recognize that your role is to help your team members thrive, you have to establish a proper level of respect. For the most part, you will earn this by doing your job (continuing to be a hard worker), communicating with your team (being honest), and admitting when you are wrong (being willing to learn).

Even if you do this well, there will arise times when you are challenged. If a team member is out of line you have to know your level of responsibility as well as the level of support. There are few things more embarrassing than laying down the law and not having the support of your supervisor so that your team sees that you have no real authority. If you have a good manager, they will help you to see when you are out of line and provide you with some guidance through this process. If you don't, you will have to be creative.

Leverage matters in life. By this, I mean that you need to understand what leverage you have in any given situation. Identify what authority and power you have so that you can operate within those boundaries. If you don't have your manager's support you have to establish what resources for the discipline you have at your disposal and to what level your authority extends before you need consent from someone above you.

I think it is important to keep a running file for personnel notes on every employee. You want to keep track of affirmation as well as discipline. This includes everything from a discussion to formal discipline. Doing so helps you be accountable to your process and make decisions objectively, based on data.

This will not be popular, but if you are part of a larger organization, you want to be careful about what information you upstream as it can be used against you later. For example, I once filled out a performance report honestly, only later to have it brought up when I requested compensation and promotion for an employee later in their development. Keep track of everything but be discerning about what you share.

At points in my career, I may not have had the authority to fire someone but I did have control over the schedule, so if there were prime assignments or we had to make tough decisions about who was working in slow periods, my employee notes were factors. Be careful not to misinterpret or abuse what I am saying, always conduct yourself (to the best of your ability) in accordance with the law and without malice or discrimination.

You will hear servant leadership often used as an effective paradigm. There is a dichotomy here of being a person in a position of leadership and yet understanding that your role and your success are directly tied to getting the best out of your team members. For many, serving your team to success has been a means of keeping yourself accountable to your role without allowing your position to go to your head.

Even if you adopt a humble method, there are times when you will be tested as a manager and you have to decide how best to respond. Whether you respond with a heavy hand, are too lenient, or nail it, your decisions will define you as a leader.

The 26th president was played so affably by comedic icon Robin Williams in the Night at the Museum movie series. Theodore "Teddy" Roosevelt was fond of repeating a West African proverb that says, "Speak softly, and carry a big stick; you will go far." This has come to mean that we should be as diplomatic as possible (speak softly), but at some point, diplomacy will be tested and at that crossroads, you will have to decide with what action (big stick) you will back your words.

I find it interesting to allow Teddy to speak further on his thoughts about this *big stick policy* which he applied both to domestic and foreign relations while he held one of the highest seats of leadership in the world,

> *"Persistently only half of this proverb has been quoted in deriding the men who wish to safeguard our national interest and honor. Persistently the effort has been made to insist that those who advocate keeping our country able to defend its rights are merely adopting 'the policy of the big stick.' In reality, **we lay equal emphasis on the fact that it is necessary to speak softly**; in other words, that it is necessary to be respectful toward all people and scrupulously to refrain from wronging them, while at the same time keeping ourselves in condition to prevent wrong being done to us. If a nation does not in this sense speak softly, then sooner or later the policy of the big stick is certain to result in war. But what befell Luxembourg six weeks ago, what has befallen China again and again during the past quarter of a century shows that no amount of speaking softly will save any people who do not carry a big stick[105]."*

As a leader who is developing their skills, remember it is not just speaking softly (being the nice manager) or only carrying a big stick (being the heavy-handed manager), but doing both that will help you keep a better balance in your approach to situations. I can remember when I started in this industry, I was working with some people who had done time in jail. I have never considered myself a tough guy, but I also work intentionally to address an issue when I feel that it needs to be addressed.

I was still young and new to the team when a fellow employee mentioned that they were going to beat me up. This person definitely could have done it and had the background to prove

---

[105] Encyclopedia Britannica. *Big Stick Policy*.
https://www.britannica.com/event/Big-Stick-policy

it. I am not sure where I mustered the response but I said, "Well, if we're going to do this let's go behind the dumpster so that it isn't on camera." After an odd silence, we both laughed and that was my schoolyard moment. Humor can go a long way to help ease tension, but your team will also test whether you stand for what you say you do.

Before you will ever be comfortable in an advanced leadership position, you need to be comfortable in your own skin and exemplary in your current role. I found it amusing that later on we brought in someone that thought they were pretty tough. This
person received a similar ritual to mine but didn't fare as well. They never were physically accosted but they also didn't settle in well with certain members of the team.

Perhaps this person was tough in past situations, but there is always someone tougher. In the workplace, your resolve is often of more value than your toughness. Meaning, you don't need to be bigger and badder than others in order to win them over. Stand your ground and learn to promote trust and the achievement of shared goals as the key binders of a team. You don't have to like everyone and they don't have to like you in order to get along and get the job done.

Some of you may wonder what kind of rodeo we were running, but I would gladly stack any of those people against any team doing similar work. We all had great pride in what we did and we did it well. We could assemble containments efficiently, you could eat on the surfaces in our worksites (embellishment), and we rarely failed a clearance (simple truth). Could some of those rougher edges have been sanded a bit smoother? Yes. I enjoyed my time with that team and I learned a lot about people, business, and leadership.

Later in my time with the same team, we brought on an employee with the deepest record of the bunch. There was a situation where a team member I respected and this person hadn't yet come into containment and I was in a supervisory role. We hadn't yet started into our work so I went back up to our staging area and reminded them both to pick up the pace.

It was probably thirty minutes later and I noticed they still weren't in containment. I had to doff my gear and go back up. They were still fiddling with their PPE and I said something to the effect of, "No more dilly-dallying, get into containment." This employee said that they were almost in containment but then they had to poop. I raised my voice and said, "Get into containment, enough is enough."

Later, when we left containment for lunch, this employee hung back and tapped on my shoulder, "Izzy, I'm not used to people talking to me like that." The implication was that there were going to be problems. Somewhere I found the strength to look them right in the eyes and say, "I'm not used to people not doing their job."

I was hot and a bit on guard. I didn't take a quick nap like I normally did for lunch that day. After our interaction I called my boss and said he needed to get this employee out of there, it wasn't the first time they had performance issues. To my manager's credit, he came right away, which in California traffic was a feat. Surprisingly, he arrived before we went back in for lunch. The employee gave him more of the same attitude and they were out of there.

I wasn't rude and I didn't pull the, "I'm your boss dang-it" card, but it was another defining moment for me. This wasn't a "big stick" moment, but walking softly wasn't going to do the trick. I couldn't use humor and I had to find a backbone. The team responded well, even though he was a friend to many of them. Because we had pride in our work they were not sad to see him leave due to this person's consistently poor performance.

The dynamic that I believe President Roosevelt was trying to convey is the process of learning who you need to be as well as what you need to do in any given situation. As a starter kit for your disciplinary process, I will share a few simple tools.

Developing a Disciplinary Process

My father-in-law introduced me to a series of questions that have been very helpful in raising our children. I have used this approach to discipline in business as well. The core of the practice is to include your team members in the process when something goes wrong. When someone acts in a way that is out of line, you start by asking them a question (Q1), "What did you do that was not in line with our vision and values?"

- If it was public and everyone saw it, you may want to do this exercise as a group. If it wasn't, it is probably best to be conducted one-on-one.
- In teams large and small, the word always gets around, so be mindful of controlling the narrative when disciplinary action is involved.

The next question (Q2) is, "How should we address this issue and/or correct this behavior?" Interestingly, the data from resources like *Insuring Tomorrow*[106] have shown leaders that younger generations (i.e. Millennials and beyond) want more immediate feedback. *KnowHow*'s research reveals that younger people want to feel like their managers are coaches, not just beating them up for doing things wrong but giving them constructive feedback and showing them how to perform better.

Every person is an individual, so if you want a fighting chance at keeping them, you have to invest in getting to know them which includes knowing how to approach them when something goes wrong as well as how best they receive encouragement.

Question 3 (Q3) consists of, "What do you think the consequence should be for this and/or if this happens again?" We have talked about the difference between an honest mistake and an obstinate one, so there may be fewer options to Q3 if this is a persistent issue. Keeping a record of disciplinary conversations with your team members helps you to make decisions with data rather than memory.

For example, you may be tempted to think, "You ALWAYS do this," when you are talking to an employee but when you reference the employee record you may realize it's not that

---

[106] https://insnerds.com/insuring-tomorrow/

consistent of an issue. Or you may realize it's much worse than you thought. When you are clear with your vision and values you can be consistent with your training and discipline so that everyone, including yourself, is accountable to uphold these standards.

What do you do when you are tested by an employee? It depends. A good friend of mine shared a funny story. They were disciplining their child and raising their voice. The kid responded, "Why are you yelling at me, this is not how adults are supposed to treat children." They were that much more upset but also were confronted with the truth.

As a parent and as a manager, it is not a weakness to admit when you are wrong. In these scenarios, it is important to admit where you are wrong while following through with disciplinary discussions and actions. You being wrong does not change the necessity for accountability.

So, what do you do when you aren't wrong and someone wants to test you? This is an important moment, whether everyone is there or no one is there, whatever you choose to do will be something that will change things from that point forward. The questions contained in this chapter can help. If something is egregiously out of line with your values more immediate action will be necessary.

Typically we want to follow a process of verbal consultation, written disciplinary action (write-up), disciplinary action (i.e. unpaid time off), and then termination or demotion. The expectations should be clear and the process should be consistent. Discipline is critical to reinforcing your culture and elevating your norms. You will need to confirm the process with your organization.

As a mid-level manager, there will be times that you feel like you are stuck in the middle. I would like to share a few thoughts for adjusting your perspective to seeing yourself as planted in the middle. Being in a position of leadership should mean that you work intentionally to:

- Serve those (internal) who serve your clients (external)

- Ensure that your communication is as clear as possible (internally and externally)
- Build consistency in your organization (internally and externally)
- Demonstrate accountability through leading by example

How do you change your mindset when you are feeling stuck in mid-level management? Think about this, according to Wikipedia, "Middle managers have a huge influence on an organization's development and success as they often have direct control over 80% of an organization's workforce." If you are a mid-level manager, you likely feel like your influence is difficult to quantify.

Mid-level managers have to do an odd dance of both leading and following to an extreme that low-level and top-level managers don't have to contend with. With those who are downstream, lead by example. Bring the team that you are responsible for into alignment with the vision, values, and goals of the organization.

Demonstrate the value of what you can bring to the table by making your team shine. If you can lead a successful team, you can garner some influence with those upstream. Credibility and influence are essential at every level.

As I share in *Be Intentional: Culture*, I can remember when I was a project manager and wanted the opportunity to test my ideas as a general manager. I wanted the next level up the "ladder". Even though I wanted the opportunity, I knew that as an estimator I had one boss, my general manager. I knew that if I reached the role of general manager, like him, I would be subject to anyone at the corporate office (they preferred to be called "Home Base") that needed something.

I felt stuck many times as a project manager. I was tempted to think that "someday" I would climb the ladder out of my current level of leadership to reach a height where I couldn't be stuck. The reality is there are plenty of people stuck in higher-level management. Stuck is a state of mind and it will follow you wherever you go if you don't develop a planted mindset.

The leadership ladder mindset, and the feeling of being stuck, will suck you in if you let it. If your desire is to make a difference, then you have to see that you have a voice and a platform. Even if you think you are just a lowly technician or a mid-level project manager who is just treading water to stay alive, you are planted where you are for a reason.

With Ben Justesen at his Enlightened Restoration Solutions (ERS) estimating course hosted

CHAPTER 15

A Few Closing Thoughts

It is not a daily increase, but a daily decrease.
Hack away at the inessentials.
Bruce Lee

Project management is a team effort. Our success as an organization is tied to each team member doing their own job (DYOJO). Yet, each individual success is interwoven with the success of the team. We have to be willing to honestly review our norms (what we do) so that we can address issues. We are constantly working to bring our activities into alignment with our expectations (or stated vision, aka what we say).

Many project managers report feeling undervalued and under-supported. In property restoration, there are so many tools for outsourcing estimating but there is not, and likely will not be, a means for outsourcing your project management. By this I mean, that removing the direct interaction between your organization and your client would be detrimental. We are in a customer service business where customer experience drives success.

If you do program work, it's what the carriers say they care most about. The service level agreements (SLAs) are driven by timelines which are key factors in producing consistent outcomes. You may not agree with that, but efficiency is essential to both achieving a happy customer as well as a profitable project.

If you do not do preferred vendor work, there is a good deal of value in building some of those same SLA benchmarks into your processes. For example, having standard operating procedures (SOPs) for who and how soon you make contact and your intake process. Develop your process to clarify and build consistency in the project life cycle.

With regards to turnover in the position, in a seven-year span with a national restoration company, we had nine project managers.

- Three project managers left the company and are self-employed
- One left and is in the same industry[107]
- Two left and are in another industry
- One was clearly let go. I say clearly because almost all departures were some level of mutual separation, and they are self-employed
- There is one outlier, actually a pretty funny story, who was "fired" but asked to stay on for about six weeks to close out some big projects.

PM	Self Employed	Same Industry	Another Industry
Left	3	1	2
Let Go	1	0	0
Both	1	0	0

On the day this project manager was "fired" they stopped by my office. We had received one of the infamous Friday emails from our manager that said something to the effect of do-better or else.

As a side note, If you are an owner or manager reading this book (or anyone who sends sternly worded emails), I would challenge you to think through what you say in your emails and really consider whether:

---

[107] I am the only one of nine that is still directly in the restoration industry. A few of those who are self-employed do some restoration work but to my knowledge it is not their focus.

- Does this need to be said?
- If it needs to be said, should it be in an email where the interpretation is up to the receiver - as opposed to an in-person discussion where I can better control the narrative and gauge the responses?
- If it needs to be said and an email is the best delivery system, does it need to be a carbon copy to everyone in the office?

This PM came by my office and showed me an email response they had drafted on their Blackberry[108] smart phone. They asked for my opinion. I said, "I don't disagree, but is it your goal to get fired?" They said, "Good point, I'll read it over and think about my wording before I send it." About halfway up the stairs they shouted an explicative and said, "Oh well Jon, I sent it."

Their response went out to the whole office in response to the email sent by the manager to the whole office. The manager had to act but it was a bit comical in how it was carried out. At the end of the day, no one had deep-rooted hard feelings, but the project manager was burned out and tired of feeling like they were to blame for the issues.

This project manager had expressed what many of us felt, that we were overworked and underappreciated. The project manager carries the pressure of executing a scope, whether it is written well or not. It is a lot of pressure. Usually, estimates are not written well. Many estimates are missing key items and the transfer of scope details from estimator to project manager (if there is one) is void of key details. As you have likely already picked up on, this is one of the main threads in my first book, *Be Intentional: Estimating.*

It seemed like project managers had about a year and a half shelf life in our company. I believe part of that was a misalignment of values, for example, hiring former contractors

---

[108] Look it up

who had high technical skills but low people skills for a role that is primarily customer service. An employee strong in one area will need assistance and time developing in those other areas. It is unfair and silly to expect someone to be a ninja-rockstar-A-player in every facet of project management. I can say that most managers have the best intentions but in the fight for which issues get our time often training and leadership development get little attention. Managers and project managers need to have ongoing discussions about their needs and work together to source realistic solutions to make progress. We will never be perfect, but we must work together.

Another issue that erodes that sense of teamwork, is being aligned with estimators who do not set the production team up for success. This happens through the communication of scope as well as the sharing in the spoils (commissions). To the latter, I will share an example in the hopes that it will help others recognize where they can better support their team members.

Play Dumb Games, Win Dumb Prizes

On one occasion, my project manager was assisting another estimator with a large commercial loss at a local university. In our organization, the estimator received the majority of the available commission and a project manager received a smaller portion of the same. The project had to meet certain criteria of profitability and be paid on time.

This estimator was a good salesperson but constantly utilized the manager to assist them with a majority of their responsibilities on these larger losses. This included completing all of their moisture documentation and dealing with third-party consultants. Part of the broader issue, in my opinion, was not allowing this estimator to operate in their realm of highest competence. Good at sales, not strong with the details.

When it came time for them to share the commission with the project manager, they excluded them without even notifying their team members face to face. We found out in the production meeting following when the check had been received. Magically the project manager's name was no longer listed in that role and the estimator had put themselves as performing both roles.

My project manager didn't want to confront the issue so I did. The estimator stated their reasoning was that they performed the "majority of the work" and the project manager wasn't onsite as much as they were. In respect to how much this person relied on others to handle the details, I thought it was hypocritical and shady to not have the conversation in a clear way so that everyone could present their case.

I called them out on their BS stating that this project manager performed the same oversight and attention to this project as they did on all of my projects (I oversaw all mitigation, except for this one special account). Furthermore, I stated, that on some of my projects I do the majority of the writing and running, on others my project manager takes on both roles. As such, we share everything; we succeed as a team and we share the commission evenly on every project. Is it worth a few hundred dollars to crap on your teammates?

As an industry, many of the organizations have the perception of making commissions harder and harder to qualify for. When you mess with people's livelihood, word gets around and it impacts our ability as a whole to attract good talent who don't want to play games when it comes to getting paid for the work that they do.

As an office in a local market, it doesn't matter how big the market is, when it comes to your industry it is a small network and word gets around. If your organization doesn't treat people well or you have people in a position of leadership with a negative reputation, you will struggle to recruit and retain good talent. There are too many options in the current market to play stupid games with good people.

Having some turnover at the entry-level positions is to be expected, but to have high-performers leave is not a sign of health. As I shared in Chapter 6 about winning a high volume client because a contractor didn't want to budge over a few hundred dollars. When you put money over the big picture, the data, and relationships you will struggle.

According to **KnowHow's** research of over one thousand one-star reviews for restoration contractors, poor communication was the number one reason for customer dissatisfaction. Over 26% of the customers who verbalized their complaint with a restoration company performing work in their home or business cited this issue of communication as top of the list[109].

If communication is the result of a project manager having clear and consistent interaction with the client, the second and third-ranking reasons were closely tied to that same core issue. Number two was poor quality workmanship and number three was project delays.

I believe there is a shared responsibility between

- The organization setting and monitoring the workload
- The project manager effectively starting and finishing projects
- Both parties building an operational project management process

We need to have clear and consistent conversations about our expectations and our norms. Do we have the right goals, do we prioritize our resources to regularly achieve those goals, and are we proactive in addressing issues that arise?

A project manager will not be accurately communicating with a client if they don't have a well-thought-out schedule and the resources to make the plan happen. If the PM makes a schedule but their own team cannibalizes the assigned assets, there will be no trust in the team or the system.

- Do we have the right people in the right seats[110]? (Chapter 13)
- Are we working together to clarify our project management process?

---

[109] KnowHow. *Delivering 5-Star Restoration Experiences.* https://www.fivestarrestorer.com/?ref=blog

[110] See *Good to Great* by Jim Collins

- Do our PMs know how to create a production plan and can they trust the board? (Chapter 8)
- Are we making progress on our goals?

One mindset and habit that I would love to see change is in the area of thinking differently about the opportunities for growth that we provide our team members. While it is important that
employees understand upward mobility, it is as important that we create avenues where professionals can operate in their realm of greatest value to their personal vision as well as the needs of the organization.

If the best thing Employee A can do is project management, they find fulfillment in this role, and this would be the best area of responsibility that they could fill for our team - why wouldn't we make this work long term? In the status quo model, they can only "grow" if they become an estimator.

I am always encouraged when I hear of owners and managers that are investing in pathways of internal growth that give preference to people already in the organization. When someone already knows your culture, it is a shame to have them go elsewhere for a promotion due to a lack of communication of an opportunity that existed within your company. People leaving is a part of life, to the best of our ability we want people to leave for the right reasons.

On the other hand, if you are a professional who is going to leave, do so on good terms and for the right reasons. You never want to burn a bridge. While it may feel good to unload all of the things that you didn't like about your place of employment, brevity is your friend. "Thank you for the opportunity here, I have found an opportunity that I must pursue. Here is my two-week notice. I look forward to helping you wrap up any loose ends within that time frame."

If you are a person in a position of leadership, understand the difference between someone leaving for negative reasons (which may reflect more on you than them) and positive reasons; keep the door open. Exit interviews are a good opportunity to get a better sense of what an employee learned and felt about their time in your organization. "What could we have done better?" may be a hard question to ask but it can be a good time to get some honest feedback.

Attrition or turnover is not an issue that is unique to our industry. Writing for *Forbes*, Kristi Hedges noted five factors for why organizations are *Losing A Whole Generation of Managers*.

Even prior to the 2020 pandemic and what many are calling the great resignation, she asked the question, is this because employees have lost their desire, or have companies killed it? The five factors for managerial turnover according to Kristi, are[111]

1. Lack of training
2. Overwork
3. Unrealistic expectations
4. Virtual everything
5. One-size-fits-all support

I find Kristi's comments on one-size-fits-all support to be on-point. She says,

"When companies do offer support for managers, rarely is it broken down by functional area, team stage, or experience. While there are similarities across all areas of leadership, the fact is that it takes a different approach to manage a team of 25-year-old developers than 40-year-old accountants. Leadership training is too often formulaic and generic, and therefore not nearly as relevant as it should be."

Whether you have been intentional in developing your understanding and empathy for current generations or not, there is going to be a variance between your perspective and those you are working with. This is true regardless of generation.

---

[111] Hedge, K. (2013, January 16) *Five Reasons We're Losing A Whole Generation of Managers*. Forbes. https://www.forbes.com/sites/work-in-progress/2013/01/16/five-reasons-were-losing-a-whole-generation-of-managers/?sh=4f2b839413a0

Support for project managers can come in a variety of ways. We talked about the importance of building and empowering a value-driven administrative team with Whitney Wiseman, who operates RFI Companies in Jupiter, Florida, for *Benchmarks of Growth*[112]. It is important that the organization clarifies roles and responsibilities so that no position is viewing themselves as more important than another. I have been in companies where estimators and project managers were allowed to treat administrative staff like doormats and I have been in others where the support staff was not very supportive.

In the relationship between an estimator and a project manager, as well as a project manager with their subcontractors and employees, each party needs to respect as well as value the other. Everyone has a job to do and the support systems should be structured around making the workflow clear, consistent, and accountable. We should all be invested in a culture of helpfulness with parameters that keep team members from abusing each other. To the best of our ability, we do not want our team members to be managing a workload that burns them out.

Combat Burnout and Increase Retention

If you agree with the processes that we have discussed regarding the project manager regularly meeting with the client and production team to ensure everyone is on the same page, you will want to do the same thing with your management team. It is important for owners and managers to listen to their team members and develop a process that helps to distribute the workload in a manner that is conducive to everyone's strengths and capacity.

Greg Smith of Eugene, Oregon, who has many years managing teams in restoration and insurance work, states it simply, "Listen to your people." He adds that often you need

---

[112] The DYOJO Podcast, Episode 62

to seek out those team members that don't always speak up. Greg says, "The challenge of a leader, in my opinion, is realizing that those that don't speak out, tend to be the ones you need to hear the most. I believe that those that tend to prop themselves up as the spokesman for all, tend to say what they need to say to advance their careers." Listening requires you to learn how your team members communicate.

If the project manager is responsible to set the right expectations with the client, the general manager has the role of setting the right expectations with the project managers. It is a team effort for a company to intake and complete projects efficiently. It is a team effort to keep a high level of quality, customer satisfaction, and profitability.

Richard Sheridan and his team at Menlo Innovations have a wonderfully simple process for demonstrating to a client how their changes will affect the project. The process first translates the agreed-upon scope into time and resource commitments in a manner that is visible and understood by all parties. When they conduct regular meetings with the client and the production team, if a change is suggested then the group discusses what items would have to be removed to keep the project on schedule and on budget without making any change orders.

This process should be replicated with project managers so that the internal team understands a PM's workload and can distribute projects accordingly. The core of this shift is first regularly having conversations beyond just the numbers (financials) and developing a process that brings our vision into alignment with our activities (norms). If we struggle with low profitability and/or low customer satisfaction, could it not be a result of the overload on our project managers and their ability to provide the level of service that we promised?

By discussing and creating objective measures for what PMs can realistically accomplish, we can be clearer about our expectations, more consistent in our approach, and increase our level of accountability. We will be more realistic in our approach but also more scientific in our training, application, and discipline. Something as simple as post-it notes or 3" x 5" index cards may go a long way to better and more consistent outcomes.

Perhaps you don't believe in burnout or that people complain too much. In an inquiry on this topic on social media, one respondent said, "I was a PM and after seven years was burned out. I loved the job, but I was burned out. 60-hour weeks and 40k miles a year take a toll on you. I had great pay and benefits but left for less money so I could get my life back. This decision hurt financially and we struggled at first, but it was so worth it for a 45-hour-a-week salary with a carrier."

Some might be tempted to think this person just couldn't hack it, but it's important to comprehend that money isn't the only motivation for many high-performing individuals. It's helpful to understand, as a group of authors in Restoration and Remediation (R&R) Magazine outlines, there are three common manifestations of burnout in our industry.

>**Exhaustion:** The feeling of being overextended and physically and emotionally drained.

>**Cynicism:** This leads to people developing a distant attitude toward work and the people surrounding them at work.

>**Professional Efficacy:** Relates to feelings of effectiveness and adequacy regarding a person's work[113].

If your people are exhausted, cynical, or beyond the point of professional efficacy, there are going to be issues. We would all do ourselves a favor to develop means to detect these

---

[113] Avila, J., Rapp, R. & Lavender, L. *(2019, November 6) Burnout in the Restoration Industry (Part 1)*. Restoration & Remediation Magazine. https://www.randrmagonline.com/articles/88683-burnout-in-the-restoration-industry-part-1

negative trends as early as possible so that we can source solutions together. This will take some tact as we also have to be savvy enough to determine whether someone is misusing the opportunity. But this reality reinforces the idea that we want to make the process visible and the metrics as objective as possible.

The study cited in R&R recognized six sources for burnout which included workload, control, reward, community, fairness, and values. In this first of a multi-part series, the authors reported, "Results of the six sources of burnout found that workload was the only source having a statistically significant effect on exhaustion for restoration professionals."

In part two, they noted factors such as adjusting incoming work during periodic spikes, number of subordinates, and expanse of territory. If your focus is revenue, you will chase every dollar that you can. If your goal is profitability and a strong reputation in your market for customer satisfaction, then these concerns will be top of mind to your team.

As a person in a position of leadership, whether you are a training manager trying to connect with your direct reports, a new project manager building relationships with your team members, or a growth-minded professional trying to advance your career, it can be exhausting trying to keep up with trends. At the risk of repeating this too much, I find it helpful to reference a sentiment from Jeff Bezos. When he was asked about how Amazon stays ahead of the curve, he mentioned that one exercise they do is to ask, "What won't change?"

He noted that at Amazon they know consumers will always want more selection, lower prices, and faster delivery. These elements won't change. It doesn't make it any easier to address those issues but rather than tire yourself out trying to be clairvoyant, you can do yourself and your team a lot of good by recognizing those universal principles. This truth applies to all of the responsibilities of the project manager including people skills, customer service, and the battle for profitability.

Professional development is often associated with career opportunities. Another area that I would encourage you to challenge the status quo with regards to the common conceptions of organizational growth. Growth within an organization is often referred to as "climbing the ladder".

Get rid of the leadership ladder.

Too often we constrain our organizational and personal development vision by conforming to the narrow mindset and habits of this leadership ladder. Think for a moment, what is the view like when everyone is on the same ladder trying to reach "the top"?

The Ladder Mindset

- On a ladder, there is a limited view and therefore limited opportunities.
- On a ladder, the perception is that there is always someone above, regardless of how far someone climbs.
- On a ladder, team members feel like they are either being stepped on or pulled down.

In the Pacific Northwest, we are so blessed to have beautiful views. Picture a local climbing trail or nearby mountain, what are the views along the upward trail from those landmarks?

The Mountain Mindset

- On a mountain, there are no limits to the views (opportunities).
- On a mountain, there are many ways to get to "the top".
- On a mountain, the more challenging the climb, the more we need our teammates to help us overcome and work through obstacles (collaboration).

A ladder is only designed to perform two functions, it either helps you get up or it helps you get down. There isn't much room for creativity or exploration while on a ladder. You can go up until you reach an obstacle. You can choose to stay until you become an obstacle for others. If you want to advance in the corporate structure you have to get on the ladder and move your way up.

The Ladder Habits

- On a ladder, there's only one "top spot", so there is little room for collaboration; it all but ensures conflict.
- On a ladder, those with unique skills, perspectives, and abilities feel limited by their chances to contribute to the mission.

What happens if there is someone else on the ladder? You have to choose to climb around them or over them; they are blocking your view and restricting your upward mobility. If there is someone below you they have to make similar decisions. The leadership ladder does not support collaboration among peers.

The Mountain Habits

- On a mountain, the "top spot" is only one of many desirable opportunities.
- On a mountain, there are unlimited success trails and collaboration enhances progress for the team.
- On a mountain, there is plenty of room for people with unique skills, perspectives, and abilities to contribute to the mission.

If your mindset, and that of everyone in your organization, is to climb as high as they can on this limited structure, you will have constant friction due to log jams. The ladder mindset does not inspire purpose, or facilitate collaboration and it does not lay a foundation for a sustainable culture. If the options are limited don't be surprised when the culture is cannibalistic and leaders create silos of information to protect their rung.

If you are in a position of leadership and you have the ladder mindset, you will have and will perpetuate:

- A limiting view of opportunities and challenges.
- A bottleneck of upward mobility and idea flow.
- A challenge in getting your team members to collaborate.

If you are in a position of leadership and you have the mountain mindset, you can:

- Create an unlimited view of opportunities where team members embrace challenges together.
- The best ideas flow throughout the organization as obstacles require that everyone works together to achieve big hairy audacious goals (BHAGs).
- Collaboration and creativity help the mission move forward.

When you are bound by the mindset of climbing the leadership ladder, you limit your perspective as well as the opportunities for your team. Success is not easy or guaranteed. But each of us has the ability to chart a path to progress. You may not have the ability to control sweeping changes, but are you making the changes that are within your control?

- In your own MINDSET are you stuck trying to climb the ladder or are you tackling the mountain?
- Are you cultivating HABITS for your team that are limiting the flow of ideas and choking collaboration or are you opening pathways to success that unlock the creativity of your team members?

Though it seems counterintuitive, if you want to carry your goals over the peak, you should start by reducing the weight of your load. According to Bruce Lee, "It is not a daily increase, but a daily decrease. Hack away at the inessentials." Prioritization helps you to embrace your identity and live your purpose.

Climbing a mountain requires preparation, dedication, and endurance. You have limited time and you have to be realistic with what you can pursue and invest in. Whittle down your priorities to the core things that matter to you. Your priorities will change as you unfold your personal and professional development.

If everything is important then nothing is. Be intentional by reducing your list of priorities to items that you can gain momentum and achieve. Focus is the key to harnessing your ability to achieve. If you want to achieve your goals you must transfer your ideas (what is in your head) into habits (action) as this is the most effective way to develop sustained positive changes.

As I said in the Preface, my goal in writing this book was to help three groups of people:

- **Construction professionals** who seek to grow their career opportunities through pursuing the role of project management.
- **Project managers** who need some guidance to better understand leadership development and execute their position.
- **Managers and owners** who are looking for some assistance in helping their team members develop in their roles and responsibilities as project managers.

If you are looking to grow your career opportunities, I believe I have done my best to share what has worked for me. Your path forward is affected most by your mindset and habits. Be honest with where you are and use these concepts to help drive yourself off the blocks and down the road to your destiny.

As you grow, make sure you leave the door open for others to follow in your path.

If you are already in the position of project management, like many, you may feel like your training has not been thorough. I believe this book will help you to identify and further pursue resources that will shape your mindset and habits for growth in your role. You alone are responsible for your development. Leadership is about leading. To be good at it, your results are best judged by those you help to rise with you.

If you are a manager who is responsible for training, the DYOJO Chart and the concepts in this book are what I have used over my twenty years in this industry. Remember, you are not stuck in the middle, you are planted there. You are uniquely positioned to help initiate positive changes from within your organization. You may have to be creative, but don't fall into the trap of blaming others for your limitations.

Keep doing good things.

AFTERWORD

Here are three life lessons to be learned from sailing:
find and follow an experienced captain who knows
what they are doing;
always chart a course but, don't be afraid to adjust;
and learn to enjoy the ride even when it's rough.
Randy Jones

With contributions from **Michael Stein** and **Mark Springer**

Find and follow an experienced captain who knows what they are doing...

My hope is that this book serves to help you have a better sense of what you are getting yourself into and how to prepare for success.

- Learn all that you can from where you are and do your best to apply what you are learning to your daily activities.
- Supplement your learning with some of the stellar resources available to intentional restorers through articles, videos, podcasts, and local meetings.
- If you discover a course that will elevate your skillset, discuss this with your employer and tie the experience to your ability to better perform for your organization (look for the win-wins).

It can be difficult to cut through the noise. Remember that you are responsible for your journey and many of those who have made something of their career have reached their station through trial and error. You are going to make mistakes, as you build your career. You must learn how to fail, learn, and repeat. It may seem like an impossible goal, but it can be done.

Always chart a course, but don't be afraid to adjust...

Michael Stein, who we introduced in Chapter 3, states that "Perseverance, developed at an early age, has been a major factor in the "success" of every aspect of my life."As a child, many of you may have dreamed about becoming a pilot, Mike actually achieved this. He now manages aircraft management services and has a consulting practice out of Moses Lake, Washington. As we were discussing the book, he shared a story from his career journey where he faced an impossible task:

In the early stages of an intense training program designed to teach me how to fly a complicated airplane (a Swearingen Metroliner, aka Metro) as its only pilot (i.e., captain), I experienced emotional highs and lows that I've never experienced before. At the beginning of my training, I'd been flying for years and considered myself an above average, competent pilot, and training on the Metro would be tough but possible. After all, other people managed to complete the same training.

My first day in the flight simulator was humiliating. I made the other occupants sick to their stomachs simply taxiing the "airplane" on the ground. My in-flight maneuvers were suitable, but my landing felt like the fire/rescue trucks would be dispatched to pull us out of the virtual wreckage. That evening, I studied my brains out, memorizing procedures, limitations, and other pertinent information.

My second day in the simulator found me performing at my peak. Every training event was completed to the highest degree of competence. I was back. That evening, I thoroughly prepared for the next day by memorizing emergency procedures and planning for contingencies.

My third day in the simulator was the worst performance of my career. During the planned onslaught of training emergencies (intentional, on the instructor's part), I couldn't hold headings or altitudes. While conducting engine failures during take-off, I nearly crashed the "plane" each time. As though my simulator session didn't go horribly enough, afterward, I was required to fly as the captain during the training session for a co-pilot.

Throughout his engine failures during take-off training, he literally crashed each time.

Midway through his training, the instructor was so mad at my performance, that he reminded me that I was still the captain, and it was my duty to ensure the plane didn't crash. He was right; if the plane was going to crash in real life and I was on it, I'd be fighting to save the plane and my own skin. The next several practice engine failures were better - not perfect, but better. I talked the co-pilot through the maneuver each time, keeping the wings level and the plane climbing away from the ground, up to relative safety.

That night, I reflected on the day's activities. I cried thinking about my performance. Despite all the flight experience I had up to that day, I couldn't imagine being able to get a job at a fast-food restaurant - who'd hire such a failure? I was literally in tears, trying to work my way through my issues. Fumbling around in my brain, I found a possible solution.

Since I wasn't the first person to ever attend training on the Metro, I decided I was going to complete my training. At the very least, I would not give up. I was determined to successfully pass this training event; I would make my instructor kick me out of training if I wasn't capable of performing - I wouldn't do it to myself.

At that moment, I made peace with myself, the flight simulator, and my personal goals.

The remainder of my training was adequate or better. I didn't get in my own way again. Weeks later, during my practical evaluation, I exceeded all stated standards by a significant margin. I successfully completed my Metro training, joining a relatively small number of pilots authorized to fly the airplane as a single pilot. I felt like I was on top of the world, and it was my perseverance that helped me achieve that outcome.

Learn to enjoy the ride even when it's rough...

The events of 2020 affected a lot of people, businesses, and organizations. I remember being excited to attend the Restoration Industry Association (RIA) Conference in Louisiana and to present a closing keynote for a local organization in my home state of Washington. The RIA Conference was going to be a celebration of the launch and momentum of the Advocacy and Government Affairs (AGA) committee and an opportunity for me to meet many of the people I had made contact with through my podcast.

I reached out to RIA President Mark Springer to ask him about what that looked like from inside the organization, to have built up so much progress and goodwill only to face an impossible situation. As you all know, everything was shut down in 2020 and we all learned more than we ever wanted to know about the joys of video conferencing. During our conversation, Mr. Springer shared the following insights:

A pivotal moment for any leader is not when you have a plan and everything is proceeding as expected. You are tested when you have a plan, you are executing the plan, everything is going according to the plan, BUT THEN, something major happens. It takes a lot of mental fortitude to work through that.

One of the things I always think that's interesting and instructive comes from the world of investing. To my knowledge, Bill O'Neil is one of the wealthiest people in the world who flies under the radar of the public eye. I took an investing course several years back from his son Scott. Scott shared his perspective that the stock market is just human emotion on parade. Primarily, it's driven by greed and fear.

That has always stuck with me, and I think there are so many applications to this outside of the stock market. Furthermore, he said the most dangerous human emotion isn't necessarily greed or fear - these are pretty obvious as to how they can be detrimental; especially in investing. Rather, the most dangerous emotion is HOPE.

I think of where we were as an association (Restoration Industry Association, RIA) coming out of 2019 and into the new year. We were all witnessing the onset of the pandemic, but I was really hopeful in March of 2020 that it would be "over" soon. Hope is dangerous when it prevents any leader (or team) from confronting the brutal facts.

Confronting the brutal facts is vital as a person in a position of leadership. I think this is true for a project manager as well.

- You can hope that the insurance company is going to send you the approval that you requested a month ago.
- You can hope that the third-party consultant is going through your entire scope and they're not going to just pick everything apart.
- You can hope that the subcontractor that you have lined up isn't going to flake out.

In the insurance claims restoration business, there are so many disruptive factors. One of the greatest areas of growth for a professional is in fighting against the impulse to ignore an issue. This is a mix of fear and hope. Fearing the unknown and hoping that it will solve itself. Problems don't solve themselves; you have to face them head-on.

With the events of 2020, I was hopeful that everything was going to be resolved and that we were going to be able to stay on our schedule for our big event in New Orleans. I was hopeful that we would continue to build on all the momentum that we had from the Advocacy and Government Affairs (AGA) Committee. Everyone was excited. But I learned, once again, that you cannot allow hope to cripple you to the point that you land in an area of inaction.

For our RIA Board of Directors, as soon as we saw those brutal facts and confronted them, we started building contingencies. We had quite a few special board meetings. In any sort of crisis, large or small, communication becomes paramount. You must fight the natural tendency to clam up or go into your shell.

When there is an issue, that's the time you must communicate the most.

We started to model what this-or-that scenario would look like? We started to build all these scenarios and every week we would adjust our strategy based on the data that we were getting. The Bible says, *"In the multitude of counselors there is safety[114]."* We gathered a lot of counsel. I was regularly picking up the phone and calling past RIA presidents, I was talking to all our board members, and to our staff.

Many of the worst-case scenarios started playing out. If we had buried our heads in the sand and relied on blind hope, it would have been even more difficult for RIA to have made it through. Because we thought through worst-case scenarios and brutal facts, we had strategies to address those events. I can't remember how many times we had to change course. I'm grateful for the group. We had excellent people that are so committed to the restoration industry.

We had a lot of vigorous debate around these issues because we understood that the stakes were so high. We didn't just operate in the hope mode; we took action. This is what project managers must be able to do. When something doesn't look great, you have to find a path. Fight against fear and don't rely on hope as a strategy, but rather take very careful and well-thought action steps.

I'm a man of faith, so I see God's hand in all of it, and how he protected us. From a human standpoint, the communication, facing the trouble together, the generosity of our members, and the resolve to push through trouble is what propelled us through. Tough situations create lifetime opportunities. When trouble hits, don't ask, "Why is this happening to me," put your boots on and get to work.

---

[114] Proverbs 11:14 KJV

Project managers are constantly dealing with the unknown. You create a plan and have to be constantly ready to adapt. Project management requires a lot of patience, or as Jon Isaacson says,

"The will, the skill, and the chill."

The Team Behind This Book

Podcastalypse 2021 with Blue Collar Nation, GMS Podcast, and The DYOJO

A big THANK YOU to everyone who agreed to review portions of the book and provide input. Many were noted in the chapters, several more contributed by challenging me to think through my process and the delivery of these concepts. The property restoration community, and the cohort of craft persons who make up the skilled trades, is full of many generous people.

About The Publisher

The DYOJO is The Do Your Own Job Dojo. We help you train your mindset and habits to become an Intentional Restorer.

This is the third book from The DYOJO as well as book 3 in the Be Intentional series.

- **Book 1. Be Intentional: Estimating** (2020). Developing the right mindset and habits for yourself and your team to succeed with estimating property insurance claims.

- **Book 2. Be Intentional: Culture** (2021). How the Small Things Enhance or Undermine Your Culture. Co-authored with Lisa Lavender, Andrew McCabe, Jeremy Watkin, Dr. Leroy Nunery, David Princeton, Luke Draeger, Christopher Stanley, Elan Pasmanick

- **Book 4. How To Suck Less At Estimating**: *Habits For Better Project Outcomes* (2022)

The DYOJO Podcast

Home of The DYOJO Nation. Podcast of The DYOJO Way for Intentional Restorers. Helping property restoration professionals to shorten their DANG learning curve by developing the mindset and habits for achieving their goals. You can watch The DYOJO Podcast on YouTube or listen on your favorite podcast medium including Spotify and iTunes.

About The Editor

Tiffany Acuff has been assisting me with editing various articles and my second book, *Be Intentional: Culture*. She is a project coordinator and property restoration technician in North Florida.

Through a chance meeting of a friend, Tiffany Acuff was brought into the restoration industry. After three years, she has seen just about every aspect of working for a restoration contractor: from extracting water into the night, to packing out a house after a fire, to coordinating projects and estimating. She is IICRC certified in Fire & Smoke Restoration (FSRT) and continues to sharpen and broaden her skills for a restoration company in North Florida. Her enjoyment of reading as a child birthed in her a love of words which she is bringing to the restoration industry through editing and writing.

About The Author

Jon Isaacson, The Intentional Restorer, is an author and host of The DYOJO Podcast. Jon speaks, writes, and coaches through his organization The DYOJO helping the start-up phase owners and growth-minded restoration professionals to shorten their DANG learning curve for personal and professional development. For over two decades Jon has been working in leadership roles with organizations in the construction, hazard abatement, and property restoration industries.

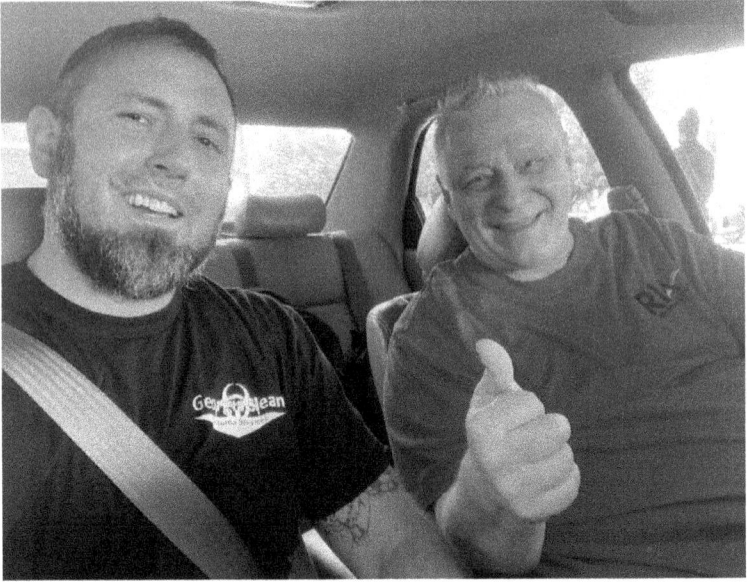

Photo of Pete Consigli, The Restoration Global Watchdog and The OG Intentional Restorer, with the author Jon Isaacson, The Intentional Restorer, on a road trip in 2021 following the RIA Convention.

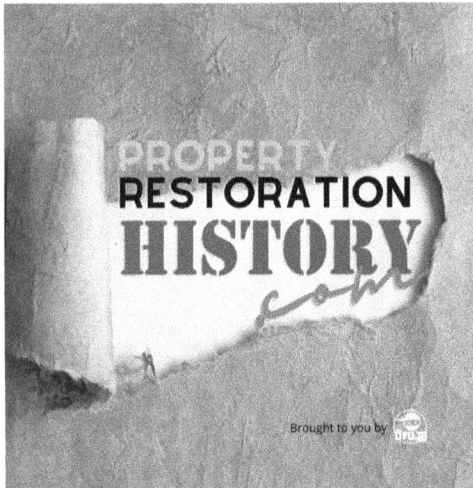

Pete is also the technical advisor for
PropertyRestorationHistory.com

www.ingramcontent.com/pod-product-compliance
Lightning Source LLC
Chambersburg PA
CBHW052123270326
41930CB00012B/2731

* 9 7 8 1 7 3 5 6 2 2 7 5 0 *